Financial Mail on Sunday

Complete Guide to Pensions and Planning Your Retirement

Financial Mail on Sunday

Complete Guide to Pensions and Planning Your Retirement

Stephen Womack

RANDOM HOUSE
BUSINESS BOOKS

Published by Business Books in 2002

1 3 5 7 9 10 8 6 4 2

First published in 2002 by Random House Business Books
The Random House Group Limited
20 Vauxhall Bridge Road, London SW1V 2SA

Random House Australia (Pty) Limited
20 Alfred Street, Milsons Point,
Sydney, New South Wales 2061, Australia

Random House New Zealand Limited
18 Poland Road, Glenfield,
Auckland 10, New Zealand

Random House (Pty) Limited
Endulini, 5a Jubilee Road, Parktown 2193, South Africa

The Random House Group Limited Reg. No. 954009

www.randomhouse.co.uk

A CIP catalogue record for this book
is available from the British Library.

Papers used by Random House are natural, recyclable
products made from wood grown in sustainable forests.
The manufacturing processes conform to the environmental
regulations of the country of origin.

ISBN 0 7126 8087 X

Typeset in Sabon by MATS, Southend-on-Sea, Essex
Printed and bound in Great Britain by
Mackays of Chatham PLC, Chatham, Kent

Dedication

To Lucy, who kept me sane throughout.

Acknowledgements:

I owe a debt of thanks to many people who have helped in the preparation of this book.

Special thanks must go to Adrian Shandley of Balmoral Associates, John Sheffield of AIS Pensions and Ronnie Lymburn of The Drawdown Advisory Bureau for looking at sections of the manuscript.

The team at Financial Mail on Sunday was always supportive and full of extra ideas. Thanks to Jeff Prestridge, Neil Simpson, Clare Hall, Toby Walne, Sally Hamilton and Cathy Simmonds. And extra thanks to Philippa Mechan for fighting through a mountain of photocopying.

The following people and organisations have also provided patient help:

Elaine Graham and John Fennessey at the Department of Work and Pensions; Jeff Newton of Standard Life; Steve Leach and Lyn Webb at Legal & General; David Marlow and Peter Quinton of The Annuity Bureau; Steve Radford at the Chartered Insurance Institute; Andrew Haxton of Bridgegate Annuities; Danny Cox of Hargreaves Lansdown; Jon Francis of Francis Walls & Richards; Sheila Longley and Andy Fleming from the National Association of Pension Funds; David Cresswell of the Financial Ombudsman Service; Chris Wheal of Wheal Associates.

Contents

Preface

How to use this book

A book on retirement planning and pensions is not everyone's idea of a light read. But don't run off for your aspirin and thinking head just yet. Admittedly, this is no beach novel. But nor is it a heavy textbook. It is a practical and accessible guide to a very important subject.

While you are very welcome to read every page, you probably don't want to. Nor do you need to. The book has been structured to give you different routes to the same information.

Rather than grouping facts and figures in a way that suits the writer or a pensions professional, this book tries to bring key information together in chapters which reflect your current situation in life. Initially, you need read only the chapters that apply to you; these may then refer you to other parts of the book but you choose to learn information that is directly relevant.

I would recommend everyone reads the first three chapters which form Part One. Chapter 1 is a brief introduction to the concepts of planning for retirement and Chapter 2 sets out the key basic principles of savings and pensions. Chapter 3 covers state pensions, which apply to everyone.

Part Two of the book carves up retirement planning according to which stage of life you have reached. Chapters focus on planning from starting out, through job changes and looming retirement right up to how you manage money after retirement.

Part Three addresses some key retirement challenges, problems and special circumstances. It touches on everything from early retirement and running your own business, to death and divorce.

Each chapter in Parts Two and Three has a useful reference box at the start so that you can quickly see if it might be relevant to your circumstances.

Part Four provides the in-depth details which you might want to refer to once you have worked through chapters specific to your circumstances. Trying to identify a particular type of pension or want a reminder of annuity rules? This is where to find help.

It would be wrong to claim that this book can answer every question possible on retirement planning. To do this, it would have to be ten times as thick and ten times the price! What it can do is help 95 per cent of readers with 95 per cent of the questions they might have – and point you in the direction of where to find answers to the rest.

This is not a book about pensions. It is a book about how to use your income today to ensure that you have the resources when you retire to make the most of your leisure time. Pensions and all the rest of it are just a mundane means to an exciting end.

Author's note:

The world of retirement planning is fluid. Rules and regulations continually change. All information in this book was correct at 31 July 2001.

PART One
Setting the Scene

CHAPTER 1

Setting the scene

What is the most valuable thing that you will ever own? Your house? A plot of land? Perhaps a particularly fine classic car? Maybe you are one of the lucky few who have a family heirloom such as a painting or a stunning jewel passed down over the generations? Good guesses, but wrong, wrong, wrong.

Almost without exception, the most valuable thing that will ever have your name on it is the pot of money, assets and linked entitlements that will support you through retirement. This pot may include the house, the car and the fine painting. It might also include cash in the bank, pension funds and share portfolios. You may not even realise that some of it exists. Pension rights and entitlements to income in retirement, especially from the state, often have no apparent cash value. Nevertheless, they are worth a fortune.

Even a couple who retire after a life on low incomes or benefit, with little money saved and who live in rented accommodation can still value their 'retirement pot' in six figures. It would cost well over £100,000 to go out and buy privately the income that a couple get from the basic state pension alone.

For a middle earner, multiply that valuation tenfold at least. For a top executive, multiply it thirty- or fortyfold.

These are quite staggering sums of money. And they need to be. That mixture of savings and entitlement to income in years to come is all that will support you for the rest of your life. It might need to last twenty, thirty or forty years. Sure, the odd person will get lucky and win the lottery. But not you and me. We have to live off this retirement pot.

New landscapes

The prospect of a leisured retirement has only been a realistic notion in Britain for the past century or so. Before then, the vast majority of people went on working until they dropped. It is only over the last few generations that significant numbers of men and women have been able to look ahead to retirement and plan for a life after work.

But this planning process has become far more complicated during the last two decades – and is likely to remain a challenge for the foreseeable future. Planning ahead sensibly for retirement has become one of the new skills needed to navigate the twenty-first century. Planning is more complex because our lives themselves have become more complex. The social patterns of work and family life have changed. No longer is it typical to join one company and stay there for many years, perhaps even for life. Our careers chop and change.

For better or for worse, family life too is unpredictable. Divorce, second marriages and step-families are on the rise. Longer lifespans mean that retirement can stretch into decades. It is an opportunity for a golden third age of your life – if you get the planning right.

Understanding how these changes might affect your future is the first step towards taking control of retirement and getting the planning right.

Changing work life

Social commentators hark back to a supposed golden age when everyone had a job for life. That is wishful thinking. There was never such a time. Companies have always gone bust. People have always lost their jobs. Others were forced out of work through accident, illness or social pressure. It is less than forty years ago that many employers – including the Civil Service – forced women to resign from their jobs when they married.

The point the commentators are trying to make is that work life used to be more predictable. You generally stayed in one job, or with one employer, longer. There was not the expectation of regularly moving job or career. Contrast this with the workplace of the twenty-first century, where sudden changes of employer or career are now the norm – whether workers like it or not.

Changing jobs can have advantages for retirement planning. If by moving job you advance more rapidly up the career ladder and boost your earnings, you are in a position to save more for retirement. But frequent changing does make planning more complicated. The more different jobs you do, the more bits of pension and savings you may collect along the way. Keeping track of them and working out how you are doing becomes a chore.

There may be downsides too. If you swap jobs too frequently you may find you lose a year or two of pension entitlement when you move. And each time you change, you may be faced with questions about what to do with pension funds. Charges for switching money around can eat into what you have saved.

Swapping jobs more frequently is only half the story. Another fundamental change in the past few years is the rise of self-employment. Around one in five of the workforce is expected to be self-employed by 2010[1] – double the number who worked for themselves in the early 1990s. Frequently, individuals will switch between being self-employed and employed and then back again. Self-employment poses its own challenges to retirement planning. It shuts the doors on some kinds of savings and pensions, and opens the doors to others.

Shorter working lives?

Different patterns of employment pose one set of challenges in retirement planning. These pale into insignificance compared with the challenge posed by a shorter working life. The value of your retirement kitty is linked directly to the number of years you spend paying into it. The more years in work, the bigger it will be. Yet at the moment, the trend is pushing us towards fewer and fewer years in work.

We start our working careers later. Go back forty years and the majority of pupils left school at fifteen. The official leaving age has inched up to sixteen, with most staying on in some form of education until eighteen. And further education is now more common. The government aims for a majority of children to go on to university. Add in the gap year many spend travelling the globe, and suddenly it is not unusual for someone to settle down to full-time work at age twenty-two or twenty-three – potentially six to eight years older than their grandparents when they joined the workforce.

At the other end of our careers, early retirement is very much in vogue. Hundreds of thousands of those in their mid-fifties are keen to retire early. When employers have to cut jobs and make redundancies, they are happy to encourage these willing individuals out of the door. What is the problem with that? In some cases nothing. But if early retirement is a genuine retirement and a person has no intention of going back into work, they need to be absolutely certain that their retirement pot will be able to sustain them comfortably over an extended dotage.

Someone who started full-time work aged fifteen and retired at sixty-five would have had a working life of fifty years. Their modern contemporary, who started work at the age of twenty-two and retired early at age fifty-seven would have had a working life of thirty-five years. That is 30 per cent less time to save for a retirement fund that is likely to have to sustain them for a much longer retirement.

The early retirement trend may be easing. Firstly, because changes in demographics and the labour force may make employers less willing to offer it. Companies will need all the staff they can get, so will not incentivise employees to quit early. Secondly, the financial reality of early retirement is catching up with people. They realise they cannot afford to go early; instead, gradual retirement involving part-time or freelance work is a growing phenomenon.

Family fortunes

Families, too, are changing. They have moved on from the husband, wife and 2.4 children who featured in our school reading books.

Divorce is completely socially acceptable. More married couples stay together than divorce, but it is becoming a close-run thing. Divorce can turn retirement plans on their head. Pension assets and entitlements are now considered as part of the break-up equation. This affects women, who are usually the beneficiaries, and men, who have to revisit their saving strategy.

But divorce also has deeper implications. There will be more single-person households in retirement in the years ahead. While it is not true that two live as cheaply as one, they can certainly subsidise each other. For example, a separated husband and wife may want two cars, whereas a couple can share. So planning for retirement as a single person means redoing the sums.

Other social trends may impact on retirement. People generally have children later in life. The average age of a mother having her first baby is now 26.9 years. Many women are not having children until after they are thirty. Go back a generation and the average first-time mum was aged twenty-two.

Starting a family later means parents may still have children dependent upon them when they are in their late forties or early fifties. Indeed, this may be the time when children need most support; for example, help with college or university costs. Yet historically these are the years when those who do save hard for retirement stash away most of the cash. Will you be able to afford to do both?

The triumph of age

One other issue has significantly changed the retirement game. Improved diet and better health care have contributed to a stunning – there is no other word for it – a stunning improvement in longevity. For the past thirty years, life expectancy has been increasing at the amazing rate of roughly two years per decade. So in just one generation, people in Britain can expect to live for six years longer than their parents.

There is no guarantee that the trend will continue at such a pace. Although, if scientists and doctors can unravel the secrets of our genetic code, there is the potential for another big advance. Table 1.1 shows two estimates of life expectancy.

In many senses this longevity represents a huge triumph for humanity. But it throws up other challenges. Longer lifespans mean longer retirements. That in turn means your retirement pot needs to be spread over a greater number of years. Couple this trend with early retirement and it is quite possible to imagine someone whose retired life is longer than their working life. This would have been unthinkable even twenty years ago.

Take the example of a woman retiring at age fifty-seven after thirty-five years in work. On the latest mortality data, on *average* she can expect twenty-nine years and eleven months of life after her fifty-seventh birthday, taking her almost to age eighty-seven. If she lives 15 per cent longer than the average and survives past her ninety-second birthday she will have been retired longer than she was in work.

Long lives are one thing. There is also the matter of how healthy you may be in the final years. Good though medical care is, it cannot yet turn back the clock on ageing. One side effect of improved health care has been to make events like heart attacks, strokes and severe cancers much more survivable. Who might look after you after such an attack? Will your retirement pot be big enough to bear the costs of long-term care, or nursing at home? These are painful questions, but they have to be faced.

Table 1.1: How long might you live?

Estimates of life expectancy can only ever be educated guesses. Actuaries can predict what might happen to an 'average person' with confidence, but it is a dangerous game to try to apply these averages to individuals. Your health, lifestyle, occupation, genetic make-up – even where you live – all have their influences on life expectancy. But in planning for retirement it is prudent to take account of general trends in life expectancy, and these are all pointing to longer lives and so longer retirements.

Below are two different statistical measures of how long the average man and woman might survive. The figures in column A are taken from the official English Life Tables, based on data collected in the 1991 Census. This measures life expectancy across the population as a whole. A new version will be produced late in 2002 after the 2001 Census, which is expected to show big increases, especially for middle-aged men.

The figures in column B come from actuaries at the Continuous Mortality Investigation Board. These are based on life insurance company claims, with an allowance for improving life expectancy. Column A is historic and shows how long people actually survived a decade ago, while column B is forward-looking and includes the impact of factors like improving medical technology to produce updated figures.

Age today	Men		Women	
	Column A	Column B	Column A	Column B
	Years of future life	Years/months of future life	Years of future life	Years/months of future life
30	44.88	55/4	49.94	58/4
31	43.92	54/4	48.86	57/4
32	42.96	53/3	47.98	56/3
33	42.00	52/2	47.00	55/3
34	41.04	51/2	46.03	54/2
35	40.09	50/1	45.06	53/1
36	39.14	49/0	44.09	52/1

Age today	Men		Women	
	Column A	Column B	Column A	Column B
	Years of future life	Years/months of future life	Years of future life	Years/months of future life
37	38.18	48/0	43.12	51/0
38	37.24	46/11	42.16	49/11
39	36.29	45/10	41.20	48/11
40	35.34	44/10	40.24	47/10
41	34.41	43/9	39.28	46/9
42	33.47	42/9	38.32	45/8
43	32.54	41/7	37.37	44/8
44	31.61	40/6	36.43	43/7
45	30.68	39/6	35.49	42/6
46	29.76	41/5	34.56	41/5
47	28.85	37/4	33.61	40/5
48	27.95	36/3	32.68	39/4
49	27.05	35/3	31.76	38/3
50	26.16	34/2	30.85	37/2
51	25.30	33/1	29.94	36/2
52	24.40	32/0	29.03	35/1
53	23.55	31/0	28.13	34/0
54	22.70	29/11	27.24	33/0
55	21.86	28/10	26.36	31/11
56	21.03	27/10	25.48	30/11
57	20.21	26/10	24.61	29/11
58	19.41	25/9	23.76	28/10
59	18.62	24/9	22.91	27/10
60	17.85	23/9	22.08	26/10
61	17.10	22/9	21.26	25/10
62	16.36	21/9	20.45	24/10
63	15.64	20/10	19.66	23/11
64	14.94	19/10	18.88	22/11
65	14.26	18/10	18.11	22/0
66	13.62	18/0	17.36	21/1
67	12.98	17/2	16.62	20/2

Age today	Men		Women	
	Column A	Column B	Column A	Column B
	Years of future life	Years/months of future life	Years of future life	Years/months of future life
68	12.36	16/3	15.90	19/3
69	11.77	15/5	15.18	18/5
70	11.19	14/7	14.49	17/7
71	10.62	13/10	13.80	16/9
72	10.08	13/1	13.13	15/11
73	9.56	12/4	12.48	15/2
74	9.06	11/7	11.85	14/5
75	8.57	10/11	11.23	13/8
76	8.11	10/3	10.63	12/11
77	7.66	9/8	10.04	12/3
78	7.23	9/1	9.48	11/7
79	6.82	8/6	8.93	11/0
80	6.44	8/0	8.41	10/5

A quick word on the state

Some of the bills in retirement will be picked up by the state. For the foreseeable future, everyone who retires will get a state pension. Don't hold your breath, though.

The growing number of demonstrations by pensioners tell you all you need to know about the state pension. It is in poor health. The basic state pension faces an uncertain future, like many of those who rely on it. On current forecasts it will dwindle to a relative pittance at some point beyond 2050. The political climate may change in the years ahead and far greater resources may be channelled into the state pension. But do not count on it; the days of a comprehensive cradle-to-grave welfare state seem numbered. Chapter 3 explains more fully what the state will deliver when you retire.

Why didn't they tell me this at school?

Making sense of all these issues is not always easy. Working towards retirement now means we have to make choices and decisions that previous generations did not have to face.

Is the average person equipped to make these choices? Probably not. This is not because we cannot understand the issues; there is nothing like talking about your own future to focus your attention. It is simply that we lack the knowledge. Retirement planning was not something we were taught at school (though increasingly this kind of personal financial planning is creeping on to the timetable). It is not something that we would automatically pick up along the way. It is possible to go for years without encountering pensions paperwork or without being aware of changing legislation. Then, when you do stumble across something, it is frequently too late to act. This book is designed to fill the gaps in your knowledge. It will equip you with the information to make your own plans, and help you take control of your own future.

In summary, we can expect:

- A changing landscape for retirement.
- Jobs and careers will be more varied, with greater self-employment.
- More divorces to pressure existing savings plans.
- A longer life.
- A reduced role for the welfare state.
- To have to take more responsibility for our own futures.

Notes

1 Henley Centre forecast, cited in Swiss Re, *The Insurance Report*, 1997.

CHAPTER 2

First steps in taking charge of your retirement

When you are heading on a long car journey you plan your trip. You will plot a route, make sure there is enough fuel in the car and estimate how long the journey might take. You may even plan where to stop and eat. As the journey progresses you adapt your plans. Bad weather or heavy traffic can slow you down. You may hear on the radio that roadworks are ahead and find an alternative route. But you have a clear destination in mind and work your way towards it.

Planning your future is a little more demanding than working out a quick route to a friend's house. But the same principles should hold true when heading for retirement. You set your goals, plot your route and then check progress every so often to see how well you are doing. Yet each year there are millions of people in Britain heading towards their retirement without the foggiest idea of what they are aiming for or what sort of income they can expect when they get there. This section explains the essential first steps in planning for retirement.

Be prepared to guess a little

Planning for retirement is not an exact science. When you are looking thirty, forty or fifty years into the future, a certain amount of guesswork is inevitable.

Our personal lives are hugely uncertain. Without a crystal ball, who can predict:

- Where you will work and how much you will earn;
- How good or bad your health will be;
- Who, if anyone, will be dependent on you;
- How long your retirement will be – five years or thirty-five years?

In the wider world, no one can be certain about the impact of inflation on our savings, about how quickly money invested in pensions might grow, or about what future governments might do to penalise or reward pensioners.

But do not let uncertainty put you off or be an excuse for doing nothing. Plans can always be modified along the way and the nearer you get towards retirement the more confident you can become in your predictions.

Key questions

Plotting a retirement plan means asking yourself some crucial questions. And then asking them again every few years to make sure you still like the answers. There are five key issues:

1 *When will you retire?* Do you have a definite age in mind? Does your employer set a retirement date? Is early retirement a realistic option? Do you want to coincide your retirement with that of a spouse or partner?

2 *How will you retire?* Is retirement going to be sudden; will you simply clock out one Friday and not return on Monday? Or can you ease into retirement, winding down from full-time to part-time work and spreading the process over several years? Much

will depend on the type of work you do and the flexibility of your employer.

3 *What do you want to do with your retirement?* Is retirement going to signal a life of leisure? Do you have specific goals of places to go or hobbies to pursue? Will retirement be the chance to do something different? Maybe some part-time work in a different job, or voluntary service. Or will retirement from one job even signal the start of a second career?

4 *What sort of income will you need?* How much will essentials like housing, food and heating cost? How much will it cost to live your retirement dreams, to see the world or to master that golf course? And what about the later years? Should you plan for the potential costs of ill health, nursing homes and medical treatment?

5 *What sort of income can you expect?* Unless you are starting out in your first job, you will already have some pension entitlement, even if it is just something from the state pension. How certain is this income? What about previous employment? What other money might come your way; for example, through inheritance? How far might all these sources of income fall short of what you will need?

Of course, the answers to these questions are linked. You may fancy the idea of quitting work at fifty-seven, for instance. But looking realistically at your income needs and expectations, you find that the sums simply don't add up. On the other hand you may be the kind of person who wants to delay retirement as long as possible, so you are keen to avoid needlessly saving too much for what you expect to be a shorter retirement.

It is useful to consider two of these questions in more detail; how much you might spend and how much income you will have.

How much will you spend in retirement?

This may seem an impossible question to answer, especially for those who are years from retirement. However, preparing a list of the day-to-day living expenses you might have after you retire can help you plan your income needs. Those on the verge of retirement can be confident that the numbers they write in won't change too much; table 2.1 shows an example list covering the most likely spending.

But for those who are ten, twenty or more years from quitting work, it is very hard to draw up a meaningful plan. You wouldn't have put down bills for satellite or cable TV on a list drawn up ten years ago, but many households now consider this essential expenditure. Who knows what else will change? You may develop new interests, give up others and see your family expand and grow. Don't worry too much at this stage. This process can only be a rough guide, so have a go and see what comes out.

When drawing up a list of potential spending, it may help to bear in mind some of the common ways in which spending patterns change in retirement. Typically, many of those who have retired will have paid off a mortgage, so housing costs are reduced. They will also have raised families and coped with the expense of children. They no longer have to make National Insurance contributions from earnings, which count for 10 per cent of most salaries. Also, they no longer need to make pension contributions, potentially another big saving.

Other expenses increase. Older people spend more on health care. Homes may need heating for longer during the day. Travel and leisure costs may rise in the early years of retirement, as active pensioners keep busy and fill their days. You may need to buy a car and pay for running costs, perhaps replacing a vehicle that came with your job. In later years, spending is likely to reduce as the typical pensioner slows down, travels less and spends more time at home. Spending may then rise again in the final years as nursing fees and home help costs become an issue.

A separate issue to consider is your attitude towards inheritance. Do you want to be able to pass on a substantial legacy to children or grandchildren? Or are you happy to run down savings and borrow against assets such as your home in retirement? The more you hope to leave, the more income you will need in retirement to avoid eating into your savings.

Table 2.1: Your income needs in retirement

Filling in this chart will help you to estimate how much income you will need in retirement. If you are unsure about costs, look at recent bank statements and credit card bills for guidance. It is unlikely that you will have something to write in every box.

Expenditure	Annual cost (£)
Day-to-day costs	
Food and household basics	
Newspapers and magazines	
Everyday clothing	
Cosmetics, toiletries and hairdressing	
House and home	
Rent or mortgage	
Utility bills: gas, electricity, oil, water	
Buildings and contents insurance	
Council tax	
Saving for repairs and maintenance	
Telephone	
Other services, e.g. satellite TV, Internet access fees	
Cost of help around home, e.g. cleaner	
Transport	
Owning a car: insurance, road tax, financing costs	
Running a car: petrol, servicing, breakdown insurance	
Bus, taxi or train fares	

Leisure and fun
Holidays and leisure travel
Eating out
Pets (including food and vets' bills)
Sports and hobbies
Drinking and smoking
Health and fitness
Dental fees
Opticians' fees and glasses
Private medical insurance
Long-term care insurance
Contribution to pay-as-you-go medical fund
Other protection insurance, e.g. accident cover, life cover
Other health costs, e.g. physiotherapy
Savings
Saving for major household items, home improvements, new car etc.
Savings for later in retirement, children or grandchildren
Giving
Presents
Regular charitable donations
Regular gifts to children/grandchildren
Any other spending

Total
Allowance for tax * — 20 per cent – multiply total by 1.25 to produce gross income
Gross income required

---

* An accurate tax calculation is impossible. No one knows what tax rules will be in force when you retire. The rate of tax will depend on your income – modest incomes will probably attract no tax, but an increasing number of pensioners are now retiring as top-rate taxpayers. For planning purposes, assume 20 per cent of

your total income might be lost to tax, so multiply your annual total by 1.25 to give the gross income required.

How big will your income be?

The flip side of spending is income. Increasingly, our income in retirement will be made up from lots of different sources. So estimating how much income you can expect once you are retired requires a bit of guesswork and a bit of legwork. Estimating income breaks down into four parts:

- Calculating what pension you are already entitled to.
- Calculating what pension you might accumulate from future working.
- Calculating how you might increase your pension going forward.
- Considering what other sources of income you might have in retirement.

Later sections of the book will explain these issues in more detail. Chapter 19 tells you how to track down pensions from previous employment. Chapter 11 explains the alternatives to pensions and what other kinds of income you might have in retirement. But it is useful to go through a quick summary of these issues to get us started.

Pensions come in different shapes and sizes. The common thread is that they are designed to take part of your income now and translate that into income once you have retired. Think of all pensions as giant piggy banks that you cannot break into until you have stopped working and you won't go far wrong.

The government deducts National Insurance from our salaries and from our employers. In exchange, we become entitled to a range of pensions and benefits when we retire. The more years of work and the more we earn, the greater the entitlement. The next chapter spotlights state pensions in detail.

Many employers run pension schemes. Employees who join

these schemes again build up an entitlement to pension benefits. Roughly speaking, the more years you belong to the scheme the higher a pension you will get. These benefits are normally not lost if you move jobs, so someone who moves jobs five or ten times in a working life may end up with several different pots of pension. Chapter 19 talks you through the ins and outs of company pensions.

You can also choose to save for yourself through a wide range of personal pensions. Here, individuals pay money directly to a pension company. They hope this will grow a fund over the years that can be converted into an income when they retire. Chapter 20 explains the technicalities of personal pensions.

Both private and company pensions aim to grow the money that we and employers pay into them. They do this by investing in a range of different assets. These investments crop up time and again throughout this book. Box 2.1 is a brief introduction to the different ways pension money can be invested.

Box 2.1: A quick word on investments

When thinking about saving for retirement it is helpful to have an idea about what happens to the money you save.

Money you put aside for retirement does not just sit there – unless your idea of saving is to stuff £10 notes under your mattress or in a box at the bottom of the garden. Your cash is invested in a variety of assets, which can help that money increase in value.

The same basic assets can be used to underpin a company or personal pension, other investments such as an Individual Savings Account (Isa), or for savings you make directly yourself.

The main types of asset are:

- Cash – also known as deposit-based investments. Your money sits in an account or fund. The capital is almost completely secure. It may earn some interest, paid monthly or annually. Money held on deposit will grow; but historically it grows more slowly than other types of investment. And it sometimes does not increase in value as quickly as prices.

- Bonds – these are issued by governments or by private organisations such as companies as a way of borrowing money. They are a kind of IOU note, issued in exchange for a lump sum payment. The issuer of a bond promises to repay the money they have borrowed at a set date in the future, plus to pay a fixed rate of annual interest between now and then. The more creditworthy the bond issuer is, the lower the rate of interest they need to offer. UK government bonds are called gilts. Bonds can be traded. Their value will fluctuate as interest rates fluctuate. But in general they provide a steady and reliable stream of income.
- Equities – also called shares. These are the most important long-term investment. Historically they have grown in value better than any other type of asset. The majority of most pension funds is invested in shares. Companies issue shares as a way of raising capital. The owners of the shares are the owners of the company. The price of the shares can rise and fall, depending on the fortunes of the business. General economic conditions also affect the value of shares. Shares are traded through stock exchanges all over the world. Shareholders may get paid an annual dividend, an income, by the company. Through your pension and other savings, you will own a small slice of many of the companies operating in the UK, plus household names from around the world such as Microsoft or Sony.
- Property – is still an important investment asset. Individuals own their own homes and possibly holiday homes or even other property they let out. But investment funds also buy commercial property; the shops, offices, factories and warehouses you see around you. The owner of a property can earn an income through rent, plus hope to see the value of the property increase.

Most of us will end up with a healthy mix of these different types of assets. It is healthy to mix, because it avoids putting all your eggs in one basket and so seeing your wealth damaged too severely if property prices fall or if the stock market plunges.

The simple truth for all these pensions is the longer you are in them the better. The more years you are putting aside some of today's income, the bigger your pension will be in retirement. Early and often should be the watchwords in saving for retirement.

Many start their pension planning in later life; decent retirement incomes are still possible if you start in your forties or early fifties, but they require you to sacrifice a much higher proportion of your earnings today to hit the targets. The examples in table 2.2 show the importance of timing.

For planning purposes you can ask the government, your employer, previous employers and personal pension companies for projections of what you have already achieved. These show your possible future pension based on your savings and employment so far.

Employers and private pension companies can also add to this a projection of what you might achieve if you go on saving into a pension at the same rate until retirement. Often, employees can choose to top up their company pension through extra voluntary saving. And personal pension customers can boost their contributions, subject to various tax rules. Again, in both cases you can obtain projections of how increasing your saving might increase your final pension.

Of course, most of us expect our earnings to increase as our careers progress. So it makes sense to build in some allowance for this in the planning process. But it is prudent not to expect too much; after all, not everyone will make it to managing director.

Table 2.2: It pays to start early

This table shows an estimate of what income a personal pension might produce at age sixty-five if you save £100 per month gross of tax into it. It clearly shows the benefits of starting saving earlier rather than later. Be aware, though, this makes no allowance for the impact of inflation.

Women get a lower pension than men because on average they live longer, so a given pot of money has to be spread over more years. Chapter 7 discusses the particular challenges facing women in saving for retirement.

Age saving starts	Forecast monthly pension at age 65 (£)	
	Man	**Women**
25	1582	1407
30	1128	1003
35	793	705
40	545	485
45	362	322
50	227	202

Assumptions: Growth of 7 per cent per year, annual charge of 0.7 per cent per year, interest rate of 6 per cent for fund conversion into income.

Source: Marks & Spencer Financial Services.

In this wired world, several pension companies and financial websites now offer on-line pension planners via the Internet. These allow you to play around with different scenarios. You can vary how much is saved each month and the age at which you retire to see how the final pension estimate changes. Sites operating free, no-obligation planners include www.landg.com and www.thisismoney.com. A few far-sighted employers also offer these interactive calculators to members of their company pension schemes.

Many savers choose to go to a financial adviser for help with their retirement planning. Advisers can help you obtain and interpret pension projections. And they can suggest ways to boost income in retirement. Chapter 12 talks about the different kinds of advisers, what advisers can do for you, and warns of the potential pitfalls. Collecting information and advice from all these sources will help you build up a much clearer picture of what sort of retirement income you are heading for. You can then decide what action, if any, to take. Your forecasts will still be a guess, but at least they will be an informed guess.

Box 2.2: There's lies, damned lies, and then there are pension projections

A word of warning. Pension projections can range from confusing to downright misleading. This is not a deliberate plot to trick the poor old saver. It is simply a reflection of the long-term guesswork involved in projecting twenty or thirty years in advance.

Projections have to make assumptions about how fast money invested in a pension will grow, about how your income might grow and about how a pension fund might be converted into an income when you retire.

For example, at the moment most personal pensions are projected forward at an annual growth rate of 7 per cent. Projections benefit from an effect called compounding. This means that each year the amount of growth projected for a pension is bigger than in previous years because you include accumulated growth too. Over long periods, this compounding effect can turn seemingly modest contributions into enormous pension funds. So £100 saved each month for thirty years, growing at 7 per cent, with annual fund charges of 1 per cent, becomes a fund of over £171,000. Not a bad pension you might think.

But these enormous fund values mask the potential impact of inflation. Rising prices mean that the value of money is reduced. Even if inflation stays low by historical standards, say an average of 3 per cent for the next thirty years, £1000 then is worth only £401 in today's value. Put another way, it would cost £1000 to buy what you could get today for £401. Faster inflation would reduce the value even more dramatically. At 5 per cent inflation, £1000 in thirty years is worth only £214.64 in today's money.

So the most useful pension projections are ones which are adjusted for inflation, also called real terms or current-value projections. In the example above, where £100 each month is invested for thirty years at 7 per cent growth and inflation is 2.5 per cent, the value of the fund in today's terms is £45,774.* Still a tidy sum, but not as exciting as £171,000.

Also, you need to be aware that the growth rates used in projections are not guaranteed. Your future is dependent on the whims of the stock market. Over the past twenty to thirty years, growth has averaged between 12 and 13 per cent a year. What happens in the future could be higher or lower than the 7 per cent projected. Some pension companies invest more effectively than others. Some get lucky. Conversely, some companies have disappointing investment growth.

If that uncertainty were not enough, there is also doubt about what kind of income your savings can produce. Many of today's pensions convert the fund built up over the years into an income through something called an annuity. You buy an annuity with some or all of the fund, handing over your piggy bank full of cash in exchange for a guaranteed income for life. Chapter 21 explains annuities. Annuities fluctuate in price. The amount of income you can get for a given sum depends on factors like how high interest rates are and how long people live. Pension projections assume standard annuity rates. The real rates may be higher or lower than those projected.

So is a projection worth the paper it is printed on? The nearer you get to retirement, the more certain you can be of the assumptions. And even looking twenty or more years into the future a projection is better than nothing, if only because it illustrates again the key lessons of retirement planning: save early, save often and review your plans regularly.

* Source: Hargreaves Lansdown pension calculators.

Why bother with a pension at all?

If pensions are complicated and it is uncertain what income they will produce when you come to retire, why bother with them at all? Why not save for retirement in other ways?

Pensions are certainly not the only game in town. They are only a part of the retirement-planning jigsaw, albeit a very important piece. Many of those who retire get an income from several different sources. Cash in the bank, other investments and property are all good ways to save. In some cases, and for some savers, they have more to offer than pensions. Chapter 11 explains the pros and cons of all these types of savings.

But pensions have three crucial advantages which make them hard to ignore. Firstly, company and personal pensions receive special tax treatment. Money paid into them is free of tax. In some cases pension contributions can be taken direct from wages before tax has been deducted. In other cases the government will actually top up your payment into a pension to refund the tax paid on this money. This tax concession can boost the value of a pension payment by as much as 40 per cent. The pension fund itself also grows free of tax, though tax has to be paid on the ultimate pension income.

Secondly, in the vast majority of cases, employers subsidise the costs of company pensions. The most generous companies cover all the costs and make all the contributions into your pension. Others share the costs with the employee. This is a valuable benefit, potentially worth up to 15 per cent of your salary. It is foolish not to join a scheme and so miss out. By not joining you are awarding yourself a pay cut.

The third advantage of a pension might be seen by some as a disadvantage. Pension assets are locked up tight until you retire. You cannot usually get your hands on them earlier, though there are exceptions such as in cases of ill health. The state pension is not available until sixty-five if you are a man and sixty if you are a woman (soon to become sixty-five). There is a little more flexibility for company and personal pensions, but again you cannot just dip into the pot willy-nilly. Tying up the cash in a pension means that savers cannot help themselves whenever temptation strikes; for example, when a big credit card bill arrives or when the car needs replacing.

In summary, by now you should be aware that:

- Planning for retirement is not an exact science.
- Plans need to be reviewed regularly.
- It is important to make realistic assumptions.
- Income in retirement will come from several sources.
- Pensions are a key part, but not the only part, of retirement planning.
- The earlier you start the better.

Inevitably, planning for retirement involves hard choices and difficult compromises. The rest of this book is devoted to helping you through these decisions.

CHAPTER 3 What you might get from the state

The good news is that you are going to get some help from the state when you retire. The bad news is that there is no guarantee what this will be and how much it might be worth. State retirement benefits have been stitched into a patchwork quilt of different pensions, allowances and handouts. Nevertheless, state pensions still provide a key component of your income in retirement and have a place in everyone's plans.

State pensions are going through great upheavals. The basic state pension is no longer the guarantee of a comfortable income that its founders once intended. Around the framework of this basic state pension, successive governments have built a series of extra payments, allowances and benefits. The result is a complicated mixture of payments, some of which everyone gets and some of which you have to qualify for. Each year the picture changes, with new rules coming into force in 2002 and 2003.

The basic state pension

The basic pension is the starting point for retirement planning. For tax year 2001/02 (that is the year that runs 6 April 2001 to 5 April 2002) it is worth a maximum of £72.50 a week (£3770 per year) for a single person. A married couple may get either the couple's rate of up to £115.90 a week (£6026.80 a year) or up to a maximum of twice the single person's rate, worth £145 a week (£7540 a year). A modest supplement worth 25p a week is paid to those who are aged eighty or over. There are also extra supplements available for any pensioners who care for children.

Table 3.1 shows how the basic state pension has changed over the past few years and will change from April 2002. Income tax is never deducted from the state pension, though it does count towards your total income, so other earnings or income may be taxed because of it. Box 3.1 explains how today's pensioners are taxed.

Table 3.1: How the basic state pension is changing

Tax year	Maximum annual pension		
	Single pension	Married couple's pension	A couple each claiming the full state pension in their own right
1999/2000	£3471	£5548.40	£6942
2000/01	£3510	£5610.80	£7020
2001/02	£3770	£6026.80	£7540
2002/03	£3926	£6276.40	£7852

Source: DWP.

You qualify for the basic state pension when you reach state retirement age. For men this is sixty-five. Women currently retire at sixty, though this will change in the near future (see below). The pension kicks in on the Monday after your birthday. Payment is not automatic. You must complete a claim form, which will be sent to you approximately four months before you reach retirement age.

The basic pension has declined in value as the nation has got richer. Since 1980 the pension has been linked to inflation. It increases each year to keep pace with rising prices. But average earnings tend to grow more quickly than inflation. This means that over the years the pension has fallen in value against the wages and salaries people receive while in work. The trend is set to continue.

In 2000 the basic pension was worth roughly 16 per cent of national average earnings. By 2030 it is expected to be worth between 7.5 and 10 per cent of average earnings, depending on how quickly wages increase.

Although the state pension has declined in value, it is still worth having. If he were trying to replicate the basic pension privately, a man aged sixty-five would need a pension fund of £52,350[1] to produce an annual income of £3770, which is guaranteed for life and which rises in line with inflation. A couple, where the man is aged sixty-five and the wife aged sixty-three, would need a fund of £104,740[2] to produce an annual income of £6027 – the couple's rate – which is guaranteed until one of them dies and linked to inflation, and then £3770 a year thereafter, also linked to inflation.

Box 3.1: How pensioners are taxed

Anyone who has retired must pay tax like the rest of us. But there are some special concessions for older taxpayers.

Each individual in Britain has a personal tax allowance. This states how much income they can have in any one tax year before having to pay income tax. For anyone aged less than sixty-five this allowance is worth £4535 a year. Those who are aged sixty-five or more qualify for an enhanced allowance of £5990 a year. At seventy-five the allowance increases again to £6260. These age-related allowances will rise by £240 a year more than inflation in April 2003; on current estimates that means the over-sixty-five allowance will become £6560 and the over-seventy-five allowance will become £6850. In future these allowances will rise in line with average earnings. However, where a pensioner has a higher income, the allowances are gradually clawed-back. On incomes over £17,600 a year they count for nothing.

What are these extra concessions worth?

Take the example of a single person with an income of £12,000 a year. Based on 2001/02 tax rates and the current allowances, someone aged under sixty-five would pay £1416.70 in income tax. A person aged over sixty-five would pay £320.10 a year less, that is £1096.60. Someone aged over seventy-five would pay £1037.20, that is £379.50 a year less in tax.

A couple each have a personal allowance, so in theory a couple both aged over sixty-five could have a combined income of £11,980 a year without paying tax. In practice, the income is not likely to be split evenly.

Some pensioners benefit from one other tax concession. Pensioner households containing someone born before 6 April 1935 still qualify for the married couple's allowance. This is worth up to £535 for a couple where one is aged less than seventy-five and up to £543 for an older couple.

The tax can be collected in a variety of ways. The basic state pension is not taxed. But personal and company pensions are usually paid net of tax, that is with tax deducted through the PAYE tax system. If you have a personal or company pension you may find this appears to be overtaxed. This is because the PAYE system is being used to collect extra tax due on other income.

If you have no PAYE income in retirement you may have to complete an annual tax return and pay any tax due twice a year in a lump sum.

Under normal circumstances the basic state pension increases in line with inflation. It is increased at the start of each tax year in April, based on the figure for inflation, the Retail Price Index, in the previous September. However, the pension for tax year 2001/02 and

2002/03 has been given an extra boost as part of a wider reform package. It has risen by more than inflation.

These recent tweaks illustrate a key point about the basic pension – and about state pensions in general. They are not guaranteed. They are vulnerable to political intervention. Governments can and do change the value of state pensions, change the rules over who gets what and change the timing of benefits. Sometimes the changes can be to your advantage; frequently they disadvantage you. The message is clear. Do not take state pension benefits for granted.

How you qualify for the basic pension

Many people are startled to discover that the basic pension is not granted automatically. It depends on how much National Insurance (NI) you have paid over your 'working life'. The full pension only goes to those who have paid the right kind of NI for at least 90 per cent of their working lives.

The Department of Work and Pensions (formerly the Department of Social Security or DSS) assumes that our working life starts the year we turn sixteen and ends at normal state retirement age. So a man has forty-nine years of working life and needs to have paid National Insurance for at least forty-four of these years to get the maximum pension. Women who retire at sixty have a working life of forty-four years, so need to have paid for at least thirty-nine years for a full pension. Women born after 5 April 1950 will have a longer working life (see below) and those who were born on or after 6 March 1955 will be subject to the same rules as men.

Those who have paid National Insurance for less than 90 per cent of their working lives get a reduced pension. Table 3.2 shows how the basic pension is reduced. The minimum level is 25 per cent, or £18.12 per week. If you do not have enough years of contributions to count for this you get no state basic pension. Instead, you will be eligible for other state help.

Women may qualify for a pension based on their husbands' NI payments. Her pension will be 60 per cent of the value of his. This pension continues if her husband dies, but is lost if she marries again. At the moment, men with a poor contributions history cannot use their wives' contribution records to boost their own pension. However, men who retire after 2010 when the system is reformed will be able to start claiming against their wives' NI payments if they are better than their own.

If you have paid sufficient contributions you get the full pension, regardless of how much other income you have. This means wealthy pensioner households can still receive up to £7500 a year from the government.

Table 3.2: How much of the basic state pension will you receive?

Number of complete years of National Insurance contributions	Percentage of the basic pension for which you qualify	
	Women born on or before 6 October 1950 *	Men plus women born after 5 October 1954
9 or less	0	0
10	26	0
11	29	25
12	31	28
13	34	30
14	36	32
15	39	35
16	42	37
17	44	39
18	47	41
19	49	44
20	52	46
21	54	48
22	57	50
23	59	53
24	62	55

25	65	57
26	67	60
27	70	62
28	72	64
29	75	66
30	77	69
31	80	71
32	83	73
33	85	75
34	88	78
35	90	80
36	93	82
37	95	85
38	98	87
39	100	89
40	100	91
41	100	94
42	100	96
43	100	98
44 or more	100	100

Source: DWP.

* Women born between 6 April 1950 and 6 March 1955 will be affected by the move to equalise state pensions. The standard female working life for NI contributions is forty-four years – this will gradually extend to forty-nine years to be the same as men. So women born before 6 October 1950 will have a working life of forty-four years, between 6/10/50 and 5/10/51 it will be forty-five years, between 6/10/51 and 5/10/52 it will be forty-six years, between 6/10/52 and 5/10/53 it will be forty-seven years, between 6/10/53 and 5/10/54 it will be forty-eight years. Those born after 5 October 1954 will be deemed to have a working life of forty-nine years.

So how much basic pension will you get?

As explained above, the value of your pension depends on the number of your National Insurance contributions. But not all NI payments count towards a pension.

There are five types of National Insurance contributions:

- Class 1 – paid by employees and employers on earnings above a set limit. These count.
- Class 1 reduced rate – paid by some women. These do not count.
- Class 2 – paid by the self-employed on the first slice of their profits. These count.
- Class 3 – voluntary contributions. These count.
- Class 4 – paid by the self-employed on higher profit levels. These do not count.

If you are working part-time, you may not earn enough to start paying National Insurance. It is currently payable only on earnings of more than £72 per week. Obviously, any casual or 'cash-in-hand' work will not count.

It is also possible to be given NI credits. These have the effect of crediting you with a year's contributions even if you did not pay anything. Credits can be awarded to:

- those claiming state unemployment, sickness or maternity benefits;
- those born after 1957 who were at school or on an approved training scheme between the ages of sixteen and eighteen;
- men who are unemployed between the ages of sixty and sixty-four, even if they are not signing on;
- someone who has taken time off work since 1978 to care for an elderly relative, or to raise children. This is called home responsibilities protection. It is automatic for those who are not working and who draw child benefit. Others will need to claim it through the DWP.

The chances are you will not have the faintest idea how many years of contributions you have paid and whether or not you have any NI credits. Don't panic. The DWP can produce an individual pension forecast based on their records for you. To obtain one of these, complete form BR19 and send it to the Retirement Pension Forecast and Advice Service. To obtain a copy of the form, call

0845 731 3233 or download it from the Internet on www.dss.gov.uk/lifeevent/penret/index.htm. It can take up to six weeks for a forecast.

Your pension forecast will not only contain details of your entitlement to basic state pension. It will also estimate other state pensions including any Graduated State Pension and State Earnings Related Pension Scheme (see below).

If you do not like the result of a forecast, there are ways to boost the value of your state pension. Women who are currently paying reduced rate Class 1 National Insurance can switch back to paying the full rate. And it is possible to make voluntary contributions to top up missed years. You can go back up to six years. For more details on these options, go to Chapter 7: Women and state pensions.

Rolling back the female retirement age

As has already been mentioned, the state retirement age for women is being changed. Between 2010 and 2020 the female state retirement age will gradually shift from sixty to sixty-five. This will equalise retirement ages for men and women.

There are two reasons for the change. Firstly, it fits with current attitudes on sexual equality. Without the change the government would have been open to charges of discrimination, both from women who want to work longer and from men who want to quit earlier. Company pensions have already been forced to equalise their retirement age. The move will also save the government money because it delays the date at which millions of women will be able to draw a pension. By the time the switch is complete, it is estimated the saving will be £5 billion a year, some of which is being used to boost other parts of the state pension scheme.

The change affects women born on or after 6 April 1950. For each month which passes, the retirement age slips back a month.

Table 3.3 gives examples of how this works. Women who were born on or after 6 March 1955 will reach state retirement age when they are sixty-five. Women who are born after April 1950 can choose to retire before they reach state retirement age, for example, if they want to retire at the same time as an older husband or partner. They will still earn NI credits for the time up until their designated retirement age, protecting the value of their pension. But they will not be able to draw any pension or other benefits from the state until they reach sixty-five (or their transitional retirement date as listed in table 3.3). So they will need to have planned an alternative source of income.

Table 3.3: How the female retirement age will change

Your date of birth between *	Your new pension age and retirement date	
	Age (Year.month)	Date
6/4–5/5/50	60.1	6/5/2010
6/6–5/7/50	60.3	6/9/2010
6/8–5/9/50	60.5	6/1/2011
6/10–5/11/50	60.7	6/5/2011
6/12/50–5/1/51	60.9	6/9/2011
6/2–5/3/51	60.11	6/1/2012
6/4–5/5/51	61.1	6/5/2012
6/6–5/7/51	61.3	6/9/2012
6/8–5/9/51	61.5	6/1/2013
6/10–5/11/51	61.7	6/5/2013
6/12/51–5/1/52	61.9	6/9/2013
6/2–5/3/52	61.11	6/1/2014
6/4–5/5/52	62.1	6/5/2014
6/6–5/7/52	62.3	6/9/2014
6/8–5/9/52	62.5	6/1/2015
6/10–5/11/52	62.7	6/5/2015

6/12/52–5/1/53	62.9	6/9/2015
6/2–5/3/53	62.11	6/1/2016
6/4–5/5/53	63.1	6/5/2016
6/6–5/7/53	63.3	6/9/2016
6/8–5/9/53	63.5	6/1/2017
6/10–5/11/53	63.7	6/5/2017
6/12/53–5/1/54	63.9	6/9/2017
6/2–5/3/54	63.11	6/1/2018
6/4–5/5/54	64.1	6/5/2018
6/6–5/7/54	64.3	6/9/2018
6/8–5/9/54	64.5	6/1/2019
6/10–5/11/54	64.7	6/5/2019
6/12/54–5/1/55	64.9	6/9/2019
6/2–5/3/55	64.11	6/1/2020
6/4/55	65	6/4/2020

* To save space, only every other month is illustrated.

Extra benefits

Getting the basic state pension qualifies you for some extra goodies from the government. The main one is the winter fuel payment. This has increased in value over the last few years. It is paid as a tax-free lump sum in the run-up to Christmas. Each household with a qualifying pensioner gets one payment. If there are two or more pensioners at that address they split the cash. For Christmas 2000 the payment was worth £200. The government has said that in future years it will be worth at least £150.

Those households with a pensioner aged over seventy-five also qualify for a free television licence. This is worth £104 a year for a colour set.

The government pledged late in 2000 that all state pensioners would qualify for concessionary local bus travel from June 2001. Prior to this, some local authorities already granted this concession.

Additional pensions

The basic state pension is not the only cash you might receive from the state when you retire. You may also qualify for one of a range of additional pensions. Whether you qualify and how much you get depends on if, and when, you paid into one of the state-run additional pension schemes. There are three different schemes to consider:

- The State Graduated Pension Scheme
- The State Earnings Related Pension Scheme (Serps)
- The State Second Pension

The idea behind all three schemes is to top up the basic pension with extra money linked to the amount someone has earned.

State Graduated pensions

This scheme ran from 1961 to 1975. Those in work during some or all of these years may have had the chance to pay extra National Insurance contributions to earn extra pension units. These pension units translate into a slightly higher pension today.

The maximum benefit under this scheme is worth around £7.54 a week for a man and about £6.31 a week for a woman. But for most people the benefits are far smaller. The payments increase in line with prices. From 2010, women's units will be calculated in the same way as men's.

Many employers were allowed to contract their staff out of the State Graduated Pension Scheme because they ran good company pension schemes instead. This means their workers did not participate in the State Graduated Pension Scheme. You can find out if you have any entitlement to a graduated pension addition by completing the BR19 pension forecast as discussed above.

The scheme ceased in 1975 because the government of the day decided to replace it with something far more generous – Serps.

The State Earnings Related Pension Scheme (Serps)

Pensions historians recognise Serps as a gem of a pension scheme. It included much of the workforce, offering generous benefits linked to the amount someone earned. In fact, so generous was the scheme that successive governments of all political hues have been chipping away at Serps over the past twenty years to try to keep costs under control. These changes have had the effect of reducing the value of one year's worth of Serps pension by a staggering 50 per cent.

What is Serps?

Serps was introduced in 1978. All employees automatically belong to Serps unless they or their employer contracts out. Contracting out means leaving Serps and putting your faith into a company or personal pension. The intention is that these personal or company pensions provide at least a similar level of pension to Serps. The self-employed and those who do not work are not part of Serps.

The value of a Serps pension is linked to what you earn. In broad terms, the more you earn, the bigger your Serps pension. However, there are limits to the maximum value of a Serps pension. Those who retire sooner will get better value from their Serps pensions than those who leave work thirty or forty years from now.

How much will a Serps pension be worth?

In theory, Serps can produce valuable pension benefits. The maximum possible Serps pension for someone retiring today would be worth more than £106 a week, rising in line with inflation. Very few will qualify for that. Someone on average earnings of £18,000 to £20,000, who has earned around the average for most of the last twenty years, will retire with a Serps pension worth between £60 and £75 a week. A low earner may get only £15 a week. Remember, these payments are in addition to the basic state pension.

But those retiring now, or who have just retired, have seen the best of Serps. Changes already introduced to the system will gradually erode the value of the Serps pension. It is estimated that the maximum possible pension for someone retiring in 2040 or later will be nearer £88 a week at current prices, compared with £106 today.

And the days of Serps itself are numbered. The scheme is due to 'close' to new contributions from April 2002. A new State Second

Pension will be introduced then. Benefits accumulated under Serps will not be lost; they will be preserved until you retire. But future years of work will start to earn credits under the new scheme.

How is Serps calculated?

For those who want to know the nitty-gritty, box 3.2 sets out the detail of how your Serps pension is calculated. In a very rough summary, the pension is linked to the amount of your salary on which you pay full Class 1 National Insurance contributions. This figure varies each year.

When you retire, each year's qualifying salary is averaged out. Depending on when you retire, the averaging is either based on one-quarter of the best twenty years of earnings, or one-fifth of average lifetime earnings, or a blend of the two methods.

Even the textbooks used to train financial advisers say that it is virtually impossible for an individual or their adviser accurately to calculate entitlement to Serps. Instead, you are forced to rely on the forecasts produced by the Benefits Agency when you submit a BR19 form.

Contracting out

Many employees are now contracted out of Serps. For each year that you are contracted out, you build up no entitlement to a Serps pension. Instead, you rely on either a company or a personal pension to grow into an alternative income to Serps. The government encourages individuals and companies to contract out of Serps by reducing the amount of National Insurance they have to pay and/or by making payments directly into a personal pension on your behalf.

Sometimes contracting out is automatic; that is, anyone who joins their company pension scheme is automatically contracted out. Other types of company pension scheme give the individual the option to contract out of Serps. If you have no pension through your employer, you can make the choice yourself as to whether or not to be part of Serps. Once you have left, it is also possible to rejoin at a later date and contract back in.

The decision whether to contract out, or to contract back in again can be finely balanced. It depends on your age, your current pension arrangements and on what you think the government might do in years to come. Chapter 21 discusses contracting out in more detail.

If you have switched jobs a lot, it is quite easy to lose track of whether you are contracted in or not. If you are in a company pension scheme, your company personnel department or pensions office can tell you. If you have a personal pension, the pension provider will also be able to tell you whether or not your pension is receiving contracted-out payments from the government. Alternatively, contact the Department of Work and Pensions directly.

Contracting out will continue once the new State Second Pension starts in April 2002.

Box 3.2: Getting under the skin of Serps

Have you got your maths head on? Then let's delve into the detail of how Serps works.

The pension is based around the amount of National Insurance employees pay during their working life, or since April 1978 for those who were employed before Serps started.

Each year the government sets lower and upper limits for earnings. Employees pay National Insurance on all earnings between these two limits. In tax year 2001/02, for example, the lower earnings limit is £72 a week and the upper earnings limit is £575 a week. This means the Serps pension for this year is calculated on earnings above £72 a week and below £575. Any earnings above £575 are ignored. Part-time workers who earn less than £72 a week will not gain any credit towards Serps.

When an individual arrives at retirement, each year's qualifying pay is totted up. The pay is revalued according to a pre-set formula to allow for how earnings have grown and so express that pay in today's money.

What happens next depends on when you reach state

retirement age. This is because Serps has been modified since the scheme was first started. Originally it was intended that pensions would be based around 25 per cent of revalued earnings over a person's twenty highest earning years. But in 1988 this was changed to save the government money. Instead, it was decided that Serps should build up at the lower rate of 20 per cent of revalued earnings averaged over your whole working life.

Those who were paying into Serps before April 1988 have their pension on earnings up to then worked out on the old basis. The pension based on earnings after April 1988 will be worked out on the new 20 per cent formula, unless you are due to reach state retirement age before April 2009. In this case special transitional arrangements apply. For example, someone retiring in tax year 2004/05 will get a pension based on 25 per cent of their pre-1988 earnings and 22.5 per cent of their earnings after 1988. Anyone joining Serps after April 1988 started on the new 20 per cent scale straight away.

So your Serps pension calculation depends on when you reach state pension age.

- If you retired before 6 April 1999: each year's earnings are averaged out and you get one-quarter of this as your annual Serps pension.
- If you retire between April 1999 and April 2009: earnings up to 1988 are averaged out and one-quarter of this counts towards your pension; earnings since 1988 are averaged and a transitional formula is applied. The two parts are added together to give an annual Serps pension.
- If you retire after 6 April 2009: each year's earnings up to 1988 are averaged out and one-quarter of this counts towards your pension; earnings after 1988 are averaged out and one-fifth of these count towards your pension. The two parts are averaged together to produce your annual Serps pension.
- If you retire after 6 April 2037: each year's earnings are

averaged out and you get one-fifth of this as your annual Serps pension.

But it can get more complicated still. Individuals may have been in and out of membership of Serps. They may have contracted out, or been in company pensions, or have been self-employed or unemployed. All these will affect the calculation.

Years in which you were contracted out or self-employed are simply ignored and do not count in the calculations. Likewise if you were earning National Insurance credits through sickness or unemployment benefits, or qualified for Home Responsibilities Protection, these years are also discounted. But if you are otherwise out of work, or working part-time and earning less than the lower earnings limit, you are still technically in the Serps scheme. These years will count against you because they count as zero years and will bring down your average lifetime earnings.

The State Second Pension

The latest evolution in state pensions is the planned introduction of the State Second Pension. This is scheduled to replace Serps in April 2002. If all goes to plan, introducing the State Second Pension will be a two-stage process, which should be complete by April 2007.

Why do we need something different?

Serps gives a reasonable top-up pension for middle- and higher-income earners who have an uninterrupted working life. But Serps does little for those people who earn low wages, who work part-time or who have long periods out of the workplace, either through unemployment or because they are caring for others. To try to assist these groups, the government thinks we need something different.

Longer term, the government is also worried about the costs of maintaining the existing Serps scheme. As people continue to live longer, it fears the costs of paying out state pensions at the current levels will become unsustainable. So under the State Second Pension, people on middle and higher earnings will be, to use the government's own term, 'strongly encouraged' to contract out and rely on private pension provision. If they do not contract out, in the longer term they will receive smaller pensions than they would have done under Serps.

Bringing pensions to more people

The big change produced by the State Second Pension will be to give more people an additional pension from the state. Those who gain will include:

- carers who are looking after young children or disabled people and who either do not work, or only earn a small amount through part-time working;
- those with long-term illnesses or disabilities which prevent them from working, or interrupt their working career;
- low earners: anyone earning less than £9500 a year;
- in the short term moderate earners: anyone earning between £9500 and £21,600.

Those who earn more than £21,600 will not gain from the scheme. In the short term they will continue to build up pension at the same rate as they would have under Serps. In the longer term they will be worse off, unless they contract out.

The self-employed will not participate in the State Second Pension.

How the State Second Pension will work

The pension will be introduced in two very different stages. In the first stage, starting April 2002, entitlement to State Second Pension will be linked to earnings. There will still be a link between paying National Insurance contributions and entitlement to an additional pension.

- Anyone earning at least National Insurance lower earnings limit (£3744 a year in tax year 2001/02) but less than a new *lower earnings threshold*, currently estimated at £9500 a year, will be treated as if they had earned £9500. They will build credit to a second pension at the rate of 40 per cent of the difference between the lower earnings threshold and the lower earnings limit.

- Earnings above this lower earnings threshold but below a *new higher earnings threshold*, estimated to be £21,600 a year, will build credit to a second pension at the rate of 10 per cent a year.
- Earnings above the higher earning threshold but below the National Insurance upper earnings limit (£29,900 in 2001/02) will build credit to a second state pension at the rate of 20 per cent a year. This is the same rate at which you currently gain credit towards a Serps pension.

The impact of this system is illustrated in table 3.4.

Qualifying carers and those on other benefits will also gain from this new approach. A qualifying carer will be someone who:

- receives child benefit for a child aged five or under, OR
- is entitled to Invalid Care Allowance, OR
- is given home responsibilities protection because they are caring for a sick or disabled relative.

All qualifying carers will be treated as if they have earned £9500 and be credited with the State Second Pension for each year that they qualify.

People who cannot work because of illness or disability will also gain. Those entitled to Incapacity Benefit or Severe Disablement Allowance who do not work will be credited with State Second Pension as if they had earned £9500. This credit is subject to a test at retirement: to qualify a person must have worked and paid class 1 National Insurance contributions for at least one-tenth of their working life since 1978.

Someone working part-time but not earning the National Insurance lower earnings limit will not participate in the State Second Pension unless they qualify under one of the concessions above. Nor will someone who is unemployed.

Table 3.4: How the State Second Pension will affect different earners

This shows how three people on different income levels will build up credit towards the State Second Pension when it is introduced from April 2002.

Case study 1: Claire, thirty, has two children aged five and three. Her husband works, earning £27,000 a year. Claire does not work.

Claire is credited with pension as if she earned £9500 a year. Her pension credit for this year is:

£9500 minus the lower earnings limit of £3744 = £5756

The £5756 is then multiplied by 40 per cent to give her credit of £2302.40

Under Serps, Claire would have got no credit for this year.

Note: this does not mean Claire gets a pension worth the equivalent of £2302.40 a year when she retires. Her credits for other years may be higher than this and when she retires all years are averaged out to give a final result.

Case study 2: Lee is nineteen. He is on an apprenticeship earning £7400 a year. His pension credit for this year is:

£9500 minus the lower earnings limit of £3744 = £5756.

The £5756 is then multiplied by 40 per cent to give his credit of £2302.40.

Under Serps Lee would have got a credit of £771.20.

Case study 3: Charlie is forty-two. He earns £16,000 a year. His pension credit for this year is:

£2302.40 for his first £9500 of earnings as worked out above, plus £16,000 minus £9500 = £6500 multiplied by 10 per cent = £650.

His total credit is £2952.40.

Under Serps, Charlie would have got a credit of £2451.20.

* For illustrative purposes, this table uses the tax year 2001/02 National Insurance lower and upper earning limits. Slightly higher limits will apply in 2002/03 when State Second Pension starts but these are not known yet. The State Second Pension lower and upper earnings thresholds may also differ.

WARNING

The lower and higher earnings thresholds for State Second Pension will change each year. They are expected to rise in line with average earnings. The levels have not yet been finalised for April 2002. The £9500 and £21,600 figures used above are the ones quoted in all the government planning and consultation paperwork. The actual figures could be different.

State Second Pension phase two

Some time after it is introduced, the State Second Pension will change. It is estimated this change will take place by April 2007, but this is not certain. It will drop the link with earnings and become a flat-rated scheme. This means everyone will earn the same entitlement to pension for each year they are in the scheme.

Following this change the pension will provide a credit of 40 per cent of the difference between the lower earnings threshold and the National Insurance lower earnings limit. This means that it will continue to benefit all those earning up to £9500 a year over the existing Serps scheme. Carers and the disabled will also continue to gain from the scheme.

But middle and higher earners will no longer get any recognition for their bigger incomes in the pension. They are likely to fare better by contracting out of the State Second Pension and taking their chances with private and company pensions. National Insurance rebates linked to earnings will continue to be paid to those who do contract out, which means the higher earners will have a bigger amount paid into their alternative pension. This fits with the government's long-term objective of moving people towards private pensions.

There is one exception to the flat-rate system. Anyone who is aged forty-five or more at the time phase two is introduced will stick with the phase one earnings-related scheme. This is because they are deemed to be too close to retirement to allow alternative pensions enough time to grow to a decent value.

Deferring state pension

It is possible to hold off taking your state pension when you reach state retirement age; for example, if you want to carry on working and have a job which allows this. Deferring allows you to claim a larger pension when you eventually retire.

If you choose to do this, you have to defer all state pensions – the basic pension plus any additional pensions such as graduated pension and Serps. If a wife expects a pension based on her husband's contributions then this has to be deferred too. For each year that you defer the pension, the sum due is increased by 7.5 per cent. You can defer the pension for a maximum of five years, i.e. until the age of seventy for a man and sixty-five for a woman retiring today.

From 2010 the rules around deferring are due to change. From then you will earn an extra 10.4 per cent for each year you delay taking the pension. And the five-year limit will be scrapped. You will be able to defer for as long as you like.

Is it worthwhile deferring? Box 3.3 works through two examples of what it means to defer. Even to consider deferring, you need to be certain of alternative income to tide you over the years until the state pension kicks in. Running down savings to achieve this might be risky if it leaves you short of cash. On the other hand, if the pension added to the other income – for example, from continuing work – is sufficient to push you into a higher tax band, it could be worthwhile holding back for a few years.

You also need to consider your health. You will be giving up income today in order to have a higher income in future years. Put bluntly, you need to feel confident of being around long enough for the higher income in the future to outweigh what you will be sacrificing in the short term. This suggests those who retire in poor health should take their pensions immediately.

Box 3.3: Deferring a state pension

Case study 1: Mary reaches sixty in March 2002. She is entitled to a full basic pension of £3770, plus an additional £1650 a year through Serps. This is a total pension of £5420. She has savings and her employer is allowing her to keep on working part-time.

Suppose she defers her state pension for three years. In today's money she will lose £5420 x 3 years = £16,260. In return, when she takes the pension in March 2005, she will receive a 7.5 per cent x 3 = 22.5 per cent higher pension. Her new pension, in today's money, will be £6639.50 a year. This is a gain of £1219.50 a year. Is waiting worthwhile?

If we divide £16,260 by £1219.50 we get 13.33. In other words, Mary needs to live for thirteen years and five months after she starts taking the pension to catch up on the lost income. The average life expectancy for a woman aged sixty-three is 19.65 years. There is no guarantee she will live that long. But, on balance, deferring looks a fair gamble.

Case study 2: Thomas turns sixty-five in March 2002. He too is entitled to the full basic pension of £3770, plus an extra £1650 a year through Serps. He has a company pension and his wife has a pension in her own right. He is not certain he needs the state pension now.

Suppose he defers his state pension for five years. In today's money he will lose £5420 x 5 years = £27,100. In return, when he takes the pension in March 2008, he will receive a 7.5 per cent x 5 years = 37.5 per cent higher pension. His new pension, in today's money, will be £7452.50 a year. This is a gain of £2032.50. Is waiting worthwhile?

If we divide £27,100 by £2032.50 we again get 13.33. So Thomas needs to live for thirteen years and five months after his seventieth birthday when the pension kicks in to catch up on the lost income. The average life expectancy for a man aged seventy is 11.2 years. Thomas may live far longer. But in his case, all other things being equal, he is better off taking the pension now.

The rules on deferring state pension are changing for those who reach retirement age after 2010. The state pension will build up at the higher rate of 10.4 per cent a year. How would that change the equation?

Suppose Thomas reached retirement age in January 2012 instead and wanted to defer for five years. Again, using today's money his lost income is £27,100. But his new pension is now £8238.40 a year because he has been compensated for missed years at a higher rate. This is a gain of £2818.40. It would take Thomas only nine years and six months to make up for this lost income. Assuming male life expectancy is unchanged (and if anything it is likely to improve) the average man would live longer than this, so deferring now looks a fair gamble.

Other state help

There are other ways in which the state helps pensioners. The two most important of these, the Minimum Income Guarantee and Pension Credits, are set out below.

Whereas other state pensions cover all income groups, these are aimed specifically at those who will have a low to middle income in retirement. If you are confident that when you retire you will have an income of more than £134 a week or, as a couple, a combined income of more than £200 a week, *and that that income will grow faster than earnings*, then skip these next two sections and go straight to the conclusion and summary at the end of this chapter. If not, read on.

The Minimum Income Guarantee

Minimum Income Guarantee, also know as MIG, has become increasingly important to the government as a way of targeting state help towards the poorest pensioners. It is not a benefit itself. The MIG is simply a target income below which, in theory, no pensioner is allowed to fall. The MIG goes to those who, for whatever reasons, have small state pensions, modest private or company pensions, and insufficient other income to support even a meagre standard of living. Those who qualify for MIG typically include older single female pensioners, who perhaps did not work in formal employment or only worked for short periods before starting families.

This tax year MIG is worth £92.15 a week (£4791.80 a year) for a single person and £140.55 (£7308.60) for a couple. It will rise again in April 2002 and from April 2003 it will be worth £100 a week (£5200 a year) for a single person and £154 a week (£8008 a year) for a couple.

MIG is not an automatic entitlement. To qualify for assistance, someone who has reached state retirement age must go through a means test. This is a regular analysis of a person's income and savings to see if they qualify for help.

At the moment help is only available to those pensioners or pensioner couples with savings of less than £12,000. Full assistance only goes to those with savings of less than £6000; those with savings of between £6000 and £12,000 get some income top-up, but are assumed to be able to draw an income from their savings too. Savings in this case is not just money in the bank. It includes all capital such as National Savings, shares, unit trusts etc. But it does not include any money you have tied up owning your own home.

If you qualify for help, then your income is topped up through income support benefit by whatever is needed to bring it up to the MIG level. Qualifying for MIG can also open the door to other benefits, such as grants to help install central heating and reduced-rate council tax. Many pensioners do not like the idea of the means test. They feel it is intrusive and carries a stigma. An estimated 300,000 to 400,000 people who are entitled to MIG do not claim it. There is now a dedicated MIG phoneline to assist people in claiming. This is 0800 028 1111. It operates Monday to Friday from 7 a.m. to 9 p.m.

From April 2003, the MIG rules will change slightly. The capital limits of £6000 and £12,000 will be scrapped. Instead, MIG will be assessed only on income, and the process of assessment will move from the weekly means test to a once-a-year check. The government also hopes to introduce the new check automatically for all those who newly retire, so that anyone in need will switch on to MIG straight away. These changes to MIG will coincide with another new benefit for retired people, the Pension Credit.

Pension Credits

This is a planned top-up payment, aimed at those who have made an effort to save and/or who have modest personal or company pensions. It is still a proposal. The government hopes to introduce it in 2003 but, at the time of writing, the appropriate legislation has not passed through Parliament.

Why a Pension Credit?

While the Minimum Income Guarantee helps poorer pensioners, it also creates a problem of fairness. People who have saved for retirement can end up barely any better off than people who have not saved. For example, someone with an income of £20 a week from a private pension may find themselves only a pound or two a week better off than someone who has not saved at all. This hardly acts as an incentive to save. To ensure that anyone who has put aside money for retirement is rewarded, the Pension Credit will boost the incomes of some low- to mid-income pensioners.

Who will benefit?

It is expected that anyone with a weekly income of less than £134 or any couple with a weekly income of less than £200 will gain, even if it is just by a few pence. Around 5 million pensioners will qualify. The intention is to ensure that anyone who has saved is clearly better off than anyone who has not saved.

The Pension Credit is designed to dovetail with the MIG. It ensures that firstly everyone will get their income topped up to a basic level. Secondly, it will reward savings income (including other pensions or earnings from part-time work) up to a certain level. A sliding scale will be used; initially each £1 per week of savings income will earn a credit of 60p. For bigger incomes the rate will drop. Crucially, the credit will be free of tax. Otherwise it would have the effect of giving with one hand and taking away with the other. Table 3.5 shows how the credit might work in practice.

Graph 3.1 shows how the credit fits together with the MIG and other income. As a person's income rises (going from left to right across the bottom scale) the MIG and the credit gradually add less and less to that income. Everyone has at least £100 a week and everyone who has saved gets some reward for it.

It is expected that the qualifying limits for the Pension Credit will rise in line with average earnings. This means that over time more people are likely to be scooped into the net. This is because many personal and company pensions only increase payments in line with inflation. And the state pension too is only set to rise in line with inflation.

So a person who retires in 2005 with a modest company pension and an income of, say, £160 a week will not qualify for any help from the Pension Credit to start with. But it is possible that ten years after they retire they will get some help because the qualifying limit for assistance has increased more quickly than their own income.

Graph 3.1

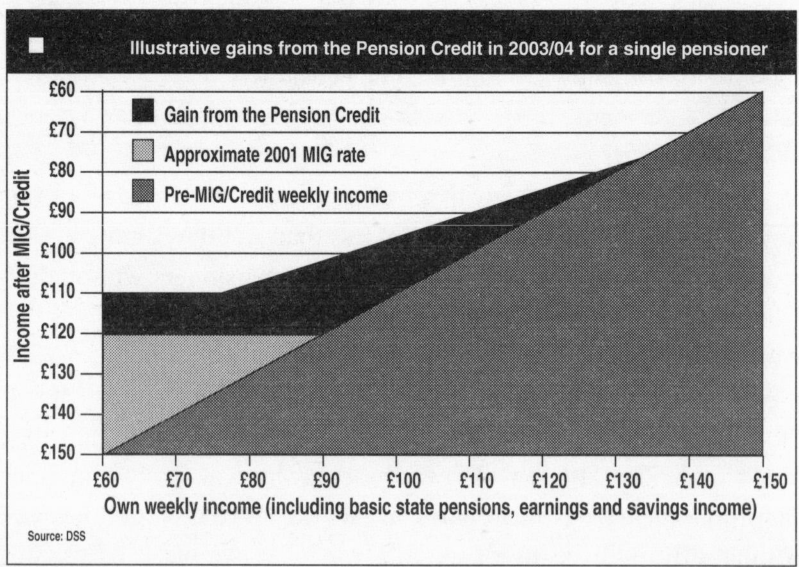

Table 3.5: How the Pension Credit might work

An illustration for tax year 2003/04 (income shown as £ per week)

Your income from savings, other pension or earnings	Your basic state pension	Your original income	Your pension credit		Your final income
			Guaranteed income top-up from MIG	Credit for saving	
0	77	77	23	-	100
10	77	87	13	6	106
20	77	97	3	12	112
30	77	107	-	11	118
40	77	117	-	7	124
50	77	127	-	3	130
60	77	137	-	-	137

Source: DWP.

WARNING

The Pension Credit is still only a proposal. Plans may change between now and 2003. The credit may be modified or scrapped altogether.

Conclusion

Congratulations on battling your way through the labyrinth of state pensions and state pension benefits. As you can tell, predicting state pensions is a little like walking on quicksand; you are never certain where the ground is firm!

What is clear is that there has been a fundamental evolution in state pensions over the past two decades. While we will all continue to get something, the value of this is uncertain and has diminished. State help is being targeted at those on the lowest incomes. But even so, it does not ensure a high standard of living, or even a comfortable one. Do you really want to be forced to get by on £5200 a year – the value of the MIG in 2003?

The basic state pension will remain for the foreseeable future. But its real value is set to keep on falling. The introduction of the State Second Pension over the next five years is likely to push the vast majority of the workforce away from relying on the state for a meaningful additional pension.

Enhanced handouts will go to the most needy. However, the message coming loud and clear from both political parties is: if you want a comfortable retirement then you are going to have to be prepared to put money aside and plan for the future.

In summary, the key messages on state pensions are:

- We will all get some form of pension from the state.
- It is not guaranteed. Rules change all the time.
- Nevertheless, the overall trend has been for state pension benefits to diminish in value.
- There is now more targeted help for those on very low incomes in retirement.
- We can all expect some basic state pension.
- Serps is being phased out and a new State Second Pension is coming in.
- Carers, the disabled and very low earners will benefit from this. The rest will be encouraged to contract out.
- The Minimum Income Guarantee and the Pension Credit will act as a safety net for the poorest.

Notes

1 Legal & General.

2 Legal & General.

PART Two
Planning Through Your Life

CHAPTER 4
Starting out

Read this chapter if:

- You are beginning work for the first time.
- You think you currently have no extra pension arrangement or retirement savings.
- You would like a general overview of the savings options.

Anyone who is in work and paying National Insurance contributions is already building entitlement to some pension from the state. Just by collecting your first pay packet you have achieved something towards retirement. However, most people in work today now realise they need to have something extra put by to enjoy a comfortable retirement. Whether you are just starting out in a job or facing up to retirement planning for the first time, there will be a moment when you decide it is time to do something extra. What should that something be? How much more should you put away? How do you go about saving more?

This section will help you deal with these questions. But first ask yourself this:

Can you afford to save extra for retirement?

This may sound a strange question. As Chapters 1 and 2 explained, you will be mainly reliant on your own savings in years to come. The earlier you start, the bigger your pot is likely to be at retirement. So surely the issue is: 'Can you afford not to save for retirement?' In the ideal world, this would be the case. We would all start squirrelling money away from our first day at work. But it is not a perfect world. There are always other calls on our cash.

This is especially true for those just starting their working life. If you have been a student, the chances are you will have taken out loans to help fund your studies. There could be a hefty bank overdraft and groaning credit card bills. Repayment of some of this debt is an obvious priority. Do you have to banish all debt? Certainly not. Many people run a regular bank overdraft and carry some debt on their credit card, while at the same time making contributions to pensions or other forms of long-term saving. But huge debts have to be cleared at some point and realistically the sooner the better.

You may also have short-term expenses which need meeting. For example, you may need new clothes for starting work or perhaps have to buy a second-hand car so that you can get to the new job. These are obvious priorities. And you may have medium-term goals such as saving for the deposit on a house or flat.

There is also the matter of an emergency fund. Financial planners recommend that you keep a savings account with ready-access cash for emergencies. These can range from suddenly losing your job to the heating system at home packing up. Emergencies do not include topping up the beer money or an extra week in the sun if you feel like it! A fund equivalent to three months' salary is the ideal, though few achieve it. Realistically, if you can keep at least half that and not dip into it you will have breathing space should the worst happen.

There are also issues of affordability for those more established in work. With a young family, there are always pressures on your budget. And once the basics of home and food and clothing are taken care of, you will face tough choices. What is more important: saving for retirement, buying adequate life and ill health insurance to protect your family, or keeping yourselves sane by having a week's holiday?

Inevitably, managing your budget will involve compromise. You may have to decide to put off retirement saving for a year or two. You may have to start very modestly – saving extra through a pension can cost as little as £10 a month. But the key issue is to be aware that you have made the compromise. Do not push retirement to the back of your mind and forget about saving; instead, hold it in your mind as an issue to return to once extra cash becomes available; for example, after a pay rise or when a loan repayment is complete.

Starting out: the choices

The state pension is the first part of your retirement pot. There are three main ways to build on it:

- saving through a company pension;
- saving through a personal pension;
- saving using other methods.

Company pensions

Company pensions, also called occupational pensions, are those available through your employment. They can be organised by individual companies, by related groups such as an industry – the printing industry runs a pension scheme, for example – or by public-sector employers such as the NHS or local authorities.

Company pensions share one basic concept. They aim to provide you with the option of a lump sum when you retire, paid free of tax, plus a regular and secure annual income in retirement.

It is very likely that your employer will have some pension arrangements in place. In many companies all staff have the option of joining an occupational pension scheme. New starters may have to wait six months or a year before joining. At the very least your employer will probably offer you access to a simple pension called stakeholder.

Company pensions can take several forms. They may be:

- *A final salary pension* – here the employer runs a pension fund designed to give you an income in retirement based on your pay in the final year or years of employment. The size of the pension is set, but the amount of money the employer (and possibly employees) pays in to achieve this may vary. This kind of pension is also known as a defined benefit scheme.
- *A money-purchase pension* – here the company (and possibly the employee) pays money which is invested in a pension fund. The fund hopefully grows in value over your years at work. The final pension depends on how well the fund grows. The size of the contribution is set but the value of the pension can vary. This is also known as a defined contribution pension.
- A *group personal pension* – this is a special form of personal pension tailored to all the people who work for a particular company. It works like a money-purchase scheme in that set contributions are invested each month with the value of the final pension dependent on how stock markets grow.
- A *stakeholder pension* – this is a new form of pension introduced from April 2001. All companies with more than five employees who do not run another kind of company pension which every staff member can join will have to give employees access to a stakeholder pension. It too is a kind of money-purchase scheme, with defined contributions invested to grow over time.

Chapter 19 explains these different pensions in much more detail. Stakeholder pensions are covered in Chapter 20. There are additional pension choices open to those who run their own businesses. Chapter 18 talks through these.

Staff handbooks and contracts of employment will usually tell you about what pension, if any, is offered through your job. If you are unsure, ask your personnel or human resources department, or speak directly to your manager or supervisor. Pay slips may also give you a clue, as they may show a deduction marked 'pension contributions'. You may be pleasantly surprised to find you already are in a company pension. Some employers automatically sign up new joiners unless the employee specifically opts out.

You cannot be forced to join a company pension scheme, but it is usually a good option. This is because:

- Employers frequently pay money into the pension too. This may be paid regardless of whether you pay in or to match contributions you make.
- The costs of running the pension are paid or at least subsidised by the employer. This can make the pension better value than other alternatives.
- There can be valuable extra benefits attached to the pension, such as money if you die or fall ill before retirement, and pensions for family members such as spouse and children.

There may be some circumstances when joining is not a good idea. For example, some pensions require you to stay working with the company for a minimum period, often two years, before giving any benefit to you. If you leave before then, contributions by the employer are lost and any money you have paid in is returned. So if you know you are only going to be working for such a company for a short period, it may be better to make alternative pension arrangements.

Who pays what?

When it comes to pensions, employers can be hugely generous, very mean, or somewhere in between. They may make big contributions towards the cost of a pension and other benefits which can be worth the equivalent of 15 or 20 per cent of the value of your salary. At the other extreme, they may pay nothing towards a pension. Generally, the bigger the employer and the longer the company or organisation has been established, the more generous the pension arrangements will be. Some newer firms, for example in the IT sector or in consulting, have deliberately decided not to set up pensions because they expect staff to move frequently. Instead, they pay higher salaries and let staff make their own pension arrangements. In many cases the employer will sit somewhere in the middle. It will pay something to a pension but leave the door open for the employee to pay more.

If you are in a final salary scheme or in an employer's money-purchase scheme, extra payments can be made through a facility called additional voluntary contributions or AVCs. These are voluntary top-up payments into the pension, made by the employee. They are typically deducted direct from your weekly or monthly pay. Chapter 19 explains more about AVCs and the related option of free-standing AVCs.

In other cases companies will invite you to make extra payments into a group personal pension or stakeholder pension, perhaps offering to match what you pay.

In cases where the employer offers to match payments that you make, not accepting the offer is tantamount to taking a voluntary pay cut. By choosing not to sacrifice some of your salary and put it into a pension you are also choosing to be paid less overall.

Box 4.1 gives three examples of the ways in which employees can boost a pension arranged through work.

There are limits to how much you can pay into a pension. This is because payments into a pension are free of income tax and the Inland Revenue wants to cap the value of this perk. However, very few people, especially in the early years of saving, come anywhere near their limits. For final salary and some money-purchase pensions, the limit is set at a flat 15 per cent of your taxable pay in any one year. This limit is *in addition* to what the employer puts into the scheme. But it includes any payments that you make into an AVC or FSAVC scheme.

For group personal pensions and stakeholder pensions, there are two ways of working out the limit. You can pay in either:

- up to £3600 gross of tax per year, or
- if higher, up to a proportion of your salary per tax year. The proportion varies with age, with older savers able to pay in more. Table 4.1 sets out the limits.

In the case of group personal pensions or stakeholder pensions, contributions by your employer count towards the annual limit.

Box 4.1: Examples of how to boost the value of a company pension

Case study 1: Peter, forty-two, works for a company offering a final salary pension scheme. As a condition of being a member of this scheme, Peter pays in 5 per cent of salary. The company more than matches this.

Peter is keen to increase the value of his pension. He decides to pay into the company's additional voluntary contribution scheme (AVC). This scheme allows him to 'buy' additional years of service, the length of time his final pension is calculated on. He decides he can afford to pay a further 5 per cent of salary. Provided he keeps paying at this rate until retirement at sixty, he will be credited with six extra years of service, increasing the value of his annual pension by six-sixtieths or one-tenth of his final salary.

Case study 2: Cathy, twenty-eight, also works for a company offering a final salary pension scheme. She too has to pay 5 per cent of her salary as a condition of membership. Again, this is more than matched by her employer.

Cathy wants to enhance her pension. She decides to pay into the company's AVC scheme. Here, her contributions are invested in a separate fund. This operates as a money-purchase fund. How Cathy's contributions grow will depend on how the stock market fares. However, when Cathy retires, the pension that this fund produces will be added to her main pension and paid as one. Cathy decides she can afford to contribute a further 3 per cent of salary and hopes for good growth.

For employees who earn less than £30,000 a year, starting a stakeholder pension is now an alternative to saving via an AVC.

Case study 3: Colin, twenty-four, works for an employer offering a group personal pension scheme. The company will match his contributions up to a maximum of 5 per cent of salary. Colin earns £18,000 a year.

Colin has come into some money this year and feels able to save hard for his pension. He accepts his company's offer and they each pay in 5 per cent of salary, a total of £1800 gross of tax. Colin then wants to put in more. Under Inland Revenue rules the maximum contribution in any one tax year for someone of his age is 17.5 per cent of salary or £3600, whichever is higher – 17.5 per cent of £18,000 is £3150, so the higher limit is £3600. Colin can pay in a further £1800. Total payments into the pension are £3600; £900 from his employer and £2700 from Colin. The actual cost to Colin is £2106 of after-tax income.

If Colin instead earned £28,000, 17.5 per cent of salary would be £4900. So the maximum that could be paid into his pension would be £4900 – £1400 from the employer and £3500 (£2,730 after tax) from Colin.

Contracting out

You will also need to check with your employer whether or not a company pension scheme has contracted out from Serps (or from the State Second Pension after April 2002).

Contracting out means giving up your rights to additional state pension in exchange for National Insurance rebates from the government, which can be invested on your behalf. There is a good chance that investing this money will give you a bigger pension than you would get from Serps or the State Second Pension. Certainly once the cash is invested in your name, it will be very difficult for future politicians to take it away, whereas entitlement to state pensions has already been removed several times by a simple vote.

But contracting out is not guaranteed to be a winner. You will move from a government-backed pension to one either supported by your employer or dependent upon the whims of the stock market. In some cases the decision on contracting out has already been made for you. Many final salary pensions are automatically contracted out and you cannot change the arrangement. Money-purchase pensions may also be automatically contracted out, but some employers leave the decision up to individuals.

In the future, as the State Second Pension takes hold, it is increasingly likely that the majority of middle to higher earners will be better off contracting out. Chapter 21 explains contracting out in more detail.

A quick word about stakeholder pensions

Stakeholder is the bare minimum of workplace pensions. This does not mean it is necessarily a poor relation to other schemes, just that it is the cheapest option for an employer to offer. Stakeholder is new. The pension only started in April 2001. By law, all companies employing five or more staff had to make a stakeholder available to all employees by October 2001, unless they already had a superior pension scheme in place. The introduction of stakeholder means that the majority of employees should have access to a pension in their workplace. Technically, stakeholder is not an occupational pension but a personal pension offered through the workplace.

Stakeholder is a simple money-purchase pension. It will usually be run by a pension company chosen, or in pension language designated, by your employer. Employers do not have to pay anything into stakeholder, though they can choose to. Employees are free to join their firm's designated stakeholder pension. Or they can join another one. Or they can ignore stakeholder altogether. Employers have to offer the facility to deduct contributions for their designated stakeholder pension direct from your salary and they must pass them on promptly. Qualifying employers who did not offer you a stakeholder option by October 2001 are breaking the law.

The costs of running stakeholder pensions are capped by law and they have to allow employees flexibility. You can pay in, stop paying or transfer your money to another pension without penalty. Chapter 20 explains stakeholder pensions in more detail.

What happens when you retire?

How you retire and what happens when you retire depends on what type of company pension you belong to. Those in a group personal pension or in a company stakeholder pension are governed by the rules on personal pensions (see page 74 below).

Those in a final salary or company-run money-purchase scheme will do things differently. The pension scheme is likely to have a target retirement age, also known as the official pensions age. It may be sixty, sixty-two or most typically sixty-five. In the past men and women could have different retirement ages, but equality laws now mean that schemes set a common age for both sexes. Some employers are more flexible, allowing men and women to retire on penalty-free terms at any age between sixty and sixty-five.

In some circumstances it may be possible to stay a member of the pension scheme beyond the official retirement age and continue working. In this case your pension is deferred.

Retiring earlier may be an option, but it is not guaranteed. It will depend on how well-funded an employer's pension is at the time and on conditions in the labour market. If new recruits are scarce, companies will be less willing to let older workers go earlier. Early retirement through ill health is almost always possible.

When you retire from a final salary scheme, your employer will pay you an annual pension from its fund. This pension will be linked to your pay over the last year or years of your employment and based on the number of years you have worked for the company. There is also usually the option of taking a lump sum on retirement and a smaller annual pension.

In a money-purchase scheme the pension will depend on how well the stock market has performed. Part of the pension fund will be earmarked with your name and, typically, the employer will buy an annuity, an annual income for life, with your portion of the fund. Again, there is usually the option to take a lump sum on retirement and a smaller annual pension.

Rules recently introduced make it possible for members of certain company pension schemes to transfer out of the scheme shortly before retirement. This can give them more flexibility on how they provide an income during retirement and particularly can improve the amount of pension left for spouses, should they die early in retirement.

All the options are discussed in more detail in Chapter 9.

Personal pensions

If you are self-employed, or work for a small company not covered by the stakeholder rules, or do not want to join a company pension, or do not work at all, you have to look elsewhere for your pension options. This means picking an alternative pension from the hundreds of different schemes on offer. There are three types of personal pension available to you:

- Individual stakeholder pension
- Traditional personal pension
- Self-invested personal pension

Individual stakeholder pensions will increasingly become the first-choice personal pension for many savers. The individual stakeholder is a close cousin of the company stakeholder pension being promoted through employers. Stakeholder pensions are sold by banks, pension companies and investment houses. You can go direct to the providers, or get started in stakeholder through an independent financial adviser.

The aim of stakeholder is to be simple and flexible. It is a pension that you can take from job to job. You can stop or vary payments without penalty. And you can swap to a different pension company, again without penalty. Charges for a stakeholder pension are capped at a maximum of 1 per cent per year of the value of your pension fund. They can be less. There may also be an extra one-off charge, levied to pay for advice in setting up the stakeholder pension. Money you pay into a stakeholder pension is invested in a fund on your behalf. You can pick from a range of different funds, or go with the pension company's default option. For the majority of savers, a stakeholder pension should do a reasonable job of providing a fund, which can then be converted into a pension on retirement.

Some savers might prefer to stick with traditional personal pensions. These were the main option before stakeholder was introduced in April 2001. Traditional personal pensions can be more complicated than stakeholder. They may have a wider choice of savings options, with investment funds that are not available to those saving through stakeholder. They may also have more comprehensive insurance benefits built in.

But traditional personal pensions may also be more expensive than stakeholder. They are not governed by the same rules as stakeholder pensions, which regulate charges. Looking ahead, if stakeholder pensions take off as expected, the number of traditional personal pension plans being marketed to new customers will probably diminish.

The third option for personal pension investors is the self-invested personal pension (SIPP). This will appeal to those who want to take direct charge of their savings. Rather than letting a pension company decide how your money is invested, a SIPP lets the saver make these decisions themselves. They can pick and choose individual shares, buy bonds or even invest the money in properties.

In the right hands, a SIPP is a very powerful pension option. But the costs of operating this type of DIY pension are relatively high, so you need to be able to afford to pay in on average between £5000 and £10,000 a year to make a SIPP economic. It is likely to appeal to higher earners and to the self-employed running a successful small business.

You can choose to pay into more than one type of personal pension, or hedge your bets by having similar schemes with two different pension companies. Chapter 20 gives more detail on each type of personal pension.

Payments into a personal pension are again governed by Inland Revenue limits. These limits are the higher of £3600 a year or a percentage of your relevant earnings. Relevant earnings are income from employment, including perks on which you can be taxed, but not income from investments such as bank interest or share dividends. The percentage limits vary with age, as set out in table 4.1. It is important to note that the limits are gross, that is, income before tax. Tax is refunded on personal pension contributions, so the actual sum you pay in will be less. For example, a basic-rate taxpayer who is capped by the £3600 a year limit will be able to pay a maximum of £2808 a year into their pension. The other £792 is paid by the government directly to the pension company.

Your employer may also be willing to make payments into a personal pension on your behalf. This is permitted, as long as total payments by both employee and employer do not exceed the Inland Revenue limits.

Table 4.1: Maximum permitted contributions into a personal pension

Age on 6 April of tax year	per cent of relevant earnings *	
	Stakeholder, traditional personal pension, GPP	Retirement annuity plans
35 or less	17.5	17.5
36 to 45	20	17.5
46 to 50	25	17.5
51 to 55	30	20
56 to 60	35	22.5
61 to 74	40	27.5

* Or £3600 per year from any income if greater. Relevant earnings are capped at £95,400. No cap applies on retirement annuity plans.

Personal pension contracting out

Those without a company pension will also have to consider their options on contracting out of Serps and the State Second Pension. If you choose to contract out, National Insurance rebates are paid by the state directly into an appropriate personal pension of your choice. This can be the same personal pension or stakeholder pension you use for your main saving or a separate scheme. You cannot have the rebate paid to you directly. Again, see Chapter 21 for detailed information on contracting out.

What happens when you retire?

Personal pensions generally offer more flexibility than company pensions on when you retire. At the moment, benefits can be drawn from a personal pension at any age between fifty and seventy-five. Some government bodies have suggested raising the younger age to fifty-five, though nothing is yet decided on this. If the change were made, it would probably be phased in over several years. Those in a few selected occupations, mainly professional sportsmen and women, can retire earlier.

You do not have to formally retire to take an income from a personal pension; for example, you could draw some income while still working part-time. There are a number of ways in which you can take a gradual income from the pension or phase retirement over several years.

On current rules, you have to use the majority of your pension fund to purchase an annuity, a guaranteed income for life, before your seventy-fifth birthday. This requirement has become increasingly controversial as annuity rates have plunged over the past decade. This has reduced the value of a pension that a fund of a specific size can provide. It is highly likely that the annuity rules will be changed within the next few years. Chapter 22 explains fully the options for converting your pension into an income.

To pension or not to pension?

Pensions are not the only way to save for retirement. There are plenty of other choices, ranging from stuffing money under the mattress through to investing in rental properties. Other savings choices include:

- Deposit accounts
- National Savings
- Individual Savings Accounts (Isas)
- Collective investments, including unit trusts and investment trusts
- Investment bonds
- Directly held shares

- Employee share schemes and save as you earn plans
- Property

Chapter 11 explains these alternatives to pensions more fully.

As was discussed in Chapter 2, pensions have some advantages for savers. They are tax-favoured: money you, or your employer, pay in is topped up by the government so that your contribution is free of tax at your highest rate. This is a valuable concession, especially for top-rate taxpayers.

Pensions also force discipline on savers. Once money is paid in, you cannot get at it until retirement, which could be thirty or more years away. By their nature they are long-term investments, which allows pension funds to capitalise on the longer-term growth potential of equities.

But there are disadvantages with pensions. They lack flexibility. It can sometimes be difficult to move a pension from job to job, whereas other savings are not linked to your employment. The requirement to buy an annuity is now seen by many as a dangerous flaw. This can lock pensioners into a lower income than their money could achieve elsewhere, albeit one that is guaranteed. And once you have retired, it is difficult to pass on money locked up in a pension or annuity to a spouse, children or grandchildren.

Other types of saving give you much more control. Some, such as Isas, also have tax advantages. In practice, most households save for retirement using a variety of means. Pensions are part of the equation, perhaps the biggest single part, but alongside other types of savings. It is wise to be aware of the other types of saving and to work to build a balanced portfolio of retirement funds. How you want to balance it will depend on your attitudes to risk, on your company and personal pension options, on your family situation and on how active a role you want to play in managing your finances.

How much should I save?

This is the crunch question. Unfortunately, there is no single answer. If you want the kind of retirement where you can expect to jet off round the world on a regular basis, you will have to be prepared to save hard for it. Allowing for the potential increases in earnings and prices over your working lifetime, you will need to build up a retirement kitty that sounds frighteningly huge in today's money. Box 4.2 gives an example of how much one young worker might need to save.

As a rule of thumb, pensions experts predict that someone saving around 15 per cent a year of their gross salary through a pension or similar tax-favoured investments from the day they start work until the day they retire might expect a pension worth roughly two-thirds of their final salary in retirement. This prediction depends on reasonable, but not excessive stock market growth and someone whose pay rises steadily throughout their career, rather than doubles in their final year of employment.

It is possible to pay less in the earlier years and then pay more in the later years to catch up. But the longer you leave it before increasing the rate of savings, the greater the increase that will be needed. If you have done no extra saving for ten or twenty years of your working life, then you would need to start saving at a much higher rate than 15 per cent of salary to reach the two-thirds target. Conversely, someone with a generous company pension scheme where the employer is paying in big contributions might only need to pop away an extra 2 or 3 per cent of their salary to hit the same target.

Box 4.2: How much do you need to save for retirement?

Mary is twenty-five. She is a newly qualified insurance underwriter, earning £24,000 a year. Mary hopes one day to get promoted to become a senior underwriter, commanding in today's money a salary of around £50,000. She is resigned to retiring at sixty-five and hopes for a pension worth two-thirds of final salary or £33,333 in today's money. No pension is provided with her job. What sort of level of saving will put Mary on track to retire in forty years' time with a pension that will be in line with her expectations?

Mary expects to get the basic state pension, currently worth £3770 a year. This will increase in line with inflation, but not earnings. This will leave Mary with a gap, *expressed in today's money*, of roughly £29,500 between her state pension and the income she thinks she will need.

If Mary starts saving £237 a month net of tax (£304 gross), and increases her pension contributions by 7 per cent each year to allow for inflation and her increasing earning power, she is forecast to have a fund worth £1.68 million when she retires. That fund, using today's annuity rates, would give Mary an annual income of £29,563.* Her initial pension contribution costs 15.2 per cent of her gross salary.

Will Mary really have the standard of living she requires when she retires? What could go wrong?

Firstly, the state pension rises in line with inflation, not earnings. If inflation is less than earnings growth, there may be a shortfall between what the state provides and what Mary has saved privately.

Secondly, stock markets may grow faster or slower than the 7 per cent a year average rate assumed in this example. Faster growth means a bigger pension fund. Slower growth means a smaller fund.

Thirdly, annuity rates may be higher or lower than today when Mary retires. This means the annual pension she can buy with her fund may be higher or lower than projected.

Fourthly, and most importantly, earnings will probably grow dramatically over the forty years to retirement. This means Mary might retire on an annual salary worth in today's money £100,000 or £125,000, not the £50,000 used. Mary will be used to this higher standard of living. This means her fund is short of the two-thirds income target. She would need to plug the gap with extra saving before retirement.

All these uncertainties emphasise the importance of reviewing your saving plans regularly.

* All figures sourced from Legal & General on-line pensions calculator. Try for yourself at www.landg.com.

Do not forget the dangers of viewing pensions in isolation. Take the example of two friends, Jenny and Geoff. They both work in the same job and earn the same salary. There is no company pension. Jenny pays nothing into a personal pension, but spends £500 a month on a mortgage to buy her own home. Geoff pays £100 a month into a personal pension and £400 a month on rent. Geoff may have the pension, but Jenny will one day own her house and that will be a valuable retirement benefit in its own right.

Obviously the more you save, the bigger the kitty you are building for retirement. And as we have already seen, the earlier you start, the easier this process is. Table 2.2 on page 23 shows the potential costs of delaying saving.

Ultimately, it is up to you to take control of your own circumstances. Retirement planning is all about balancing today's needs and desires with future needs and desires. It genuinely might come down to sacrificing a week's holiday this year so that you might have enough income in retirement to allow you to go on holiday then. We each have to decide if that sacrifice is worthwhile.

Some final thoughts

This section has been an introduction to savings and pension strategies. If you are just starting out or thinking seriously about retirement planning for the first time, do not worry if your own position is very different from the model set out here. You are probably not going to be able to accelerate from nothing to the ideal savings position in one go. You need to advance in steps.

Try to follow a routine. Get into the habit of reviewing your saving regularly, perhaps when you receive pay increases. Often the most painless way to boost your savings is to earmark a portion of any pay rise. That way you do not get used to having the extra money coming through your monthly budgets and then have to adapt to losing it when you increase your saving.

In summary:

- Be realistic about how much you can afford to save.
- Check whether or not you have the option of a pension with your job.
- If so, make the effort to understand what it might be worth to you.
- If not, consider the personal pension alternatives.
- Do not overlook other ways to save.
- Think about what the ideal amount of saving might be.
- Be prepared to work towards it step by step.

CHAPTER 5 Changing times: new jobs and new employers

Read this chapter if:

- You are changing job.
- You are thinking of changing job.
- You have recently changed job and want to know what to do about your pension from a previous employer.
- You have been made redundant or redundancy is looming.
- Your company is being taken over.

Switching to a new job can be one of the most exhilarating and one of the most terrifying moments in our working careers. There is the excitement of a new location, new colleagues, new challenges and hopefully a better-paid job. There can also be the fear of the unknown, especially if the job change has been forced upon you by circumstances beyond your control.

In all the excitement, pensions and retirement planning can easily be overlooked. Sometimes this is not a problem. But sometimes it can be a costly mistake. Indeed, it is possible for someone to switch jobs thinking they are getting a better deal and end up effectively worse off than before. The difference in pension provision can more than overshadow a 5 or even 10 per cent rise in basic pay.

Know what you are worth

Company pensions are one of those perks of a job which people often take for granted. It is a frightening truth that many middle managers switching jobs are far more concerned about the accessories on their new company car than about what pension benefits the new role may or may not have.

Ideally, before you even think about switching job, it makes sense to have a clear view of what you are being paid now. This sounds obvious, but a staggering number of employees have no idea what their salary and benefits package is actually worth. Valuing a pension is not always easy. In general, money-purchase schemes, where you know what an employer is paying in, are easiest to value. All other things being equal, a scheme to which the employer contributes 10 per cent of your salary is worth more than one to which it contributes 5 per cent of salary. But valuing a final salary pension, where the employer may be paying in variable contributions, is harder. Yet final salary schemes often deliver the biggest pensions.

One way to try to value the final salary scheme is to project forward to retirement and work out how much your pension might be worth. You can then count back and look at what it would cost to provide this income privately, and so what a new employer would have to do to make sure you are not worse off. The process involves making assumptions about how your earnings will grow and what will happen to inflation. But it is better than nothing. Box 5.1 shows an example of this process.

Box 5.1: Calculating the value of a final salary pension scheme

Jeannette is forty-two. She earns £32,000 a year as a jewellery buyer for a high-street store. She has worked at the same company for ten years. Jeannette is thinking of changing jobs and wants a rough idea of what her company pension is worth to make sure she does not end up worse off.

Her final salary company pension is a one-sixtieth scheme. That means that her pension grows by one-sixtieth of salary for each year of service. She has to pay 5 per cent of salary as her share of the pension contribution. The company's official retirement age is sixty-two.

Assuming Jeannette stays with her employer until retirement, and that her salary increases by an average of 5 per cent a year, we can calculate her final pension as follows: when she retires, her final salary will be today's salary multiplied by an allowance for her earnings growth. Figures for this allowance are listed in the earnings growth calculator (Appendix 1a, page 405). In Jeannette's case, the figure for 5 per cent a year over twenty years is 2.653. So her final salary might be £32,000 x 2.653 = £84,896.

At sixty-two she will have thirty years of pensionable service. At one-sixtieth per year that produces a pension of thirty-sixtieths or one-half of final salary. So her pension is estimated at £42,448 a year.

So how much would it cost to produce a comparable income in other ways?

To start with, even if Jeannette were to quit her job now, she has still banked ten years of service with her current employer. This will produce a pension based on one-sixtieth times ten years (one-sixth) of her current salary, uprated for inflation until she retires. That is £5333 a year, uprated for inflation at 3 per cent a year until she retires, which equals £9631 a year. So she needs to fund the gap between £9631 and £42,448 a year – that is a pension of £32,817 a year.

For a woman aged sixty-two to buy an index-linked annuity income of £32,817 at today's rates, she would need a fund of around £549,000. And to build that fund over twenty years through a personal pension would cost £853 a month if she started contributing today and the fund grew at 9 per cent a year.*

The monthly contribution looks huge today. But we have forecast that Jeannette's earnings will rise at 5 per cent a year, so it becomes a smaller portion of salary over time. In practice, she would start saving at a lower rate and then ramp up over the years. The calculation may seem quite drawn-out, but it shows how valuable Jeannette's pension fund is. More importantly, it shows the kind of pay increase or company pension contribution from a new employer that Jeannette would need to ensure that her new job does not leave her worse off.

*Source: Hargreaves Lansdown.

On top of the retirement pension, membership of a company pension might confer other useful benefits. These include life insurance, an ill health pension and widows' or widowers' pensions. Again, the best way to value these is to find out the cost if you had to buy these extra benefits yourself.

For example, take the case of a man aged thirty earning £30,000 whose workplace pension entitled his next of kin to four times salary if he died. It would cost between £15 and £25 a month out of after-tax income for that person to buy life cover of £120,000 until the age of sixty. The price varies depending on his state of health, his occupation and whether he smokes.

Valuing a pension and benefits package is not an exact science. However, even a ballpark figure will equip you with better information when you go out to hunt for another job. And if someone approaches you and offers a new position, you are immediately in a stronger situation to negotiate a better package. Table 5.1 suggests key questions to ask a potential new employer.

Table 5.1: Key questions to ask a prospective employer

- Do you run an occupational pension scheme?
- If so, what kind of scheme is it?
- How much does the employer pay into the pension?
- And how much, if anything, is the employee expected to pay?
- What exactly is the pension based on? Basic salary, or are extras like overtime and bonuses included?
- Are there additional benefits attached to membership of the company pension?
- Can it accept transfers in from my existing pension?
- If so, how will a transfer be calculated?
- If there is no company pension, would the employer be prepared to pay anything towards a stakeholder or personal pension in my name?

Making the move

Once you have accepted a new job and made the move, there are still important decisions to be made. Broadly, these fall into two categories:

- What to do about retirement saving going forward in your new employment.
- What to do about past saving and pensions attached to your previous employment.

Saving going forward means deciding what method or methods you will use to build up a pension in your new employment. It can include joining your new employer's pension, starting a new personal pension or stakeholder pension, or continuing with an existing personal pension. What you do about previous saving will partly depend on whether your employer offers a company pension and how you were saving previously. For example, it may be possible to keep a previous personal pension going or you may want to transfer out of your original company pension into your new employer's company pension. Table 5.2 sets out the possible options. These are explained in more detail below.

Saving going forward

Once you have started building up a retirement kitty, it is vital to keep the momentum going. This is particularly important if you move from a job which had a good company pension scheme to one with no employer pension. It will then be up to you to make alternative private pension arrangements, or risk slipping off course in your retirement plans. Even waiting a year or two before starting an alternative pension could delay your eventual retirement date or knock as much as 10 per cent off your income in retirement.

As was outlined in Chapter 4, there are three possible ways of saving for retirement: the company pension, the personal pension (including stakeholder) and alternative methods such as Isas.

Where your new employer offers a company pension scheme, it is likely to be sound advice to join it. The employer may well make contributions into the scheme or at least subsidise the running costs of the pension. As mentioned earlier, there may also be other benefits, such as life or health insurance.

Until April 2001 you were not allowed to have both a company pension and a personal pension running on the same income. So those who had saved using a personal pension had to stop this if they joined a company scheme. Only if they had a second job or freelance earnings could they carry on paying into the personal pension. However, the introduction of stakeholder pensions has changed all this. Provided you earn less than £30,000 a year, you can continue to pay up to £3600 a year into a stakeholder or personal pension, regardless of how much is being paid into your company scheme. This means that you can keep a stakeholder or personal pension running through various jobs, if you choose.

Those who earn more than £30,000 or who are controlling directors of a company do not benefit from this concession. They cannot have a stakeholder pension or personal pension running alongside their company pension, unless they have a second job or freelance income.

If your new employer has no company pension, the choice is between paying into a personal pension, paying into a stakeholder pension or saving elsewhere. Chapter 20 explains these personal pensions in detail.

Where your new employer has five or more staff and no alternative pension arrangements, it will have to offer you access to its chosen or designated stakeholder pension. This makes it easy for you to continue saving, with pension contributions deducted direct from salary. But there is no obligation for the employer to pay anything into this pension and there is no obligation on you to join. You can continue paying into an existing stakeholder pension or personal pension, for example.

Don't forget the top-up

Hopefully, your new job will mean a pay rise. When you are planning how to spend this new-found wealth do not forget about retirement saving. If, for example, you are aiming to stash away 10 per cent of income in your pension, you will want to ensure this continues under the new salary and new savings arrangements.

If you do not top up your savings, you risk the value of your pension falling behind your salary. Take the example of Mark. He earns £24,000 a year in his job as a printer. There is no company pension, but he wants to save 5 per cent per year of his salary towards retirement. So he pays £100 a month into a stakeholder pension. Mark then is offered a new, more senior role at another printing firm. In this job, too, there is no company pension. Mark's salary is boosted to £30,000 a year. He needs to increase his pension contributions to £125 a month to maintain his saving at the same rate. If he does not, then the pension fund he builds up in retirement will not be sufficient to support the higher standard of living he has got used to on his new salary.

Options for your historic pension

It is important not to forget about any pension connected with your previous employment. You need to consider two issues:

- Can you continue saving using this pension?
- If not, what should you do with it?

Most of those who were using a stakeholder pension, a personal pension or who participated in a group personal pension will at least have the option of continuing to pay into this, despite the change of job. Whether you will want to continue paying is another matter.

If there is no company pension in the new employment, then keeping going with the existing scheme may well be the best option. As mentioned above, you might want to review the contribution levels, to ensure you are still saving the appropriate amounts. You might also investigate whether a newer form of personal pension or a stakeholder pension offers lower charges and better value.

Generally, though, provided you have sufficient income, you can carry on paying into the pensions as before. While any contributions made by your old employer will cease, the new employer may wade in with payments of its own.

There may also be minor changes in the way in which your pension is collected; for example, if you had chosen to be in a previous employer's designated stakeholder pension, contributions would have been collected direct through payroll. Your new employer may not be willing to deduct payments for this pension direct from salary, so you would need to arrange separate direct debits from your bank account. This will not affect how much goes in, simply where the money is paid from.

If there is a new company pension scheme, however, you will need to think hard about whether it is worthwhile carrying on paying into an existing personal pension or stakeholder.

If voluntary payments you make into the company pension scheme are matched by extra money from the employer, you would be wise to channel scarce cash into a company pension rather than continuing payments into a personal pension or stakeholder. If you can afford to do both, great.

The equation becomes more complicated if voluntary extra payments by the employee into a company pension are not matched by the employer. Extra payments by the employee, called additional voluntary contributions or AVCs, may attract lower charges and so grow faster in an employer's pension than in a personal pension. But there is less flexibility in when you can retire and how you can take your money in a company AVC than in a personal pension. Chapter 19 explains AVCs in more detail.

However, in many cases continuing saving with an existing pension will not be an option. This applies to those who were previously in a company pension, employees who earn more than £30,000 and have joined a company pension or those who were saving into a rebate-only contracted-out personal pension and have now joined a contracted-out company pension. Here, the two most common options are to leave the money from the historic pension where it is, or to move it to a new pension. A move is called a transfer. Transfers come in a variety of shapes and sizes, and need some explaining. But depending upon the previous pension scheme, your age and how long you have been in the pension, other options may be available or even forced on you.

Preserved or deferred pensions

If you leave your money (or accumulated pension rights) in the previous pension, you become what is known as a deferred pensioner. Other common terms are preserved pension, frozen pension or paid-up pension. All mean the same thing: your rights to a pension are not lost. You will still be entitled to a pension when you retire. But the value of the pension will not increase in line with salary, earnings or age.

Preserved pensions differ according to the type of pension.

For a final salary company pension the principle behind preserved pensions is that you must be given a fair share of the pension that you would have received if you had stayed with that scheme until retirement. An example of how this works is shown in box 5.2.

With a money-purchase company pension your preserved

pension is easier to define. It is simply your share of the assets in the pension fund at the point at which the pension was preserved or made paid-up. No new money can be paid in. The value of these assets may rise or fall over time, dependent upon how the stock market fares. The value may also be reduced by charges levied to pay for the running of the pension fund.

Payment of this preserved pension is usually made when you reach your former employer's normal retirement age. This may not be the same time as you retire from other work. Your pension will be the annual income this preserved fund can buy, less any tax-free cash you choose to take.

The value of paid-up or preserved personal pension or stakeholder pension is calculated in a similar way. There is a fund of assets with your name on it. No new money goes in, but the value of the fund may increase with stock market growth. Ongoing management charges will continue to be levied against this fund. These will offset the effect of growth and may reduce the overall fund in a year of slow or no growth. And where the pension fund is relatively small, these charges may actually severely erode the value of the fund. In such cases transfer may be a better option. Retirement age is more flexible. Under current rules you can take a preserved personal pension at any age from fifty to seventy-five. Taking the pension is not tied to any other retirement dates.

There are special rules for preserved pensions where an individual or company has contracted out of Serps. The portion of a pension made up of National Insurance rebates to compensate for not being in Serps must be increased in value with earnings. Chapter 21 on contracting out explains this fully.

If you decide to leave your pension where it is, be sure to keep in touch with the office administering it. They will need to know about any change of address, or about changes in your personal circumstances like marriage, divorce or changes in next of kin.

Box 5.2: How a final salary pension can be preserved

The idea of preserving a final salary pension is to give you when you retire an exact share of the pension entitlement which you had earned at the point when you left employment.

The value of a preserved pension will depend on how long you had worked for a company before you left and on your salary when you left.

Take the example of a final salary pension which builds up at one-eightieth of salary each year. Someone who had worked for that company and been a member of the pension for fifteen years would be entitled to a preserved pension of fifteen-eightieths of their salary when they left. This pension would be paid at the original employer's normal retirement date.

To guard against rising prices, Inland Revenue rules state the value of this preserved pension must be increased by inflation each year, up to a maximum of 5 per cent a year averaged over the whole period until retirement.

Once the pension is paid, it must be treated exactly the same as pensions paid to those who stayed with the company the whole time. That means it must increase each year in line with other pensions in payment and any widows' or widowers' benefits must apply.

If the pension scheme was contracted out from Serps, special rules apply to those benefits. Chapter 21 explains these fully.

Case study: Brenda, thirty-two, has spent twelve years working for a bank. The final salary company pension builds up at one-sixtieth a year. She moves to another job and decides to preserve her pension with the bank.

When she leaves, she is earning £25,000 a year. Her preserved pension is based on $\frac{12}{60}$th x £25,000 = £5000 a year. This is then increased in line with inflation, which averages 3 per cent a year over the thirty-three years until Brenda reaches sixty-five.

The final value of her preserved pension is £13,260 a year. This has the same buying power as £5000 a year did when she moved jobs thirty-three years previously.

Transfers

The alternative to leaving a preserved pension is to make a transfer. This involves your former pension scheme paying a lump sum to a new pension scheme. This lump sum buys you rights in the new final salary pension scheme or is moved over as a big payment to jump-start a new money-purchase pension or personal pension.

All company pension schemes must allow people moving jobs to transfer out. This transfer can be to a new employer's pension, provided that scheme is willing to accept it. It can also be to a new personal pension, new stakeholder pension or to other specialist pension plans. Table 5.2 summarises the options, which are discussed more fully below.

There are special conditions for those who transfer between two public-sector pension schemes.

Table 5.2: What you can do with a pension when you change jobs

Form of pension saving in previous employment	Options in new employment	
	New employer offers a pension	New employer has no company pension
Company/occupational pension	Become a deferred pensioner	Become a deferred pensioner
	Transfer into new employer's pension	

	Transfer to a personal pension	Transfer to a personal pension
	Transfer to an S32 plan*	Transfer to an S32 plan*
Group personal pension	Continue saving into GPP	Continue saving into GPP
	Transfer into new employer's pension	
	Transfer to a personal pension	Transfer to a personal pension
	Make the pension paid-up	Make the pension paid-up
	Join new employer's pension and continue GPP	
Personal pension	Continue saving into personal pension	Continue saving into personal pension
	Join new employer's pension and make personal pension paid-up	
	Transfer pension into new employer's pension	
	Transfer into a new personal pension or stakeholder pension	Transfer into a new personal pension or stakeholder pension
	Join new employer's pension and continue paying into personal pension	
Stakeholder pension	Continue saving into stakeholder	Continue saving into stakeholder
	Join new company scheme and continue saving into stakeholder	

	Transfer stakeholder into new employer's pension	Transfer into a new stakeholder pension
	Join new company pension and make stakeholder paid-up	

* If previous company pension scheme was contracted out and if earnings are under £30,000.

Special situations

There are two alternatives to preserving a pension or transferring which may arise. If you have been a member of a company pension for only a short period – typically less than two years – the employer can refuse to conduct a transfer or give you a preserved pension. Instead, the employee gets any contributions they have made into the pension returned to them as a lump sum. Contributions made by the employer on your behalf are not returned. Such returned contributions are reduced by a 20 per cent tax charge – remember, the money was originally paid in free of tax. They may also be reduced further if the company pension was contracted out and the employer has to make a payment to the DSS to buy you back into Serps or the State Second Pension.

If you are aged fifty or over, it may be possible to take early retirement from a company pension or personal pension. Rather than preserving or transferring pension benefits, you start drawing them down immediately. Early retirement is discussed more fully in Chapter 13. However, issues to consider if you plan to 'retire early' from a historic pension include:

- The value of a final salary pension may be reduced by an early-retirement penalty. Typically, this could cut a pension by 20 per cent for someone quitting five years ahead of the normal scheme retirement age.
- A money-purchase company pension or personal pension will also be smaller if you retire early because an annuity is being purchased at a younger age – in other words your pension pot is being spread more thinly over more years of retirement.

- If you carry on working in other employment, you may end up paying unnecessary income tax on your early pension because this extra income carries you into a higher tax band.

Generally, if you move jobs and carry on working, preserving or transferring benefits is usually a better option than early retirement from the previous scheme.

To transfer or not to transfer; that is the question

Deciding whether to transfer a historic pension, or to leave it where it is, can be one of the most confusing decisions in pensions. This next section can set out general principles, but no two cases are the same. To work out what is best, you will need:

- information from the scheme you are thinking of leaving as to how a preserved pension is calculated and what that might be worth;
- an estimate of the transfer value of your pension;
- information from the scheme you are thinking of joining of what that transfer value might buy.

You will also need independent advice. For high-value-fund transfers, it may even be worth paying a consulting actuary to act on your behalf, though as this will cost several hundred pounds it will not always be economic. Financial advisers have to sit a special exam called G60 to be able to advise on pension transfers. The Society of Financial Advisers (SOFA) will be able to put you in touch with a local adviser who is qualified. For more information on advisers, see Chapter 12.

In general, transfers between two schemes rarely preserve the full value of your pension. There may be charges, reductions and fees, which eat into the pension. And in final salary schemes the actuaries who run the original pension will err on the side of caution in producing a transfer value to protect their fund against an overgenerous pay-out.

But there can be advantages to transfers too. The main advantage is that it keeps all your pension in one place, rather than having separate chunks. This means your money all becomes available on a single retirement date, rather than in dribs and drabs at different retirement ages.

The rest of this section summarises the main issues arising out of particular kinds of transfer.

Transfers from final salary company pensions

The transfer value from a final salary scheme will be worked out by the actuary who advises the scheme. They will look at the future benefits to which you are entitled. They then estimate a lump sum that can be paid out and invested elsewhere to grow over the years to your retirement date to buy a pension of equivalent value.

Transfers from a final salary scheme to personal pensions, including to a stakeholder pension, are rarely recommended. This is because:

- You are giving up guaranteed pension benefits for something which is less certain, and dependent upon stock market growth and variable annuity rates.
- You will have to bear the running costs of a pension, something currently paid for by the former employer.
- You may lose other benefits such as a pension for dependants.
- The transfer value you will get is linked to the guaranteed pension. Some company pension schemes also make further discretionary payments, such as extra increases to annual pension once you have retired. If you transfer, you will miss out on these.

There can be some advantages. Personal pensions give you more freedom to retire how and when you want to. But this flexibility usually comes at a high price. The pension mis-selling problems of the late 1980s were largely the result of people being advised to transfer out of superior final salary pension schemes into inferior personal pension schemes.

The case against transfers from a final salary company pension to another final salary pension is less clear-cut. Such transfers can be advantageous and certainly have the benefit of securing all your pension benefits in one pot. Here, the two schemes may both provide guaranteed pensions and are both likely to have additional benefits such as spouses' pensions.

Factors you need to compare include the different pension scheme retirement dates and perhaps different attitudes towards early retirement, as well as the detail of how the new company scheme will treat a transfer in. Remember, your new employer can also decline to accept a transfer into its pension.

Where the transfer is to another final salary scheme, the new employer's pension can handle it in a number of ways. It can use the transfer to:

- provide a fixed cash sum pension. This is a defined pension paid at retirement on top of the pension built up over years of service for the new employer;
- buy additional years. These are extra years of service credited to a new employee's work record, effectively giving the new company pension a jump-start;
- create a separate money-purchase fund in your name, which sits alongside the new company pension. This will operate in a similar way to an AVC.

The additional years option can be especially confusing. It is explained separately in box 5.3.

Transfers between final salary pensions in the public sector – for example, someone moving from local government to the police service – often operate through a special mechanism called a transfer club. The effect of this is to give the person transferring the same number of years of service in their new pension as they had in the old one.

Transfers from a final salary scheme to money-purchase company pensions are used to build up an immediate pension fund in your name with the new employer. The final value of the pension will depend on how this money grows over the years to retirement. However, some money-purchase company pensions will also build in limited guarantees about what pension this lump sum will produce at retirement.

Whichever of these options is used, it is important to remember that once you have transferred in, you are bound by the rules of the new pension. These will govern when you can retire and what pension you will get.

Where a company pension scheme has been contracted out of Serps, there is also the option to move some or all of the pension into a Section 32 plan, also called S32 plan or buy-out bond. This is a special type of personal pension specifically designed to preserve rights to the guaranteed minimum pension (GMP) provided instead of Serps. Unlike other personal pensions, with a Section 32 plan the pension provider takes the investment risk on the GMP, not the individual. This can make such plans attractive in some cases (see Chapter 20 for more details on Section 32 plans).

Box 5.3: How a transfer can buy you added years

One way that final salary pension schemes can handle a transfer is to use a lump sum payment from the old scheme to buy you added years in the new pension scheme. This has the effect of crediting you with a longer work record at the new employer than you actually have, boosting the pension you would otherwise get.

Nevertheless, this can confuse someone who transfers because the number of years you are credited with in the new scheme is rarely the same number of years' service as you had in the old scheme. Usually it is fewer years.

This is because the old pension scheme only has to pay you a pension based on your salary when you stopped working for that company. A new pension has to undertake to pay you a pension based on your salary at retirement, which could be thirty or more years away. Growth in earnings is likely to make that a far more expensive undertaking.

Case study 1: Rebecca is moving from one accountancy firm to another. She wants to transfer her pension too so that she has all her benefits in one place. She has twenty-six years to go before the normal retirement date with her new employer.

She has ten years of service in the old scheme. This built up pension at one-sixtieth of salary a year. The new scheme also accrues pension at one-sixtieth of salary a year. But Rebecca is only given four years of service in the new scheme. This is because her salary in twenty-six years when she is due to retire is forecast to be two and a half times as much as the salary she was earning when she left her old job. The four-sixtieths of this larger salary are worth as much as ten-sixtieths of her original salary.

Case study 2: Marcus is also switching from one final salary scheme to another. He is ten years from retirement. He had twenty-one years of service in his previous employer's scheme, which built-up at the rate of one-sixtieth of salary each year.

Marcus's new pension accrues at the lower rate of one-eightieth of salary each year and it has less generous payments for death in service, ill health and dependants' pensions. He is credited with twenty-five years of service in the new scheme to balance out for these differences.

Transfers from money-purchase company pension schemes

Here the transfer value from a pension is based directly on the value of the pension fund that has built up in your name. The transfer must reflect the contributions that you and/or your employer have paid in, plus any investment growth. But, depending on how the pension is invested, there may then be early-surrender charges applied to the fund. These can reduce the value of the transfer, in some cases by up to 20 per cent compared with the quoted fund value. The size of these surrender charges, which are levied by the investment company or insurance company that manages the pension, can often be large enough to make the whole transfer a bad idea.

On top of this the new pension fund, if it is also a money-purchase scheme, may levy initial or entry charges on a new investment made through a transfer.

Again, if considering a transfer to a new employer's pension scheme, compare the standard retirement age and options for early retirement. You may find that pension in the new company scheme can only be taken from the age of sixty-five, whereas you are entitled to a pension from the old scheme at sixty. This alone may deter you from making the transfer.

When the transfer is being made to a final salary scheme, the new scheme can again treat the injection of cash in a number of ways. As discussed in the section above, it can use the transfer to buy you added years of service with the new employer, to secure a fixed and guaranteed pension on retirement or to buy top-up money-purchase benefits which run alongside the main pension scheme.

If the new company pension is not contracted out of Serps and the State Second Pension you cannot transfer the protected-rights section of your previous pension. This either has to go to a new personal pension or must stay as a deferred pension in the old scheme.

The case against transferring a money-purchase company pension to a personal pension is not as strong as that against transferring a final salary pension into a personal pension. Here, neither the company nor the personal pension produces guaranteed benefits. Moving the money into a personal or stakeholder pension will give you more flexibility over when you can retire and how you structure your retirement income. But you have to be sure that this flexibility is worth the price of any surrender charges or exit fees on the company pension.

Transfers from a personal pension

You have the right to transfer out of any personal pension. Whether this is a good idea depends on a number of factors. It will usually come down to an assessment of whether any costs you have to pay to move are outweighed by the chance to move to a better pension or the chance to secure guaranteed pension rights.

If you are thinking of moving from a pension started between 1988 and 1998, there will almost certainly be charges for transferring out, which may be very high. Some of these charges, or early-surrender fees, can be punishing. In the worst cases you may get nothing back and have a nil transfer value. Pensions started more recently generally offer higher transfer values. Stakeholder pensions, which have been available since April 2001, have to permit transfers at no charge.

Where there is a charge, it is taken by quoting a lower transfer value than the face value of the money invested in your personal pension. See Chapter 20 for detail on the different types of personal pension and how their charges are structured.

Nevertheless, there can be circumstances when it makes sense to bite the bullet on a transfer charge and switch the money anyway. Reasons for a transfer might include:

- You have the option of joining a final salary company pension scheme, which pays near-guaranteed benefits and is willing to give you credit for a transfer from a personal pension.
- You want to unify all pensions in one place to simplify planning.
- You want to improve the investment performance of a pension fund which has consistently lagged behind the market.
- Where ongoing management charges will erode the value of the preserved pension to an unacceptable degree.

Table 5.2 summarises the transfer options for personal pensions.

Where you are transferring in to a final salary company pension, the transfer can be treated in the three ways outlined above: as added years of service, to buy a fixed amount of extra pension when you retire, or as a separate money-purchase investment running alongside the main pension.

When you transfer into a money-purchase company scheme, or another type of personal pension, you will use the transfer lump sum to kick-start your investment in this scheme.

One final word of warning. If you try to transfer from a particular type of long-standing personal pension called a retirement annuity plan you will not be able to replace the pension with a similar product. Retirement annuities, which were sold until 1988, allow a higher level of contributions and have different rules on when you can retire (see Chapter 20). If it is important to be able to capitalise on the higher contribution rules, then a transfer might not make sense.

A forced change of job: redundancy, takeovers and worse

In all the circumstances described above, a change of job has been your move. But there are times when a move can be forced on you, notably when you are made redundant. Even worse, you may be fired or your employer may go bust. And businesses are constantly being taken over. What are the implications for your pension and retirement planning then?

Redundancy

There are strict legal definitions of what it means to be made redundant, even though people generally use the term to cover a wide range of circumstances in which they leave a job. For example, someone who is asked to leave employment for sub-standard work and paid a sum of money in lieu of notice has not been made redundant. Officially, redundancy covers those occasions when your individual job no longer exists; where a reorganisation is sharing existing work between fewer people; or when the whole location where you work is being closed.

Where genuine redundancy is on the cards, employers often use their pension schemes as a way of softening the blow to individuals of losing their jobs. At the same time this cuts the immediate costs to the employer of making redundancies. A final salary pension which is showing a healthy cash surplus can use some of that surplus to pay enhanced pension terms as part of a redundancy deal.

If you are aged fifty or more and in a final salary pension, a redundancy offer may include the option to retire immediately and early without any penalty. This contrasts with voluntary retirement before the normal pension age, where the amount paid will be reduced to reflect the fact that you are starting your pension early.

In addition, in redundancy you may be credited with extra years of service to boost the value of your pension still further. A typical model is to give you an extra six months' pensionable service for each year between now and the normal retirement age. So where normal retirement age is sixty-five, a man aged fifty-seven would get four years' extra service credited to reflect the eight years he could have worked if he had not been made redundant. However, there is no allowance for how your salary might have grown over the years between now and retirement.

Those aged under fifty are not allowed to retire early, but may still be credited with extra years of service in the pension scheme. This would give them a larger preserved pension or a bigger transfer value.

Where the company runs a money-purchase pension scheme, they may make an extra lump sum payment to the scheme as part of a redundancy package. Likewise, the same may apply where an employer is already contributing to a personal pension, group personal pension or stakeholder pension. It is more tax effective for an employer to make payments into a pension scheme than direct to a worker, so if redundancy is looming for you do not be afraid to make the suggestion to your employer.

Where the employer does not run a company pension or does not already pay into a group personal pension, personal pension or stakeholder pension, an extra pension payment will not usually be part of any redundancy package.

Depending on your circumstances, you might also want to think about how to use any lump sum redundancy settlements. If you are able to find another job quickly and so do not need the money for day-to-day living expenses, some of the cash could well be used to boost retirement savings, either through voluntary extra pension payments or other means. New rules introduced in April 2001 allow you to use the value of earnings you had in work to pay into a personal or stakeholder pension for up to five years after that work ceases. So even if you move into a lower-paid job or part-time work after redundancy, you can use some of the lump sum redundancy payment to fund contributions into a personal pension at a higher rate than current income justifies. Box 5.4 shows an example of this.

Once you have been declared redundant from the original employment, the issues around whether to transfer or whether to retain a deferred pension are similar to any other leaver.

Box 5.4: Redundancy and retirement planning

David, fifty-three, is a quality control manager. He has worked for his current employer for eighteen years and is a member of the company's final salary pension scheme. He earns £30,000 a year. The scheme's normal retirement age is sixty.

As part of his redundancy package David is paid £30,000. His pension is made available immediately if he wants it and his pensionable service is increased from eighteen years to twenty-one and a half years (seven years to normal retirement times half a year's service). This means his pension will be based on twenty-one-and-a-half-sixtieths of final salary.

David decides to keep working. He becomes self-employed, offering quality assurance advice to several different companies. In his first year working for himself he manages to earn £20,000.

He wants to keep saving to boost his retirement income, so decides to pay into a personal pension, using some of the £15,000 of the redundancy lump sum still left in the bank. His maximum possible pension contribution, if based on his income of £20,000, is £6000 (30 per cent of salary for someone aged fifty-four as David now is). But for the next five years he can instead base the contribution on his previous year's income of £30,000 and so is able to pay up to £9000 into his personal pension.

Getting fired

If you get fired from a job you will lose an income, you will lose dignity and you may lose friends. But you will not lose your pension. Personal pensions, including stakeholder, belong to you. Once you, or your employer, have paid into this, money cannot be taken out to be refunded to either party. So any money your employer has paid into your pension is safe.

Likewise, once you have clocked up entitlement to a company pension, this cannot be taken away from you. While an employer who is sacking you will not soften the blow by crediting your pension with extra years of service or an extra lump sum, it cannot take away what has already been earned. So you will retain the right to a deferred pension from that employer or to a transfer into an alternative fund. And you cannot be discriminated against; so your pension in retirement would have to increase in line with other former workers and would share the same entitlement to any widows' benefits or pensions for dependent children.

What if the company goes bust?

The pensions picture may be more gloomy if your employer goes bust and you lose your job because of it. Depending on the financial circumstances of the company when receivers are called in or when the business is put into liquidation, there are a number of possibilities.

If the company has been managed with an eye to the welfare of the workers, management may call it a day before the business goes completely under. This means they may be able to sell the company as a going concern, or at least have some funds left to wind up the business in an orderly fashion, pay redundancy etc.

At the other extreme, and unfortunately more common, creditors or banks may force the closure of the business and there is little left for the staff, who may not even get paid wages they are owed.

Fortunately, there are some legal protections for pensions. Where the company has been sponsoring a stakeholder pension, group personal pension or paying money into a personal pension, the funds belong to the individual not the employer. The money is held by a third-party trustee and cannot be called on by creditors of the company except in very special circumstances (usually where the directors of a firm have been stuffing money into their own pensions and not paying other bills such as VAT and tax). Such money-purchase pensions are normally relatively unaffected by a firm going bust. Obviously there will be no more payments-in by an employer. But the money already in the pension is secure.

Occasionally there can be problems when businesses on the brink of failure have not passed on contributions to one of the above pension schemes. They may have deducted money from salary and then failed to pay it into the pension. There are clear rules which require payments to be passed on by the nineteenth day of the month after they are deducted from salary. But employers may hold on to the money to help their own cash flow, even though they are breaking the law and directors can be prosecuted. If the business then goes bust, these contributions may be lost for good.

Where a firm that has run a money-purchase company pension scheme goes bust, again the vast bulk of money already paid into the scheme is safe. This is invested with insurance or investment companies and monitored by independent trustees who guard the assets on behalf of individual employees. However, in some cases there may be some loss of promised future benefit. Some money-purchase pensions target contributions to achieve a particular level of pension. This is backed up by the undertaking that an employer may top up the fund when you retire, if necessary, to hit this mark. If the employer goes bust then this pledge cannot be fulfilled.

There is also the possibility that the employer may have deducted contributions from wages but delayed passing them to the money-purchase scheme. Again, this is illegal but it can happen and may cost employees contributions missed in the two or three months before the firm goes bust.

Final salary schemes

In the past there have been cases where members of final salary pension funds have seen a company go under and discovered that their pensions have suffered. This is because final salary pensions are based on funds of money largely controlled by company management, not by third parties. The most notorious example was the Maxwell scandal when company pension funds controlled by the media tycoon Robert Maxwell were systematically looted of hundreds of millions of pounds in the early 1990s. The money was used to support the business empire and, when it failed, there was no cash left for the pensions.

That affair triggered a fundamental overhaul of pension fund regulation. It means that pension fund trustees and the advisers whom they employ have specific duties to report any suspicions. They can be prosecuted if they do not. Members of final salary pensions now have greater rights to information about the scheme, including exactly where the money is.

And in 1995 rules were introduced to make sure that companies were paying sufficient into their pension funds to meet any likely liabilities. This minimum funding requirement has meant some companies having to raise their payments into their pensions – although it has prompted others to abandon final salary schemes altogether.

The new funding rules were intended to be phased in over ten years starting in 1997, which would have meant that by 2007 every single pension scheme was adequately funded according to a common formula. However, in March 2001 the Chancellor announced that the MFR rules would be abolished and a new way of ensuring schemes were solvent would be introduced. This will be more tailored to the circumstances of each scheme. But it will require new legislation, so at the time of writing, the MFR rules still stand.

So what does all this mean?

It is far less likely that employers going bust today will have gaping holes in their final salary pension schemes. But there is still no absolute guarantee that every single penny of pension is totally secure when a final salary scheme is forced to wind up. Where an employer is forced to cease trading, the usual practice is to freeze the pension scheme. Typically, your pension earned until this point is then secured by using money in the fund to buy a deferred annuity from an insurance company. This is purchased on your behalf now and is designed to start paying an income when you retire. The process of winding up a scheme can take months or even years.

What happens if your employer is taken over?

Company mergers and takeovers are an increasingly common part of business life. These events can have a significant impact on company pensions and employees' retirement plans.

When a company merges or is taken over, the new management has several choices about how it handles pensions for staff of the original company:

- They can leave pension provision as it is. This means that any company pension scheme continues to run, with benefits unchanged and original employee entitlements preserved. If there is no company pension, but it has been the employer's habit to make payments into personal pensions on your behalf, this may also continue.
- They can merge pension arrangements across the new enlarged company: this might mean transferring all members of the old pension scheme into the buying company's own pension. Or, more rarely, employees of the predator company may move into the scheme run by the firm which has been sold.
- They can leave historic pensions untouched, preserving original benefits and entitlements for service up to the date of merger and bring in new unified pension arrangements for both sets of employees going forward.

Exactly what happens will depend on the circumstances of the merger or sale and the existing pension arrangements. *There is no legal requirement for a new employer to preserve or maintain pension benefits or to match an existing pension scheme, except for specified cases where public-sector jobs are being privatised or contracted out.*

Where you are paying into a personal pension or stakeholder

pension, or saving using other means, change of ownership by itself should have minimal effect. But there may be knock-on effects because of this, e.g. redundancy, relocation or a new higher-paid role. There are special considerations for directors and owners of a company which is sold (see Chapter 18).

Where a company is being taken over and retains its original identity, location etc., preserving a separate pension scheme is often the simplest option. But where a new owner wants to integrate a company in its wider business empire it is likely that a pension scheme will eventually be absorbed or merged into the bigger company's scheme. If this is on the agenda, employees of the old firm may find themselves joining a new scheme with inferior benefits; for example, a money-purchase scheme instead of a final salary scheme. Though legally there is no obligation to match benefits, to smooth the merger process and to pre-empt industrial relations problems the new employer may offer additional guarantees, such as 'no one will be worse off'. Unless these are written into contracts, though, the guarantees are effectively worthless – they will depend on the attitudes of future managers a possible twenty or thirty years later.

In summary:

- Try to understand what your company pension is worth.
- Use this knowledge to your advantage when changing jobs.
- When you move jobs try to keep your savings momentum going.
- You can preserve a pension or transfer it. Seek independent help if you feel transfer is on your agenda.
- Pensions are often boosted to soften the blow of redundancy.

CHAPTER 6

A routine service

Read this chapter if:

- You are already saving towards retirement and you want advice on giving yourself a regular check-up.
- You have recently received annual pension benefit statements and want help interpreting them.

Sensible motorists give their car a regular service. And sensible savers give their retirement plans a regular once-over. It is vital to get into the habit of regular reviews of pensions and other savings plans. Time and again people start a pension or an AVC, then assume, 'That's it. My pension is sorted.' They forget about it, get on with life and, unfortunately, can end up sadly disappointed when they arrive at retirement.

This sort of behaviour is understandable. It can be a real effort to go through the paperwork of arranging a pension, especially if you are doing it for yourself, rather than through a friendly employer. It is natural to want to put it to one side and relax once it is done. But starting saving is only half the battle.

Why review?

Reviewing retirement plans is simply a matter of asking yourself, 'How am I doing?' It makes sense to ask this question on a regular basis because:

- Your circumstances change as the years go by.
- Your hopes for retirement might change too.
- What you can expect from the state may change.
- Performance of existing investments may be disappointing.
- New ways to save and new pension options become available.
- You can act promptly to head off potential problems, rather than finding out about them when it is too late.

Sometimes, very little will have changed between reviews. You may be happy with the way your plans are progressing and decide nothing needs altering. But at other times your life may evolve rapidly: marriage, children, a new home and a new job can all follow in rapid succession. These changes may mean retirement plans need rewriting.

How often should you review?

There are no hard and fast rules. A reassessment every year is probably unnecessary unless you are only a couple of years from retirement; leaving it longer than every five years is dangerous. Most advisers recommend sitting down and going through all the paperwork once every two or three years, then switching to an annual review in the final five years before retirement. You may also do a one-off review if something fundamental changes, like moving to a new job or getting married.

How to review?

It is worth setting aside time to do a review properly, certainly sitting down with a financial adviser if you have one. You can prepare for a review by making sure you have up-to-date information, including recent annual statements from company and personal pensions, details of other savings and the appropriate policy documentation and company pension handbooks. If you cannot lay your hands on this material ask for duplicate copies. You might also want to ask the DWP for an estimate of your state pension in retirement. Details of how to do this are on page 35 in Chapter 3.

The government wants to try to encourage more regular reviews of pension planning. It plans to introduce annual pension statements, which would contain easy to understand forecasts of what state pension you are on target to achieve and what company pension you might get. Trials have already taken place with employers on pilot schemes, but there is no date fixed yet for when these will be introduced for everyone. And even so, these statements from an employer will not include personal pensions or historic pensions with previous employers. The self-employed, too, would miss out.

The review itself involves going through the same sort of questions and issues that were discussed in Chapter 2. You need to think again about how much income you will need in retirement, how much you might get from existing savings and pensions and about whether you might need to do more.

The difference with regular reviews is that you can compare the value of existing pensions and savings today with what they were at the last review. This will give you a better feel for how they might develop going forward.

You might also get a shock, especially if you have not paid much attention to annual benefit forecasts for a few years. Money-purchase pension schemes, including personal pensions, have to project forward how your contributions and funds might grow according to a standard method.

In 1999 the rates of growth that could be used in these projections were reduced. This means a pension that in 1998 projected a fund value of £100,000 at retirement in 2015 might today project only £85,000. This is despite the fact that you have continued paying in since 1998 and that the real value of the fund has increased. These projections are only estimates. The final value of your fund may be more or less than this. But projection rates have been lowered for a reason and you may want to think about increasing the amount you save in response to this. Box 6.1 explains more about interpreting annual pension statements and about how the rules on projections have changed.

Box 6.1: Making sense of annual pension statements

When you invest a new sum into a pension, or often when you get annual statements, you will get a projection of what sort of pension your investment is on target to produce. Projections vary between personal pensions and company pensions.

Personal pensions

The projections used for personal pensions have to conform to standard rules. Pension companies can forecast how your fund may grow using three different annual growth rates: a lower rate, a middle rate and an upper rate. In the summer of 1999 these rates were cut from 6, 9 and 12 per cent a year to 5, 7 and 9 per cent a year. Financial regulators enforced this change because they expect lower stock market growth and lower interest rates in future. This means that investments are likely to grow in value more slowly and so it is important to give savers realistic projections of what their saving might achieve. Some pension firms project using all three rates. Some project using only the middle rate of 7 per cent a year.

The effect of moving to lower projection rates has been to give some savers a nasty shock. When they read annual statements it appears that their fund has lost value. This is not the case. The projections are only estimates of what your fund might be worth in the future. The actual value when you retire might be higher or lower. All that has happened is that your pension company is making a less optimistic guess.

Forecasts of lower growth may prompt you to review how much you are paying in yourself. If your money will grow more slowly, you will need to pay higher contributions to achieve the same income in retirement.

Pension companies also have to use standardised annuity rates when they estimate how much income you can take from a pension. Generally, they use their current annuity rates. Again, it is only an estimate, though the closer to retirement you are, the more accurate is the guess.

Personal pensions based on contracted-out income from Serps or the State Second Pension will be shown separately. This is because the pension has to be delivered in a particular way, increasing at 3 per cent a year. Your pension company will show these projections in cash terms, i.e. the number of pounds in a fund when you retire. It may also choose to show the estimated value of your pension in today's money by building in an allowance for inflation. Such real-terms projections can give a much clearer idea of what your pension income might buy.

Company pensions

At the moment, there are no standardised rules on how company pension schemes show estimates of future benefits to their members.

With final salary schemes, members will get an annual report from the scheme's trustees and an update on any changes to benefits. This does not always include an estimate of final pension, though some do. If you know the scheme rules and want to guess what your pension might be, you can do the calculations yourself. You need to estimate your salary at retirement, work out how many years of service you will have by then and calculate your pension using your scheme's accrual rate, for example one-eightieth of salary per year of service. But if you are looking several years ahead, it is hard to guess the impact of pay rises and promotions on your pay.

Where you are a member of a money-purchase company

pension you will get an update each year of the value of your fund. There may also be a projection of how this might grow between now and retirement, and what kind of pension that would provide. If the scheme is being run by an outside organisation, such as an insurance or pension company, the projections are likely to be made using that company's standard format and so will be very similar to those for a personal pension. But each company scheme is free to make projections in whatever way it wants, so they vary widely.

The government's aim is for everyone in a company pension to get a statement once a year. This would tell them in a standardised format exactly what pension they were on target to achieve, expressed in real terms, that is today's money. It would include their employer's pension, plus the state pension. At the time of writing the government was consulting on this with a view to introducing it from April 2002. Included in the proposals were plans to force money-purchase company pensions to project forward using a standardised rate. The plan may or may not come into force in 2002.

Benchmarking your pension – investment performance

One key aspect of any review is to consider where your pension and savings are being invested, and to check how they are doing against rivals. The buzzword for this is benchmarking.

If you are in a final salary pension, you probably have no choice over where your pension is invested. There is a single fund. Here it is up to the employer to make sure that the pension fund hits its targets, so the issue on fund performance is not the same. Some money-purchase company pensions give their members a limited choice of where they can invest. Though the pension provider is fixed, you might be able to choose between two or three different funds.

With personal pensions of all types, including stakeholder, and often with company AVCs or free-standing AVC schemes, there is a far broader choice. Not only is there usually a wide choice of funds available from your pension company, but there are dozens of rival companies to consider too. As your final pension is dependent on how well your money grows, the long-term investment performance of your fund is crucial. Box 2.1 on page 20 provides a general explanation of the different types of investment if you want a reminder of this.

Your annual statement should make it clear which pension fund or funds your money is being invested in. Consider how these funds have performed against

- other funds run by the same company;
- the same kind of funds run by other companies.

You are trying to judge whether it is right to leave your money where it is; whether to leave the existing fund where it is, but to switch new payments into a different fund; whether to move the whole lot into another fund; or even whether you should transfer to a different pension company altogether. Unless you have a crystal ball, there are no absolutely right answers. You sometimes need to go on judgement and instinct.

Beware of reading too much into one set of figures or one year's investment performance. Try to gather as much data as you can. Magazines such as *Money Management*, available through newsagents, carry detailed performance histories of pension funds. These help you to compare one pension against another. You can also get up-to-date information from the Internet. Be prepared to take figures for past investment performance with a pinch of salt (see box 6.2).

What you are trying to do is to gauge the fitness of your pension manager against those who are working in the same arena. You want to satisfy yourself that you are giving your money a reasonable chance of growing well in the years ahead.

As well as considering overall growth, that is how much your fund has gone up or down in value, think about consistency. The ideal is a fund that is constantly above average, not one that is top of the charts for a year or two, then down in the doldrums for another couple of years, before bouncing back. And try to make your judgement forward-looking – what might happen to your fund in the years to come? Pension companies run customer relations units. Don't be shy of calling them up and asking why performance has been poor and what is being done to correct it. It is your money and your future at stake, so you have every right to ask.

Box 6.2: Past performance, future illusion?

The small print at the bottom of adverts for pensions and other investment products warns: 'Past performance is no guide to future performance.' This is a wise warning. How your money has gained or lost in value in one year gives you little guide to how it might gain in value in future years. World stock markets are volatile animals. The region or sector which is top of the pops one month may be languishing in the doldrums the next. Yesterday's 'dog' fund becomes tomorrow's 'star'. Some compare using past-performance figures to help you decide between funds with trying to navigate a car using a road map which only tells you where you have already been.

So can we disregard past performance altogether? Probably not. While different nations and types of fund will thrive in different economic climates, some pension companies undoubtedly have better investment managers than others. Comparing a fund with similar funds run by other companies at least gives you a feeling of how a firm is doing against its peers. Where your company consistently appears to be lagging across different types of investment funds and over different timescales you can rightly be alarmed.

To measure your funds against like rivals, ignore absolute performance, that is how much a fund has grown or dropped in a given time period. Instead, see which performance quartile a fund is in. Top quartile simply means the best 25 per cent of funds of the same type. Bottom quartile funds are the most sluggish 25 per cent. A fund which is frequently third or fourth quartile, say three or more years out of five, is a below-par performer. Unless there is good evidence to show that it has changed its ways – for example, a new fund management team – it could be time to consider a move.

Most personal pensions make it relatively straightforward to switch from one fund to another. In some cases this is free; sometimes there are one or two free switches a year; in other cases a nominal charge, say £20, may be levied to switch. In some cases there may also be some automatic switching going on; if you have selected a lifestyle investment option, or are in a stakeholder default fund, your money will gradually be moved from higher- to lower-risk investments as you near your planned retirement date. This is to lock in past gains against future stock market falls (see Chapter 8).

If you decide that drastic action is necessary and that you want to transfer your money elsewhere, be aware that the transfer value might be reduced by a surrender penalty. Transfers from a stakeholder pension will be free of charge, but transfers from personal and group personal pensions and free-standing AVCs will not. The surrender fees may then be on top of any charges levied for buying into a new pension fund.

These charges may deter you from the transfer. In itself, that is not all bad. Reckless switching of funds as you chase the tail of higher growth is likely to be as harmful to your long-term prospects as leaving the money in a duff fund. But do not let the charges become a ball and chain, trapping you in the fund. Think long-term. If you are convinced this is not the right place for your money, sacrifice some cash now rather than see it seep away over the years until retirement.

Benchmarking your pension – charges

It is also vital to benchmark your current pension on another key criterion: charges. The impact of annual charges, policy fees, ticking time bombs called capital units and other deductions could do more harm to the long-term value of your fund than below-average investment growth. Personal pensions in particular have evolved dramatically over the past few years. The introduction of stakeholder pensions, with strict limits on charging, has forced the pensions industry to become far more competitive and cut fees and charges.

However, in the vast majority of cases these reductions only apply to new customers and to pensions sold going forward. Pension plans already in force are still running on the old basis, where charges can reduce the final value of your pension by up to 25–30 per cent. And these nasty charges can still apply if you increase the value of a regular monthly payment into the pension or make an extra lump sum contribution. Box 6.3 gives a quick summary of the different kinds of charges you may encounter. Fuller details are contained in Chapter 20.

Charges do have a role. Pension companies are in the business to make money and they have a right to a profit. But with far more efficient and fairer pensions on sale today, those who have the old-style contracts with hidden charges must think very hard before upping their contributions.

The alternative is to take out a new pension, such as a stakeholder scheme, to run alongside your old one. Take the example of Sheila. She saves £120 a month into a personal pension that she started in 1994. Under this scheme, the first two years' payments of any increase in contribution are used to buy capital units. These units run with a punitive 5 per cent annual management fee until retirement date. This makes them poor value. Thereafter, the money she pays in buys units with a much lower ½ per cent charge.

Sheila wants to increase her saving to £150 a month. Rather than paying into her existing pension, she opens a new stakeholder scheme, which can run in parallel. She pays £30 a month into this and continues to pay £120 a month into the original scheme.

Box 6.3: Pension charges at a glance

These are some of the common charges that can be levied on personal pensions. Not all pensions will have all charges. Stakeholder pensions, for example, have to levy only a single annual management charge of 1 per cent or less. Chapter 20 contains more details on the fine print of personal pensions.

Annual management charge:	A yearly charge set against the whole value of your fund, for example 0.75 per cent a year. This is used to pay for the costs of administering the funds and paying the fund manager.
Bid/offer spread:	This is the difference between the buying price (the offer price) and the lower price (the bid price) at which units in a fund are sold back to the investor. This is normally 5 per cent.
Capital unit:	This is a special kind of unit in an investment fund. Typically, all your money invested in the first year or two years would go to buy capital units. These units then carry a higher annual management charge for the whole lifetime of the pension.
Initial or set-up charge:	A one-off charge levied at the outset of the pension or taken

	out of the first year's contributions. Often a fixed sum, i.e. £50, rather than a percentage of contributions.
Policy fee:	A fixed sum, charged monthly or annually, supposedly to cover the administration expenses of running the pension.
Surrender charge:	A charge levied if you want to transfer your pension before normal retirement date.
Unit allocation/allocation rate:	The proportion of a monthly or single payment which is actually invested in your pension. For example, with a 97 per cent allocation rate, £97 out of every £100 you pay might go into the fund. But the allocation may be a percentage of your contribution *after* other charges have been deducted. So a 97 per cent rate may also mean that only £90 out of £100 goes in.

It may seem quite difficult to compare all the different types of charges, especially if you are trying to compare a pension of ten years ago with one today. There is one useful tip. Ask your current pension provider to do you a forecast of what you will get from increasing contributions, say, by £50 a month. You will be sent a mass of paperwork and projections. Somewhere in this will be a figure for something called reduction in yield. What this is trying to measure is the impact of all the charges added together. It will be quoted as a percentage figure, for example 1.3 per cent. It may be expressed formally as reduction in yield (RIY) or in a phrase such as 'these charges would have the same effect as bringing the investment return used down from x per cent to y per cent'.

What an RIY of 1.3 per cent means is that if your fund were to grow by an average of 8 per cent each year, the charges would have the effect of reducing that growth to 6.7 per cent each year. You can compare a reduction in yield figure from increasing contributions to an existing pension with one for a new personal pension, GPP or stakeholder pension. The lower the figure, the cheaper the pension. One-off lump sum payments may be charged for in different ways from regular monthly premiums, so be sure to compare like with like.

If you discover that your existing pension seems uncompetitive on charges, should you consider transferring elsewhere? Possibly. In some cases the damage is already done. If you have an old-style pension, where the charges are loaded towards the early years of the policy, you have probably paid the bulk of the money. There is nothing you can do to get that back. Going forward, the pension may actually be good value and compare well with the alternative of starting afresh. Provided you do not increase contributions into the pension you might be better off staying put.

Other issues for review

There are two other pension topics worth double-checking. The first is your contracting-out status – are you currently in Serps or the State Second Pension, or have you opted out?

It is possible that if you opted out at some point in the past, it might now make sense to contract back in. This was particularly the case under the Serps when older workers were generally advised to contract back into the state scheme. The arrival of the State Second Pension from 2002 will gradually switch the balance once again. Once this moves into its second phase, expected to be from April 2007, contracting out will be the recommended option for all those on middle to higher earnings. Chapter 21 explains contracting out in more detail.

The other topic for review is the status of your historic pensions; any preserved or deferred pension that you have. Aside from checking the valuation of these pensions and making sure the schemes have your up-to-date personal details, it is also worth ensuring that you are still happy for the money to stay where it is.

It may be that since you last thought about this and decided not to transfer, conditions have changed. For example, you may have now joined a generous company pension scheme into which a transfer might be accepted. And there will be new alternatives such as stakeholder, which did not exist when you last considered a transfer. The actual decision on whether or not to transfer will still be governed by the arguments set out in the previous chapter.

Box 6.4: How would illness affect your retirement plans?

You can make arrangements to save hard for retirement. You can plan to have a comfortable standard of living. But an accident or illness which stops you working for an extended period can suddenly throw these plans awry. If income is not coming in, it is very hard to keep on making payments to a pension or other savings plan.

Part of any regular review of your retirement saving should be to consider how you might guard against illness.

There are several ways that you can draw a safety net around your savings. You may already have some protection through employment. If you are off work sick for a few months, you will get some level of sick pay. How much you get and how long this is paid for depends on your contract.

Being on sick pay may mean that for a few months contributions into a money-purchase company pension dip. But that is not a huge problem long term if you get back into work. If you are in a final salary scheme, a few months off ill will not break your qualifying pension service and so should not affect the final value of the pension. Payments into an AVC may suffer, though.

If the illness is severe and persists for a prolonged period, or you have an irreversible condition, you may not be able to return to work. At this point your sick pay may be stopped and you could be offered early retirement on the grounds of ill health. Chapter 15 explains this more fully.

For those saving through a personal pension, where the value of the fund depends on you continuing to pay in, the situation is slightly different. You will probably be able to maintain payments through a short illness, using your sick pay and other savings. But longer term you will need other solutions.

One option is to pay for waiver-of-premium insurance with your pension. This kicks in after a set period, typically six months. It will pay your usual pension contributions if you cannot because of ill health. Crucially, it will continue to pay these contributions until your normal retirement date. Some waiver-of-premium insurance also gives you the option of having contributions increase each year.

There is also a more expensive option called 'super waiver'. Rather than paying your premiums, it pays now the pension that you would have been forecast to get if you had carried on saving until retirement.

From April 2001 it has also been possible to include some unemployment insurance as part of waiver of premium. This will keep premiums going for a set period, usually one or two years, if you cannot pay because you are unemployed.

With a stakeholder pension you have to pay for waiver-of-premium cover as a separate charge over and above your monthly contribution. With a personal pension the cost of the insurance can be paid separately, or deducted from your fund each year.

Waiver-of-premium insurance is surprisingly cheap and should be seriously considered by all those who start a regular-premium personal pension.

An alternative is to take out more wide-ranging insurance against the financial impact of ill health. Income replacement insurance, also called permanent health cover, will provide a regular income if you cannot work because of ill health. This income is usually paid monthly. It kicks in after a set number of months, called a deferred period, and is paid for as long as the illness persists until you reach your specified retirement date. You pick the deferred period, usually anything from three months to two years. The longer the wait for money, the cheaper the insurance will be. You specify how much income you want to insure for. The benefit is paid free of tax, so it is not usually possible to insure for more than 75 per cent of your gross income.

The cost of cover varies according to your age, occupation and where you live. You also need to decide whether you want to insure against not being able to do your own job, or not being able to do any job at all. Insurance which pays out if you cannot follow your own occupation is more expensive, because it will pay even if you might be able to do other work. For example, a surgeon who suffers from arthritis may not be able to operate on patients any more, but might be fit enough to work collecting trolleys in a supermarket.

Under previous rules, money from income replacement insurance did not qualify as earnings for pension contributions. But since April 2001 it has been possible to pay up to £3600 a year into a pension regardless of where the money came from. Alternatives to pensions, such as Isas, can be used to save more than £3600 a year for retirement.

Depending on your age, you may also choose to retire early through ill health and start drawing your personal pension then. Chapter 15 discusses this in more detail.

Non-pension saving

Any thorough review of planning for retirement should also bring in other savings that you have earmarked for use when you stop work. You will want to check the value of these other savings and investments. But you also need to consider whether or not any changes you make to your pension savings will have an impact on other investments.

Take the example of Iain who is saving for retirement using a combination of company pension, free-standing AVC and a series of equity Isas. His company pension invests in a middle-of-the-road managed fund, his AVC in a UK blue-chip growth fund and the Isas are used for more adventurous investments including North American funds and technology funds. If Iain decides to reposition the AVC and moves the money into a more aggressive fund, perhaps one also investing into the US, he may want to rebalance some of the Isa investments to keep his overall portfolio diversified.

Alternatively, consider the case of Martha. She decides to transfer a historic personal pension into a final salary company scheme because she likes the appeal of more certain retirement benefits. However, in making this move she has lost some flexibility about when she can cash in her retirement pot; she is now governed by the final salary pension rules and can only draw the full value of her pension by staying in work to the scheme's normal retirement age. So she decides to beef up her saving through an Isa and through National Savings. This will allow Martha to build a smaller supplementary kitty that might allow her to take early retirement even if she cannot yet claim her full company pension.

In some cases you may also decide that boosting another form of saving is a better value alternative to boosting your pension saving. This may well be the case if you are near retirement and take a dim view of the current annuity rules. Box 11.2 on page 208 compares the pros and cons of topping up savings using a stakeholder pension and an Isa. Chapters 9 and 22 explain more about annuities.

This regular review process may seem like too much work to be bothered with. But think about this: how much time would you spend choosing, planning and arranging an annual summer holiday? You would certainly compare brochures, benchmark different hotels and resorts, and then shop around for the best deal. Surely it is worthwhile once every few years to put that much effort into planning for your retirement – hopefully the longest holiday of your life.

In summary:

- Regular reviews are essential to keep on track for the retirement you want.
- Make time and prepare for the review.
- Revisit the basic questions: when do I want to retire and how much do I need to make this happen?
- Be prepared to benchmark your current pensions to make sure they are still delivering value.
- Where they are not, investigate the options for change.
- Do not overlook other forms of saving.

CHAPTER 7 Women and retirement

Read this chapter if:

- You are a woman.
- You want to know more about the special issues women face when planning for their retirement.

Saving for a comfortable retirement can be a tough challenge in its own right. But women face unique hurdles which make it doubly difficult to secure a reasonable income when they retire. Changes in pension legislation and updated working practices over the past two decades have improved the situation. However, female savers are still hampered by basic facts of biology and demographics, which penalise them in the savings race.

General planning issues

The fundamental problem is that women can expect a longer retirement than their male counterparts, but usually have fewer years in work to build up the necessary savings. It is a double-edged sword, which almost inevitably condemns a woman to a lower income in retirement than a man who earns the same salary when they both retire.

All the demographic evidence points to women outliving men and so enjoying a longer retirement than men. As table 1.1 on page 9 shows, a woman who retires at sixty-five can expect to live on average for another twenty-two years. A man retiring at the same age can expect eighteen years of life. And though sixty-five will eventually become the common state retirement age, until that happens in 2020 women will still retire earlier than men, further lengthening their years in retirement. Stretched retirements mean women have to spread a finite pot of pensions savings over more years than men.

At the same time many women have a broken career and work history. In taking time out of the workplace to have children and raise a family, they lose years of income and years of membership in both state and company pension schemes. Even when they come back into work, it may be on a part-time basis, or in a lower-paid job. On average, a man in full-time work earns £453.30 a week before tax.[1] For women the figure is £337.60 a week. Career breaks mean that it is rare for a woman to retire on as high a salary as male colleagues.

This traditional pattern is changing. A greater proportion of women than ever before work. A growing number of women, especially younger professionals, are delaying families until later, when they are more established in their career and it is easier to go back into higher-grade jobs. Men are taking a bigger role in childcare, though only a tiny minority give up their work to raise children.

Nevertheless, on average, it is still women who bear the brunt of family responsibilities and whose jobs and earning capacity suffer for it. And for those women who are now in their late forties and early fifties, the changes may well come too late. They have suffered already from rules in the 1960s and 1970s, which effectively institutionalised pensions discrimination against women.

What are the implications of all this? Firstly, it means being aware that, as a woman, you face a steeper pension mountain to climb than your male counterparts. You may have to be prepared to save a higher proportion of earnings or accept a lower income in retirement (see box 7.1).

Secondly, it means making sure you do not pass up any opportunity that comes your way to maximise income in retirement. There are some specific ideas, discussed below, which may boost your pension and are well worth investigating.

There is good news for women, too. Recent legal changes have helped even out the retirement balance. Pension assets must now be taken into account in divorce cases, for example, which will usually benefit women. The new State Second Pension will give some limited credit for the early years a woman takes off work to raise a family. And the equalisation of retirement ages will give a woman more time in work to build a retirement fund.

Box 7.1: It's hard to be a woman

Longer female life expectancy means that money-purchase pensions pay women a lower annual income than men when they retire. Add this to the potential for earlier retirement and interrupted careers, and it is clear that a woman needs to save harder while she is working to hit the same pension target as a man. How much harder?

The three examples set out below show the different amounts a man and a woman need to save into a personal or company money-purchase pension to achieve similar pensions when they retire.

Example 1: A man and a woman, both aged twenty-five, who work continuously and retire at sixty. They both start saving £150 a month net of tax. Contributions rise at 5 per cent a year. In today's money, that is forecast to give:

- the man a pension of £921.68 a month;
- the woman a pension of £842.84 a month.

If she wants the same pension as the man, she needs to start saving at the slightly higher rate of £164 a month, net of tax.

Example 2: A man and a woman, both aged twenty-five. They work continuously, but she retires at sixty, he goes on until sixty-five. They both start saving £150 a month net of tax. Contributions rise at 5 per cent a year. In today's money, that is forecast to give:

- the man a pension of £1297.39 a month;
- the woman a pension of £842.84 a month, although she will receive this reduced sum five years earlier than the man.

If she wants the same pension as the man when she retires five years earlier, she needs to start saving at the much higher rate of £230.20 a month, net of tax.

Example 3: A man starts saving for his pension at twenty-five. But, since she is not working because of bringing up children, the woman does not start saving until she is thirty-five. Both work continuously and retire at sixty. They both start saving £150 a month net of tax. Contributions rise at 5 per cent a year. In today's money, that is forecast to give:

- the man a pension of £921.68 a month;
- the woman a pension of £505.12 a month.

If she want the same pension as the man, she needs to start saving at the higher rate of £272.65 a month, net of tax.

All these forecasts assume that the money saved grows at 7 per cent a year.

Source: Legal & General pension forecasting calculators. Try these sums for yourself at www.landg.com or at www.thisismoney.com.

Women and state pensions

The basic state pension is not granted automatically, as Chapter 3 explained. It depends on your track record of National Insurance contributions. The more years you have in work paying the correct type of contributions, the higher your entitlement to the basic state pension. And do not forget that the basic pension is paid regardless of other income or assets.

Women frequently have incomplete National Insurance contribution records. This is because:

- they have taken time out of the workplace;
- they have raised children;
- they have earned modest sums in part-time or casual jobs where no National Insurance has been paid;
- they have lived outside the UK for a period of time, perhaps while their husbands were posted overseas;
- they have at some point in the past opted to pay a reduced-rate National Insurance contribution open to married women. This option was available up to April 1977.

Even those in relatively well-paid jobs may be surprised at how patchy their NI track record is. This is because no matter how much you earn in one year, that cannot make up for missed years earlier.

You can get a forecast of your state pension entitlement from the DWP Retirement Pension Forecast and Advice Service (see page 35). It may be possible to boost the value of this state pension. If you are paying the reduced-rate National Insurance contributions, also called reduced-liability contributions, you can opt to switch back to the full rate. The lower rate is 3.85 per cent of qualifying earnings, the higher rate is 10 per cent of qualifying earnings, so this is a big difference. For a woman earning £20,000 a year, the extra National Insurance charge would be around £1000 a year. Box 7.2 illustrates this example in more detail so that those who want to can do the calculation for their own circumstances.

As well as building credits to the state pension, paying higher NI means you also become entitled to other state benefits, such as

Jobseekers Allowance. Once you have made the switch, you can no longer opt back on to the lower rate.

Is a switch back to higher rate worthwhile? This will depend on your circumstances. Many women opted for the lower rate because they expected instead to get a pension based on their husband's National Insurance records. A woman who does not qualify for a pension in her own right gets 60 per cent of the pension that her husband's contributions entitle him to. This is paid once he has reached state retirement age.

For many women in their late forties and fifties, even if they switched back to paying the higher rate, they would not build up entitlement to a pension of their own which would be larger than the pension they could claim through their husbands. Younger women will probably still have enough years of work ahead of them to build up a decent entitlement. But as you had to be married and in work before April 1977 to start the reduced rate, there are very few women to whom this applies.

If you divorce before state retirement age, the picture might change. A woman who does not remarry can still claim against her former husband's NI record. If she remarries, she then can claim against her new husband's NI record. Cohabitation does not count as marriage, either for claiming against a partner's NI record in the first place or for losing entitlement to claim against a former husband's record.

If you do not have sufficient entitlement of your own and you are single or your husband has a patchy contributions record too, then you will have to fall back on state benefits such as the Minimum Income Guarantee if you qualify for them.

What you decide to do about switching to the higher rate will depend on your age. It will also depend on how important you feel it is to have savings and entitlements which are independent of a husband or partner (see box 7.3).

The other way to boost a state pension is to pay voluntary National Insurance contributions, called Class 3 contributions. You can pay these going back up to six years to plug any holes in your NI track record; for example, the years you were at university if you pay soon enough. You are charged at a flat rate, currently £6.75 a week. Payments can be made quarterly or in a lump sum. Paying this may be a wise move for younger women who expect to have a long working life and who are likely to be building sizeable pension entitlements in their own name. Men too can pay voluntary contributions.

Box 7.2 The costs of switching back to full-rate National Insurance

Employees pay National Insurance on all earnings between £72 a week and £575 a week (£3744 and £29,900 a year). The full rate is 10 per cent. The married woman's reduced rate is 3.85 per cent. How much will it cost a woman on the reduced rate to switch back to the higher rate?

Louisa earns £20,000 a year. At the moment she pays the reduced rate. Her NI bill is £20,000 minus £3744 = £16,256 x 3.85 per cent = £625.86 a year.

If she moves back to the higher rate, she will pay £20,000 minus £3744 = £16,256 x 10 per cent = £1625.60. This is an increase of almost £1000 a year. Is this worthwhile?

Louisa is fifty, ten years from state retirement age. She currently has fifteen years of NI contributions credited. If she opts to pay the higher rate she will have twenty-five years of NI credits by the time she retires (see table 3.2, page 33). This means she would be entitled to 65 per cent of the basic state pension. This is only 5 per cent more (£3.62 a week at today's rate) than she would get using her husband's contribution record, which would entitle her to 60 per cent.

She decides the extra pension is not worth the higher NI payments and chooses to save £1000 a year into a stakeholder pension in the hope of a better return.

But if Louisa only earned £8000 a year, the calculation would be very different. She would face an increased NI bill of only £262 a year. Yet her increase in basic state pension would be the same. She might then think it is worth paying the higher payment for a slightly higher pension.

The State Second Pension

This was explained in detail in Chapter 3. It is a new top-up to the state pension based partly on earnings. It comes into effect from April 2002. This is an important development for women because:

- It boosts the pension available for lower earners and part-time workers, the majority of whom are women.
- It treats women who are not working because they are caring for small children or elderly relatives as if they earned £9500 a year and credits their state pension accordingly.

See page 44 if you want to be reminded of more details on the State Second Pension.

Box 7.3: Are you planning for one or for two?

A key decision to make if you are married or a couple cohabiting is whether you are planning jointly for retirement or whether you want to keep your plans separate. As more and more women have incomes and pensions of their own, this issue is growing in importance.

Treating all savings and pensions as a joint kitty can appear easier than trying to keep things separate. Much of the pension system is still set up on the traditional model of a working man who provided for a non-working wife. Terms such as widow's benefit and wife's pension litter the paperwork. And it is possible for spouses to share each other's National Insurance contribution record and get bigger state pensions than individually they might be entitled to.

But keeping pensions and savings separate can have its advantages too. Firstly, it is a way to double up on tax allowances. Each person has separate allowances on how much they can pay into savings and pensions. The new contribution rules, which took effect in April 2001, mean that you no longer need to be working to pay into a personal pension. This opens the door for a couple who juggle their allowances to save more through individual plans than if they lump all savings together. A non-working wife can now use some of her husband's income to buy a pension. Having separate plans also means that both husband and wife have income to use up their annual income tax allowances when they retire, which increases a couple's tax-free income.

The second advantage of independent pensions is that it does make a wife or husband less dependent on a higher-earning partner. With divorce and family break-up now common, independent planning does have a place.

In practice, a prudent approach is to plan for retirement jointly, with a couple planning to retire at the same time etc., but then letting each person build up a separate pot of retirement cash in their own name.

Changing retirement ages

You become entitled to any state pensions at the normal state retirement age. This is currently sixty for women. As Chapter 3 explained, it is moving back gradually to sixty-five over the ten years between 2010 and 2020. Women born after 5 April 1950 will qualify for state retirement benefits at an older age. Anyone, male or female, born on or after 6 October 1954 will not get their state pension until they are sixty-five (see page 36).

The state is catching up with the vast majority of company pensions, which have already equalised retirement ages for men and women.

Equal treatment from company pensions

Since January 1996, company pensions have been compelled to offer equal treatment to male and female employees. This requirement has been reinforced by a series of court cases, both in British courts and in the European courts. Some of the legal cases are still running. Broadly, the issues split into two areas:

- The availability of pensions and the treatment of women now and in the future.
- The past availability of company pensions.

Equal pensions going forward

Equal treatment going forward is relatively straightforward. It means that women are entitled to the same pension benefits, employer contributions, dependants' benefits etc. as their male colleagues. It also means that pensions should be available to all workers in a company's employment, including part-timers.

Some aspects of equality may not appeal to women, particularly if the company pension shifts the retirement age for women to the male age of sixty-five. They may not like the idea of having to go on working longer than they had expected. In such cases early retirement may still be possible for women who joined the pension before the change. But the value of part of their pension may be scaled back.

This is a complex area; essentially, pension earned in the years since the retirement ages were equalised is treated on the new basis. It can be scaled back if a woman quits early, using the pension scheme's normal early retirement rules. But pension earned in the years before retirement age was equalised cannot be scaled back; the original scheme rules apply and a woman is entitled in full to her pension from these years. Box 7.4 shows an example of how this might work in practice.

There are also some aspects of company pensions where men and women are permitted to be treated differently. This is where actuarial factors of life expectancy come into play. For example:

- A woman who transfers out of a final salary company pension can be given a higher transfer value than a man with the same salary and length of service. This is because it costs more to provide an annual pension to a woman, who is expected to live longer.

- A man may have to give up more annual pension than a woman for a specified cash lump sum when he retires. Again, this reflects the different costs of providing a pension.
- A woman who retires with a money-purchase pension fund may receive a smaller annual pension than a man who retires with a fund of equal value. This reflects the different costs of providing annuities for men and women.

Box 7.4: Early retirement from a pension which has changed female retirement date

Jean, fifty-five, has worked in a building society branch for twenty-eight years. The building society runs a final salary pension scheme, with pension building up at one-sixtieth of salary per year of service.

Five years ago, the society changed the female retirement age in its occupational pension. Whereas women used to retire at sixty, now the normal retirement age is the same as for men at sixty-five. But Jean wants to stop at sixty, because this is when her husband is scheduled to retire too.

The scheme rules say that pension is reduced by 5 per cent for each year you retire early.

What will Jean get when she retires at sixty?

Jean has thirty-three years of service, twenty-three years under the old scheme rules and ten years under the new retirement date. Her pension is split into two parts. She receives the full value of her first twenty-three, that is twenty-three-sixtieths of final salary.

Her ten years of service under the revised scheme are scaled back because of the early retirement charge. The pension is trimmed by 5 per cent each year, a total of 25 per cent. So the ten years counts as seven and a half years, or seven-and-a-half-sixtieths of final salary.

Jean's total pension is thirty-and-a-half-sixtieths of final salary.

Equal pensions in the past

The issues around the past availability of company pensions for women are more complex. In the past, many companies would not let part-time workers, the majority of whom are women, join their pension schemes. The European Court of Justice has ruled that this was tantamount to sex discrimination. It says that women who were excluded from company pensions in the past may be able to claim backdated membership. In spring 2001 the House of Lords confirmed the European Court of Justice's rulings. The Lords said that part-timers who had not been allowed to join an employer's pension were being discriminated against and could bring a claim under industrial tribunal laws.

However, new claims against employers have to be filed while an employee is still working for the same company or within six months of leaving. Unfortunately, many of those who were excluded from pensions have long since left employment and cannot claim.

Claims which were previously filed, and which were held up pending the legal hearings, are now gradually being heard.

Where a claim for reinstatement into a pension is successful, employees would have to pay their share of contributions – backdated over twenty or more years, this could amount to a substantial lump sum. However, employers too would pay their backdated contributions and the total package could be very valuable to former part-time staff. In some cases it could make sense for former employees to take out a loan to pay their backdated pension contributions. This would then entitle them to an annual pension and a tax-free lump sum payment. This payment could be used to repay the loan.

Pension rights and maternity

It may be possible to keep some or all of your pension saving going while taking time off work to raise a family. As mentioned earlier, the new State Second Pension will provide some limited benefits for mothers who have children aged five or under. If you are a member of a final salary company pension and are on official maternity leave, then this time off may count as a break in service. Once you return to work, your days of pensionable service then continue to increase.

Those who are in a money-purchase company pension, where contributions depend on salary, may see payments into their pension dip on maternity leave. It depends on how generous the employer is with maternity pay.

Previously, women who were not in work had no way of saving anything extra into a pension. But the new contribution rules, which came into force from April 2001, mean that it is possible to pay at least £3600 a year, possibly more, into a personal or stakeholder pension, even if you have no income of your own. This money could come from other savings or a spouse's or partner's earnings. This concession may help some women on a career break to keep their pension plans ticking over.

Divorce

Historically, pension rights have been overlooked when divorce settlements are negotiated. Women have usually been the ones who have suffered because of this; their husbands have taken the entire pension pot at the time of divorce, or the women's share of the pension is conditional on when the former husbands retire.

Two sets of reforms have come into force during the past five years, most recently in December 2000. These have transformed attitudes on how pensions are carved up during divorce. Women should be the main beneficiaries of change as for the first time they permit genuine clean-break divorce settlements.

The issues of pension and retirement planning and divorce are so important that they are explained separately in Chapter 14.

In summary:

- Women face more problems accumulating a comfortable income for retirement than men.
- They may have to save harder for the same sized pension.
- The state retirement age for women is moving from sixty to sixty-five.
- Several recent changes have started to level the pensions playing field for women.
- Unfortunately these changes may come too late for older women who have already suffered from pension discrimination twenty or more years ago.
- Women need to decide to what extent they want to be independent from partners in their pension planning.

Notes

1 Government labour market survey, April 2000.

CHAPTER 8

Retirement on the horizon

Read this chapter if:

- You are due to retire within five years.
- You are contemplating early retirement soon.

Athletes running a long-distance race have a bell to mark their last lap. Its chime is the signal for one last effort, with the finishing line now in sight.

The final five years in employment represent the last lap in the retirement race. Reaching the birthday five years before your planned retirement age is the signal to up the tempo of preparation. It is time to work out what sort of pension you are on target to achieve, whether you can indeed retire as planned, and to start thinking about how you will go about converting your savings into an income for the future.

If you have been planning hard for retirement already, the five-year signal will simply mark a natural extension to your work. But if you are one of the many who have come to retirement planning later, the five-year deadline can seem a frightening warning. Relax. Remember, for both types of saver there is still time to make a real difference to the quality of retirement you enjoy, provided you are willing to act quickly.

Revisit those basic questions

Chapter 2 introduced five sets of questions behind every retirement plan. With five years to go, it is time to ask some of them again. The difference now, with only five years to go, is that you should be able to be far more confident about the answers you are giving. One or two things may change, but the basics of job, lifestyle and income are unlikely to alter much in the final few years of your career. The key questions are:

1. *When will you retire?* Do you have a definite age in mind? Does your employer set a retirement date? Is early retirement a realistic option? Do you want to coincide your retirement with that of a spouse or partner?
2. *How you will retire?* Is retirement going to be sudden; will you simply clock out one Friday and not return on Monday? Or can you ease into retirement, winding down from full-time to part-time work and spreading the process over several years? Much will depend on the type of work you do and the flexibility of your employer.
3. *What do you want to do with your retirement?* Is retirement going to signal a life of leisure? Do you have specific goals of places to go or hobbies to pursue? Will retirement be the chance to do something different, maybe some part-time work in a different job, or voluntary service? Or will retirement from one job even signal the start of a second career?
4. *What sort of income will you need?* How much will essentials like housing, food and heating cost? How much will it cost to live your retirement dreams, to see the world or to master that golf course? And what about the later years? Should you plan for

the potential costs of ill health, nursing homes and medical treatment?

5 *What sort of income can you expect?* You will already have some pension entitlement, even if it is just something from the state pension. How certain is this income? What about previous employment? What other money might come your way, for example, through inheritance? How far might all these sources of income fall short of what you will need?

Table 8.1 sets out again the planner that you can use to estimate your income needs in retirement. The numbers you write in here should now be well-founded guesses. If you want to be cautious in how you plan, increase all your costs by 15 per cent to allow for some price increases over the next five years. Remember, too, that inflation probably will not stop after you retire, so these costs will escalate through your retirement. However, you should also be able to plan for your income to increase – see the next chapter for more information on this.

Likewise, with only five years to go, you can start to be more confident in your forecasts for likely pension and other income in retirement. If you have seen funds handsomely increase in value over the years of saving, it may be time to lock in some gains (see below).

Following the review process outlined in Chapter 6 will give you a fair indication of how you are placed in the retirement race – well up with the pace, or lagging at the back of the pack.

From now until retirement these reviews should be conducted every twelve months as you fine-tune your plans for life after work.

Table 8.1: Your income needs in retirement

Filling in this chart will help you to estimate how much income you will need in retirement. If you are unsure about costs, look at recent bank statements and credit card bills for guidance. It is unlikely that you will have something to write in every box.

Expenditure	Annual cost (£)
Day-to-day costs	
Food and household basics	
Newspapers and magazines	
Everyday clothing	
Cosmetics, toiletries and hairdressing	
House and home	
Rent or mortgage	
Utility bills: gas, electricity, oil, water	
Buildings and contents insurance	
Council tax	
Saving for repairs and maintenance	
Telephone	
Other services, e.g. satellite TV, Internet access fees	
Cost of help around home, e.g. cleaner	
Transport	
Owning a car: insurance, road tax, financing costs	
Running a car: petrol, servicing, breakdown insurance	
Bus, taxi or train fares	
Leisure and fun	
Holidays and leisure travel	
Eating out	
Pets (including food and vets' bills)	
Sports and hobbies	
Drinking and smoking	
Health and fitness	
Dental fees	
Opticians' fees and glasses	
Private medical insurance	
Long-term care insurance	
Contribution to pay-as-you-go medical fund	

Other protection insurance, e.g. accident cover, life cover	
Other health costs, e.g. physiotherapy	
Savings	
Saving for major household items, home improvements, new car etc.	
Savings for later in retirement, children or grandchildren	
Giving	
Presents	
Regular charitable donations	
Regular gifts to children/grandchildren	
Any other spending	
Total	
Allowance for tax *	20 per cent – multiply total by 1.25 to produce gross income
Gross income required	

* An accurate tax calculation is impossible. No one knows what tax rules will be in force when you retire. And the rate of tax will depend on your income – modest incomes will probably attract no tax, but an increasing number of pensioners are now retiring as top-rate taxpayers. For planning purposes, assume 20 per cent of your total income might be lost to tax, so multiply your annual total by 1.25 to give the gross income required.

What if you do not like the result – coping with a shortfall

The last few years before you expect to retire are where reality bites. It is quite possible that you will find a shortfall between what you estimate as your income needed for a comfortable retirement and what sort of income you are likely to have. Few of us end up with as much money as we expect. Previously, you may have glossed over some of the funding gap, telling yourself that your investments will grow faster and you will be able to save more in future. But now, with the clock ticking down, it is time to face up to retirement reality. Where you have not conducted a full review before, the numbers may seem quite shocking.

There are three main ways to try to bridge the gap between expected income and expected spending in retirement. You can

- save more;
- delay retirement so that you have longer to save and/or make your move into retirement a more gradual process, perhaps working part-time for a while;
- reduce your outgoings in retirement.

In practice, many people do all three to help balance the retirement books.

Saving more

Increasing saving is the first and obvious response to boosting retirement income. Fortunately, there is some outside help for those who are trying to maximise their retirement saving during the last lap.

The taxman recognises that many of us cannot afford to make big savings in the early years of work, while we are raising families and buying homes. So there are more generous allowances granted to allow people to boost their pension saving in their fifties and sixties.

Where you are saving into a personal pension, group personal pension or a stakeholder pension, a person aged fifty-one to fifty-five can save up to 30 per cent of their gross salary. Someone aged fifty-six to sixty can save up to 35 per cent. Someone aged sixty-one or more can save a full 40 per cent of salary. The amount of qualifying salary is capped (£95,400 in tax year 2001/02) but this still permits a huge amount to be saved.

Alternatively, anyone can save up to £3600 a year of gross income into one of these pensions, even if they have no earnings.

Remember, payments into a pension are tax-favoured.

Depending on your circumstances, they are either paid from income before tax or the government tops up your contribution by the equivalent of the tax you have paid.

Unfortunately, contribution limits do not rise with age for those who are members of an occupational or company pension scheme. They are fixed at a maximum of 15 per cent of earnings. This figure includes any extra payments being made into AVC or FSAVC top-up pensions. But members of a company scheme who earn less than £30,000 a year can also save into a stakeholder or personal pension. And if they are at their saving limits there is nothing to stop them passing some of their income on to a non-working spouse so that he or she can invest instead. Box 8.1 shows two examples of how couples can maximise their pension savings.

What sort of difference might this extra saving make? Money invested in the final years before retirement will not grow as much as money saved for twenty or thirty years. But it can still represent a useful increase in income. Legal & General estimates that a man aged fifty-seven who saved an additional £5000 per year gross of tax until he retired at sixty-two would have increased his income in retirement by £260 per month. To achieve the same result by stashing the money in the bank and living off the interest, you would need to be certain of receiving 11 per cent a year in interest up to and throughout retirement.

If you are in a final salary company pension and your AVC contributions buy extra years of service, then every penny you pay in today will have just as much effect on increasing the final pension as money saved thirty years previously. It is an opportunity too good to miss.

Not all savings have to be made using a pension. Individual Savings Accounts, Isas, are also tax-advantaged. Here money paid in grows free of income or capital gains tax and then can be paid out with no tax liability. Each adult can pay up to £7000 a tax year into an Isa.

Cash can also be invested in unit trusts, investment trusts, with-profit bonds, directly into equities or into a bank or building society. Chapter 11 explains all these options in more detail.

Maximising your saving may mean making tough choices and sacrificing other spending that you were planning for today. It may well come down to a choice between funding the pension and having a holiday; between paying into an Isa or replacing the car this year. These are choices and decisions that only you can make.

Depending on your circumstances, your finances may also be getting a timely boost. Those in their fifties and sixties have usually seen children grow up and leave home. Mortgages start getting paid off and investments, such as endowments, linked to homebuying start to mature. Many also inherit from their parents during these years. Consider whether it makes sense to apply some of this extra spending power towards retirement saving.

Box 8.1: Maximising retirement savings

Example 1

Howard is fifty-eight. He earns £46,000 a year as a senior manager of a tyre company. His wife Hilda, fifty-six, does not work. Howard wants to boost the couple's pension saving. He already has a personal pension.

This year Howard can save a maximum of 35 per cent of his salary into his pension, that is £16,100 gross of tax. This costs him £9660 of taxed income.

In addition, he can gift Hilda a further £2808, which she can use to invest in a stakeholder pension. When basic-rate tax is refunded on this, it equates to the maximum permitted investment of £3600.

For a total cost of £12,468 of take-home pay, Howard and Hilda can together save £19,700 into pensions.

The couple can also invest up to £7000 each into an Isa. This would boost their total retirement saving to £33,700 – a staggering 73 per cent of Howard's income. Whether they can afford to save at this level is another matter.

Example 2

Patricia and Roy, both fifty-seven, want to save as much as they can into their pensions. Patricia earns £23,000 from her job at a bank. Roy, who was made redundant two years ago, now works part-time behind the bar of the local golf club, earning £6000 a year.

Patricia is in her bank's pension scheme and already pays 5 per cent of her salary towards a pension. Using the bank's AVC scheme, she can increase this to the maximum 15 per cent. This translates to a pension payment of £3450, costing her £2691 of taxed income.

Roy can pay up to £2808 (£3600 gross of tax) into a stakeholder or personal pension. Patricia can give Roy money to help make these payments if necessary.

They too can each save up to £7000 a year into Isas.

Delaying retirement

Most of us set our hearts on retiring as early as possible. But financial reality means we frequently have to put the retirement dream on hold.

Where someone has planned to retire early, delaying for a year or two often makes the sums look far more appealing. They gain additional time to save, increasing their overall retirement pot. At the same time they reduce the likely length of their retirement, cutting the number of years over which the pot has to be spread.

Technically it is possible to delay retirement up until the age of seventy-five, when income from personal and company pensions has to be taken. Members of some kinds of company pensions may not find their pension is enhanced any further if they keep working beyond a certain age because there are rules about the maximum benefit you can earn from a company pension. Box 8.2 shows an example of how delaying retirement bolsters the finances.

In some cases delay may not be possible. Some employers set absolute retirement ages and refuse any requests for staff to work beyond them. Other organisations are more flexible. The more senior you are, the more clout you will have in pushing to stay on. Some organisations may rehire you after official retirement to work part-time, or be willing to use you as an adviser or consultant.

Attitudes towards older workers in general are changing. As quality staff become rarer, a growing number of organisations are not only encouraging staff to stay on longer, but are also recruiting those who have retired from other work. So if you are forced to leave one job, it may be possible to find some other employment. Even if this is not as lucrative as a previous job, it can help bridge the gap and buy a couple of years before you need to start drawing down on the main retirement savings.

Box 8.2: Delaying retirement

Jake, aged fifty-eight, is hoping to retire at sixty. He works in the finance office of a local authority and is a member of a final salary occupational pension scheme. His pension is based around one-sixtieth of salary for every year of service.

He calculates that he and his wife Mary will need around £21,000 a year before tax to support themselves in retirement. They own their own home, have a recent car but want to be sure they can travel to visit their daughter in Australia at least once a year.

Jake earns £29,000 a year, which he expects will rise to around £29,800 by the time he is sixty. By then he will have twenty-eight years of pensionable service. This means he can expect a pension of around £13,906. This will rise with inflation.

Other savings and investments should provide Jake and Mary with roughly £2500 a year in income. A pension from previous employment is expected to be worth another £800 a year. Mary and he will claim a couple's state pension worth another £6026 a year once he reaches sixty-five. This means total income will be around £17,200, rising to £23,232 once the state pension kicks in.

This is too close for comfort. Jake does not want to have to run down savings for five years until the state pension is paid. Rather than risk compromising his family visits, Jake decides to carry on working for another three years and aims to retire at sixty-three. By then, his salary is expected to be £31,450 and he will have accumulated thirty-one years of service. His pension on this higher salary and longer service will then be £16,249 a year. Estimated total income is then over £19,549 a year, rising to nearer £26,000 once Jake reaches sixty-five.

Jake and Mary could buy even more breathing space by making additional savings during the next five years.

Reducing outgoings

The third way to make retirement sums add up is to cut back on what you were planning to spend after giving up work.

Most pensions provide you with both a regular income in retirement, plus a tax-free cash lump sum when you retire up to certain limits. Many people earmark this lump sum for specific treats when they retire: to buy the new car, to fund the round-the-world trip or to extend their home. This is the first obvious way to reduce spending. By reducing the size of the lump sum you take, you can boost the amount of regular income. Alternatively, take the lump sum but then invest a portion of it to provide income, rather than spending it all. Either way, it means lowering your sights on the retirement dream; for example, cruising the Mediterranean not the Caribbean. Chapters 9, 19 and 20 explain lump sums in more detail.

Many of us plan to reduce outgoings in retirement anyway. We may want to move to a smaller home, which is easier to look after and cheaper to run. Trading down on the property market can also release money tied up in your home, which can then be used as part of the general retirement kitty.

Likewise, when one or both of a couple give up work, it is frequently possible to make economies elsewhere; for instance, running one car instead of two. But beware of expecting that you can cut back too much. Some costs increase in retirement. You are likely to have to heat a home for longer with people around during the day, and there is increased leisure time, which you will want to fill with something more stimulating than daytime TV.

Investment strategies

Worrying about potential shortfalls is only half the battle. It is also vitally important not to forget about savings and investments already accumulated on the road to retirement. In particular, with only five years to go to retirement you need to think hard about where your money is invested and whether you are happy with the level of risk you are taking.

You may need to start making decisions where you have some say, or choice, over how your pension or other funds are invested. This certainly means those with any form of personal pension, including stakeholder, possibly those in some money-purchase company pensions and probably those with AVC or FSAVC top-up pension schemes.

The chances are the bulk of your money will be invested in equities, that is, in company shares. (For a reminder on the different types of investment refer to box 2.1 on page 20.) Shares have historically shown the most potential for growth, so they are an important part of everyone's retirement plans. But investing in shares is also volatile. Prices can go down as well as up – and sometimes very rapidly. One or two shares in your fund falling is not usually a problem. Others will probably be rising at the same time to counterbalance this.

What you need to guard against is a sudden dip in world stock markets just ahead of your retirement. This can dramatically reduce the value of your retirement kitty and hence the income you can produce with it. Most pension strategists recommend that in the run-up to retirement you gradually switch the majority of your pension assets into less volatile, lower-risk funds, typically fixed-interest funds, which invest in a combination of government and company bonds, and cash. This is a way to try to lock in gains you have made on the markets over the previous years. Fixed-interest funds are not likely to grow as quickly as equity funds, so there is a danger that you might miss out on some growth over the next few years. But equally, they are less likely to drop 10 or 20 per cent overnight, so your funds will be safer.

Typically, a saver might hedge their bets by moving one-fifth of their assets from equities to fixed-interest funds each year over the five years to retirement. So gradually you move the bulk of the funds into lower-risk investments. You do not need to go to a new pension provider; virtually all pension companies have lower-risk fixed-interest or managed funds and switching into them is either free or at marginal cost.

Some pensions, including many stakeholder funds, are sold with the facility to do this switching for you. Often called a lifestyle, or default, option, your investments are automatically moved to less risky funds in the run-up towards retirement.

Similar principles can be applied to non-pension investments, such as Peps and Isas. If you are expecting to draw an income from these investments, they can be gradually switched into lower-risk funds which generate a higher income. You do not have to draw the income straight away. It can be reinvested and left to roll up until such time as you need the money.

This switching process is most important for those savers who want to convert their fund into an income as soon as they retire by purchasing an annuity. There are other options available, including phased retirement and income drawdown. These are ways of deferring buying an annuity and taking an income from your accumulated funds. Here the money remains invested, mainly in equity funds, so the gradual switch to fixed interest in the run-up to retirement may not be appropriate. The next chapter explains the concepts behind annuities, drawdown and phased retirement in more detail.

You do not have to battle through this process alone. The majority of savers turn to financial advisers to help steer them through the countdown to retirement. Chapter 12 tells you more about the different advisers and what they can do for you.

In summary:

- The final five years of work are the last chance to bolster retirement funds.
- Review the situation each year.
- There are generous allowances available to encourage saving – if you can afford it.
- Be prepared for some hard choices; it may be prudent to delay retirement or plan for a second job after you formally retire.
- Think about switching existing investments to less risky funds to guard against a fall in the stock market.

CHAPTER 9 What to do when you retire

> Read this chapter if:
>
> - You are on the verge of retirement, with six months or less to go.
> - You have just retired.
> - You want to know more about how to convert a pension into an income.

It is only natural to be caught up in a whirl of mixed emotions when you retire. There may be sadness at leaving work friends and colleagues. You will be excited at the opportunities ahead in retirement – at last, time to call your own. And perhaps there is a little fear: what will the future hold? How will you manage over the next twenty or thirty years?

Amidst these emotions and distractions, you will be asked to make some vital financial decisions. You may have to decide the best way to convert your pension fund into income. It is likely you will have to decide whether to take tax-free cash from a pension and, if so, what to do with it. You may want to rearrange other savings so as to maximise your income and reduce your tax bill. And you must not forget to claim any state pensions to which you are entitled.

Increasingly, retirement is not always a single event. More and more people are gradually switching from work to not working, perhaps winding down to two or three days a week, or doing consulting work after formally retiring from a job. Even then, there will be decisions to make; how are you going to adapt to a reduced income? Do you want to claim any pension yet, or will you live off other savings?

This chapter will help you to understand what happens when you retire and to make the right choices.

Start planning in advance

Making the right decisions and completing the paperwork cannot be done overnight. It is wise to give yourself at least three months and ideally six months before a planned retirement date to pull together everything you will need.

Dealing with personal pensions and pensions from your existing employer will on average take three to four months. Company pensions from previous employers may take a little longer to claim. Allow three months to process claims for the state pension.

If you are relying on other investments, such as maturing endowments or savings plans, to provide income, it will take several weeks to collect money from these and then to decide how and where to reinvest it.

It may be possible to rush paperwork through more quickly. But you risk hurrying vital and sometimes irreversible decisions. So allow yourself the time to think things through and to seek a second opinion.

How to claim your state pension

Though everyone will be entitled to some state help in retirement, you will have to claim what you are due.

The Benefits Agency, part of the Department of Work & Pensions, should write to you four months or so before you reach state retirement age. This is sixty-five for a man and between sixty and sixty-five for a women, depending on when she was born (see Chapter 3). This Retirement Pack should contain a form BR1, which you complete to claim your state pensions.

Alternatively, call a Benefits Agency centralised telephone service to make your claim. It is open from 7 a.m. to 7 p.m. Monday to Friday on 0845 300 1084.

If you have not received a letter and Retirement Pack ten to twelve weeks before your birthday, chase matters up yourself. The Benefits Agency may not have an up-to-date address for you. Write to your local Benefits Agency office or visit in person. Quote your National Insurance number. Do not call the centralised claims service; they can only help if you have already been sent a Retirement Pack.

If you are thinking about deferring your state pension, as discussed in Chapter 3, now is the time to do so. Those who reach retirement age before 2010 can defer up to five years.

When you claim your pension you will have to decide how you want it paid. It can be collected weekly in cash by order book at your local post office, or paid monthly or quarterly direct to a bank or building society account you nominate.

Pensions you collect weekly are paid in mainly in advance; the pensions week runs from Sunday to Saturday and money usually can be collected on the Monday. Transfers to a bank or building society are made in arrears, i.e. at the end of a four-week or thirteen-week period. So if you opt for the convenience of payment to your bank, be sure you will have sufficient funds to get through the first month or three months without your state pension.

You can switch from collecting your pension weekly to monthly or quarterly transfer and vice versa.

You will not miss out if the paperwork has not been processed by the time you reach official retirement age. State pension can be backdated up to twelve months, so it is possible to claim it after your official retirement birthday. But pension a husband claims on behalf of his wife can only be backdated by six months.

Delivery of state pensions is set to change from 2003. All order book payments via the post office will be scrapped and everything will have to be paid by automated credit transfer. However, there are plans for new types of bank account, which will mean that those who get these credit transfers can still access them as cash at post offices.

Box 9.1 explains the special circumstances if you plan to retire overseas.

How to claim company pensions

You will need to be in contact with employers, both past and present, about three months before the date at which you expect to claim a company pension.

Pension schemes that you join through work usually have defined retirement ages; for example sixty, sixty-two or sixty-five. These ages are now the same for both men and women, although women may be able to retire earlier without too large a reduction in their pension (see Chapter 7). Early retirement is discussed in detail in Chapter 13. A few occupational pensions are flexible and allow you to nominate when you retire between set ages, typically sixty and sixty-five. Benefits that have been obtained through contracting out of Serps cannot normally be taken until the age of sixty.

If you have moved jobs several times, it is possible that you may have a company pension which starts paying when you are sixty, one that falls due at age sixty-two and some pension which you cannot claim until you are sixty-five. You will need to decide how you juggle these ages and when you actually can afford to stop working.

When you have not heard from an employer or former

employer with three months to go before you expect to collect a company pension, make the first move and get in touch yourself.

If you are not certain what has happened to an employer you once worked for and that you think owes you a pension, write to the Opra Pension Schemes Registry (see Contact Information). They may be able to track down the company and give you the appropriate contact details. Do not be shy of phoning a former employer to ask whom to contact or to get more information. You have every right to ask for a pension you are entitled to.

You will usually have to complete a separate set of claim forms for each company pension. Depending on the size of the pension involved and your circumstances, you may want to meet someone from the company pension office face to face to make sure you understand all the issues.

Key questions to ask about each company pension include:

- What annual pension am I entitled to? How will that increase in future years?
- What size of tax-free lump sum will I get?
- Can I get a bigger annual pension by reducing the amount of tax-free cash I take?
- Is there a pension paid for a spouse or partner after I die? How big is this? Is this automatic, or do I have a choice about it? If there is a choice, how might my own pension be reduced if I opt for a partner's pension?
- Do other dependants, such as children, qualify for money when I die?
- How is the pension paid? Do I get any choice about how frequently it is paid?

Your pension may be boosted by any additional voluntary contributions (AVCs) you have made. If these have been paid to an in-house AVC scheme, the extra pension should be paid automatically at the same time as you retire. AVC benefits cannot be taken as tax-free cash and must all go towards providing a pension, unless the AVC started before 1987.

If the AVC contributions have been invested in a money-purchase fund, this will have to be converted to income. Depending on how the scheme works, you may need to get involved in choosing and purchasing an annuity with this money.

The Inland Revenue rules on in-house AVCs have recently changed. This means company pension funds can rewrite their rules to allow the pension from an AVC to be taken at a different time from the main pension. This would aid partial retirement. But few company pension schemes have bothered to relax their rules; most still insist that the AVC is taken alongside the main pension.

The rules are different when your extra contributions have been invested in a free-standing AVC scheme (FSAVC) with an independent pension company. Here the retirement age is whatever you have chosen it to be, which may be before or after you take the main company pension.

If you have been saving into a money-purchase company pension, you may be able to defer taking an income from the whole fund and instead run an occupation income drawdown scheme (see below for more information on annuities and drawdown). Proceeds from an AVC or FSAVC can also be used to fund income draw-down.

The proceeds of company pensions are usually paid direct to your bank. In some cases it is still possible to ask for a cheque to be sent to you each month or quarter. The pension will be taxed through the PAYE system. However, you may need either to claim back tax or pay additional tax through the annual self-assessment process.

Where a company pension is classed as trivial – that is, worth less than £260 a year – it can be paid in a single lump sum. This saves paperwork all round. The arrangement usually applies to historic company pensions where people have only spent a few years in a particular job, perhaps thirty years or more ago when earnings were much lower. The lump sum is taxed at a flat rate of 20 per cent. The tax cannot be reclaimed.

Box 9.1: Retiring to the sun

Thousands of people retire overseas each year – either to escape to the sun or to be nearer to family.

It is possible to arrange for your pensions – both state and private – to be paid to you in your new destination. However, you may have to accept a reduced income, particularly from state pensions.

The state pension

If you plan to be away for only part of a year, then you have some choices. If you will be away for less than three months at a time and are collecting your pension weekly, you can simply collect it in one lump when you return.

If you go away for longer you can tell the Benefits Agency who will keep the pension for you until you return. Alternatively, you can have the money paid into a bank account in the UK and can then arrange for it to be transferred to a bank abroad. The value of your pension may fluctuate because of exchange rate movements.

If you are going to settle overseas, payment direct abroad is likely to be the most sensible option. However, you are not guaranteed to receive future increases in the value of the state pension. These are only paid if you live in certain countries, including another European Union state, or a dozen or so other states with which the UK has a special agreement for increasing pensions. For example, the UK will keep increasing the pensions of those who live in the USA, Bosnia, Croatia and the Channel Islands. But it does not have an agreement to keep increasing pensions for those who live in popular retirement destinations like Canada, Australia and New Zealand.

The Department of Work & Pensions has a comprehensive range of leaflets on pensions and benefits in specific overseas nations. Contact your local office or look at the DWP website www.dwp.gov.uk.

Company and personal pensions

You will be able to claim the full value of any existing personal or company pensions, regardless of where you live. And future increases in these pensions will be paid too.

How you actually collect the money may depend on the rules of the pension scheme or the company that you have purchased an annuity from.

Some annuities, for example, can only be paid into a UK bank account. You will then need to arrange a transfer onward to a bank in the nation of your choice. Other insurance companies will happily make the payment to an overseas bank direct. But there could be a small extra fee to cover the higher bank charges involved. Cheques can also be sent, but as these will be drawn on a UK bank, they may be difficult to cash where you are living.

Likewise, a company may be willing to arrange pension payments overseas, especially if it is a bigger firm with international operations. If it is not, again the pension can be paid to a UK bank and you can arrange for an onward transfer.

Tax

A quick word on taxation. Personal and occupational pensions are usually paid out to you after UK tax has been deducted. The organisation paying the pension will take its lead from the Inland Revenue and deduct tax at whatever rate your personal tax code indicates. If you go overseas permanently, you run the risk of being taxed twice on your pension – once in the UK and once in your new country of residence. The UK has a series of arrangements with individual nations, called double taxation treaties, to iron out such problems.

Be sure to inform the UK tax authorities before you go and then tell the tax authorities in your new home. Depending on where you are going and on your personal circumstances, you may get your pension paid without UK tax deducted and pay tax on the income in your new home. Alternatively, your pension may be taxed at UK rates, but this tax is taken into account by your new home nation.

How to claim personal pensions

Generally, you can start taking benefits from your personal pension at any time after the age of fifty. You must 'retire' by the age of seventy-five. Older-style personal pensions, including self-employed deferred annuities (sold until April 1970) and Section 226 pensions (sold until June 1988) have different rules. Here the normal retirement ages are between sixty and seventy-five. For full details on the different types of personal pension, including historic contracts, see Chapter 20.

When you started your pension, you may have been asked to nominate an estimated retirement age. In some cases this age was merely to assist projections of the value of your pension fund. But on a few, older-style pensions, retiring before this age may mean paying extra penalty charges.

The other exception to the age rules is what are called protected rights; funds which have accumulated because you contracted out of Serps or the State Second Pension. These funds can only be used when you reach sixty – the same age for both men and women.

To claim a personal pension get in touch with the pension provider. If you have nominated a target retirement age, the pension company will get in touch with you anyway. You need to be in contact about three months before you want to start drawing a pension. Remember, you do not have to retire to take a personal pension. You can draw an income and carry on working. Beware, however, as this extra income may take you into a higher tax band and mean you pay unnecessary extra tax.

The key questions to ask are similar to those asked of a company scheme. They include:

- What is the value of my pension fund?

- What sort of income will this fund buy if I take a pension from you?
- Can I arrange for that income to increase in future years? What will that cost?
- Do I qualify for a guaranteed annuity rate (see below)?
- What is the maximum size of tax-free lump sum I am entitled to?
- How much extra pension could I get by reducing the tax-free lump sum?
- Can I arrange for a pension to be paid to my spouse after I die? Again, what will the cost be?
- How is the pension paid? Do I get any choice about how frequently it is paid?
- What are the other options, such as income drawdown?

But there is one other question which is vital. With personal pensions you do not have to draw an annual income from the company that has invested your money in the years to retirement. You can take what is called an open-market option and transfer your money elsewhere if that will buy you a bigger pension. You cannot be penalised for moving elsewhere. Only around one-third of those who could use the open-market option to shop for a better annuity actually do so. The rest frequently end up with smaller pensions than they could buy elsewhere.

Using your open-market option: shopping for an annuity and the alternatives

This section is designed to give an overview of how you can convert a pension fund into an income. It will cover the basic issues and summarise the different types of product available. Chapter 22 goes over the same ground in much more detail and contains more technical information.

When you ask your pension company for the current open-market value on a personal pension, you will have four options.

- You can leave the money where it is to carry on growing and defer your retirement.
- You can buy the annuity that is being offered by your current pension company. The forms you are sent may not mention the word annuity. They may say 'your fund will buy you an annual pension of £xyz'.
- You can shop around elsewhere to see if you can get a more generous annuity, which pays a higher pension than you are being offered.
- You can consider the alternatives of income drawdown or phased retirement.

Whatever you choose to do, on current rules you will have to use your fund to buy an annuity by your seventy-fifth birthday.

What is an annuity?

An annuity converts a lump sum into an income. This income is guaranteed until you die. Only insurance companies are allowed to sell annuities. The business is closely regulated to ensure that there is sufficient money to honour these promises. Another way to think about an annuity is like life insurance in reverse. With insurance, you pay a regular monthly premium, which produces a lump sum on your death. With the annuity, you give the insurer the lump sum and it pays this back in monthly instalments. The longer you live, the more the insurer has to pay back. But once you buy an annuity, your capital is gone for good.

How much income an annuity produces depends on several factors, not least the size of your pension fund. Bigger funds give bigger incomes. The next most important issue is age. The older you are, the more income you will get because your life expectancy is lower. Men get higher incomes than women of the same age because they are expected to die sooner.

Annuities are also affected by general economic conditions, such as long-term interest rates. The lower rates are, the more it costs an insurer to provide the absolute guarantee of future income. The size of income an annuity will produce is also affected by the added extras a pensioner can build into their annuity.

A basic annuity will give the person who buys it a set income from now until the day they die. The income will not increase; the same will be paid every year. Annuity rates change all the time. Table 9.1 sets out some example rates for what income a saver can buy with their pension fund. It is important to note that income from a pension annuity will automatically be taxed. The numbers in the table are gross income, that is, before tax.

Table 9.1: What sort of income will a pension fund buy?

This list gives a taste of the kind of income that your pension fund might buy. All the cases quoted below are the initial income that a fund of £100,000 can provide. The money is paid monthly, in arrears. The income quoted is gross of tax.

Where an annuity is level, the income will remain the same each year. Where it is 5 per cent escalation, it means the income increases each year by 5 per cent. A guarantee means the income will be paid out for at least five years, even if the holder dies.

Personal details and annuity type	Annual gross income
Male, 60, level income, no guarantee	£7926
Female, 60, level income, no guarantee	£7445
Male, 60, 5 per cent escalation, five-year guarantee	£4598
Female 60, 5 per cent escalation, five-year guarantee	£4093
Male, 65, female, 62, level income, no guarantee, 50 per cent survivor's pension	£8094
Male, 65, female, 62, 5 per cent escalation, five-year guarantee, 50 per cent survivor's pension	£4545

Male, 75, level income, no guarantee	£12,753
Female, 75, level income, no guarantee	£11,211
Male, 75, 5 per cent escalation, five-year guarantee	£8938
Female, 75, 5 per cent escalation, five-year guarantee	£7617

All figures rounded to nearest pound. Rates provided by The Annuity Bureau in July 2001.

Indicative annuity rates are published regularly in *Financial Mail* on the 'Facts and Figures' pages. Alternatively, log on to the *Financial Mail* website www.thisismoney.com or try www.annuity-bureau.co.uk.

Those retiring can shop around and obtain alternative quotes for their annuities through independent financial advisers. A number of firms specialise in this market including Annuity Direct and The Annuity Bureau in London and Bridgegate Annuities in Chester.

There is a range of different options that can be chosen to customise an annuity to a buyer's needs. These include:

- Guarantees – a period over which the annuity is guaranteed to pay out, even if the holder dies. This guards against the danger of someone handing over tens of thousands of pounds and then dying a few weeks later with very little return. Guarantees are typically for five or ten years. The cost depends on age. The older you are, the more expensive the guarantee. For example, a five-year guarantee for a man aged sixty would cost around 1 per cent of income (i.e. his annual income is reduced by 1 per cent). This would rise to 3 per cent for a man aged seventy. Do not confuse guarantees with guaranteed annuity rates, offered by some types of personal pension (see below).
- Income in advance or arrears – you can pick whether you get paid in advance or at the end of a period. Being paid in advance reduces the income; an income paid annually in advance is likely to be around 8 per cent less than one paid annually in arrears.
- Frequency of income – you can also pick how often you are paid an income. Options are usually monthly, quarterly, half-

yearly or annually. Being paid monthly in arrears gives you 4 per cent less than being paid annually in arrears.

- Escalation or inflation proofing – the basic option is a level annuity, where the income is unchanged from year to year. Alternatively, you can pick an annuity where income will increase each year. Typically, you can nominate any level of increase between nothing and 8.5 per cent a year. You can also pick the Retail Price Index, which matches increases to inflation, or a Limited Price Index increase. LPI is the lower of inflation or 5 per cent a year. All these annual increases are guaranteed. But they are costly. On average a man aged sixty opting for 5 per cent a year increases would receive a 40 per cent lower income at the start than for a level annuity.
- A spouse's or partner's pension – you have the option to extend your annuity to cover two lives, not just one. This means that when one partner dies, the annuity goes on paying out until the second death. Though sometimes called spouse's pension or widow's pension, it can cover a partner of any sex. You can pick different levels of pension for a spouse, from nothing through to 100 per cent of what the main annuitant gets. Most couples opt for between one-third and two-thirds of the original pension. The cost of providing a partner's pension depends on their age. The younger they are, the more expensive it will be. A man aged sixty-five, with a wife of sixty-two, would see his income fall by around 14 per cent if he opted for a 50 per cent widow's pension.
- A dependant's pension – similar to the partner's pension but for other dependants, such as children or aged relatives. Costs vary dramatically, depending on the age of the dependants.

There are special annuity rates paid to those in poor health, who are smokers or who live in certain areas of the UK and work in certain occupations. All these groups have statistically much shorter life expectancy, so can qualify for more generous incomes.

There is one other important type of annuity. This is the investment annuity. Here the money you give to an insurer is invested for growth. The amount of income you receive is not normally guaranteed, but depends on how well stock markets grow. Investment annuities are not usually available to those investing in a money-purchase company pension.

Investment annuities come in two versions; unit-linked and with-profit. For both, if the markets do well and the funds grow, the income can increase each year from its original level. But if the investment growth is poor, or there are losses, the income may fall in subsequent years. This type of annuity will appeal most to savers who are willing to accept an income which is fluctuating, but which has the potential to grow to higher levels than can be produced by a conventional annuity. Chapter 22 explains these products fully. It is strongly recommended that you take financial advice before buying an investment annuity.

Guaranteed annuity rates

Some insurance companies have in the past sold pensions with a guaranteed annuity rate. This promises savers that their pension fund will be converted into an income at a pre-set rate. A common guarantee for men is an income of one-ninth of the fund value per year. For women, the most common number used is one-eleventh of the fund value per year. But for both sexes guarantees can be higher.

When the guarantees were first written they were less generous than prevailing annuity rates. However, as annuity rates have fallen, the guarantees have become more and more valuable. The guarantees can now produce an income 20 or 30 per cent higher than a similar fund could buy on the open market.

Where a pension has a guaranteed annuity rate attached to it, shopping around and using the open-market option may not be a wise move. However, it is not completely black and white. Frequently the guarantees only apply to certain types of annuity. So the guarantee may apply to a single-life annuity for the pension holder, but not to a joint-life annuity to give their spouse an income after they die. In such circumstances the open-market option might appeal. It can even make sense to split the fund and use some of it to make the most of the guarantee and some of it to shop around for another annuity. Again, specialist advice is essential to capitalise on a guarantee.

Companies that have sold pensions in the past with guaranteed annuity rates include:

Company name	Years when pensions with guarantees were sold
Axa Sun Life/Axa Equity & Law	Early 1970s to mid-1980s
Equitable Life	1956 to 1988
Legal & General	Early 1970s to 1987
Scottish Amicable	1970 to 1987
Scottish Equitable	1960 to 1988
Scottish Mutual	Early 1970s to mid-1980s
Scottish Widows	1983 to 1994
Standard Life	Early 1970s to 1989

Alternatives to annuities

Annuities have a number of advantages for those in retirement. In particular, the income is usually absolutely guaranteed. It will go on being paid until the day you die. If you like, you can consider an annuity as insurance against the cost of a very long life-span. Many insurers have annuities that they have been paying for more than forty years.

But critics point to a number of drawbacks. They say that annuities offer poor value. Certainly, the income that a given fund can produce has fallen dramatically over the last decade. A fund which could produce a gross annuity income of over £10,000 a year in 1990 will produce less than £6000 a year today. Moreover, critics argue that an annuity is not an efficient investment because you lose control of your capital. There is nothing left to pass on to dependants. Critics say that, with retirements lasting thirty or so years, it is foolish to lock yourself into an income level determined by the economic conditions at the particular moment you retire.

There is a growing campaign for the compulsory annuity purchase rules to be scrapped. Many investors would rather take their chances with some of the alternatives to annuities.

Some reform of annuity rules is likely in the next few years. For the moment, pensioners can use other methods to produce an income from their pensions before they have to bite the bullet and get an annuity when they become seventy-five.

The two main alternatives to an annuity before age 75 are income drawdown and phased retirement.

Income drawdown

This is an option for those with personal pensions and for some types of money-purchase company pensions. It may also be possible to arrange a transfer out of other types of company pension into a personal pension and then go into income drawdown from that second pension. But the charges you face to do this might be prohibitive.

In brief, with income drawdown, the bulk of a pension fund remains invested in the pension. You can take your entitlement of tax-free cash. The remainder of your pension fund is then reinvested to carry on growing. Each year you are allowed to draw an income from this fund. The amount of income is strictly regulated. It must lie between 35 per cent and 100 per cent of the income you would get from a single-life, level annuity for a person of your age with your fund.

Every three years the drawdown plan is reviewed, at extra cost to yourself. If investment growth has been poor, the fund value will have been eroded and the amount of income you will be allowed to take in future years is reduced. Conversely, if your money has grown well, or if general annuity rates have improved, you may be allowed to take a higher income.

If you die while your fund is in drawdown, the value of your fund at death is taxed at 35 per cent. The remainder can form part of your estate and be passed on to a spouse or partner. Drawdown funds can also be written in trust to avoid inheritance tax.

Drawdown is not normally recommended for those with pension funds of less than £200,000 to £250,000. This is because you need a reasonable-sized fund to bear the administration costs of drawdown and to provide a good spread of different investments.

Among others, drawdown may appeal to:

- those who do not want to buy an annuity;
- those who are going into semi-retirement or part-time work and do not need to collect a full income from their pension. They would draw as much as they needed and leave the rest to grow;
- those who are retiring at a young age and want to defer buying an annuity until they are older and will get a higher annuity income;
- those who are already running a self-invested personal pension or a small self-administered pension scheme and who want to continue to be involved in investing their own funds.

It will not appeal to those who are risk-averse or who want absolute security of income.

Phased retirement

This is an alternative to income drawdown, or can be used alongside drawdown to give complete control over how you convert a fund into income. It is suitable for those who are invested in a personal pension plan. To move into phased retirement from a company pension you would have first to transfer into a personal pension. The combination of charges may make this poor value.

Put simply, with phased retirement you split a pension fund into many separate segments. Typically 1000 segments are used. Each year you 'retire', or vest, a certain number of segments. Each segment gives the saver a chunk of tax-free cash and money to be invested in an annuity or in a drawdown plan.

In the early years the majority of your income comes from tax-free cash and only a little from the annuities. But as more money is used to purchase annuities or goes into drawdown, the value of the annuity or drawdown income increases.

The rest of the pension which has not been vested remains invested and hopefully continues to grow free of tax. By the time you reach seventy-five, all the funds must be converted into an annuity.

Phased retirement will appeal to those with substantial pension funds and for similar reasons to those listed for income drawdown. There are a few crucial differences between phased retirement and drawdown though. With phased retirement:

- Tax-free cash is released gradually, rather than up front.
- It is possible to carry on paying into a phased retirement pension if you are still working.
- If you die before the whole fund is vested, whatever is left passes to your spouse with no tax charge. If you have no spouse, it forms part of your estate.

Again, phased retirement is not suited to those who are nervous of stock market risk or who want a guaranteed income. The value of the income produced in future years depends on how well your fund grows and on what happens to future annuity rates.

In theory, a wealthy saver who has two or three different personal pensions could use one to provide a guaranteed income and then use either drawdown or phased retirement with the rest.

What about your tax-free lump sum?

The vast majority of savers who have been using pensions to plan for retirement will have the option of taking a tax-free lump sum when they stop working. Frequently, this represents the largest sum of cash that a person has have ever had in one go. For lucky pensioners it can be the ticket to a round-the-world trip, or the keys to a new car.

Up to 25 per cent of the final fund value of a modern personal pension plan can be taken as tax-free cash. The figure varies for older types of plan. On money-purchase company pensions the rules on how big the lump sum can be vary depending on when you joined the scheme. For example, someone who joined after 1989 can have the greater of three-eightieths of salary per year of service or two and a quarter times their initial pension. Similar rules apply to most company final salary schemes. Public-sector final salary pension schemes tend to offer a tax-free lump sum of three times your initial pension.

The lump sum can be swapped in all, or in part, for a bigger annual pension. However, advisers usually recommend that most retirees take the maximum tax-free cash they can, even if they need their fund or pension to produce as much income as possible. This is because the lump sum can be invested in tax-efficient ways, to produce an after-tax income that is bigger than you would get from taking it as a pension.

Non-pension investments are discussed in detail in Chapter 11. Options for tax-efficient income include:

- Individual savings accounts (Isas) – each person can invest up to £7000 a tax year. The income produced is free of tax and so is any capital growth. A retiring pensioner can gift some of their lump sum to a spouse or partner, so that he or she can also invest, doubling the annual Isa investment to £14,000.
- National Savings products – several of these pay income free of tax, including the fixed-interest savings certificates, index-linked savings certificates and Premium Bonds. Gross rate of interest may appeal to higher-rate taxpayers.
- Investment bonds – higher-rate taxpayers can draw up to 5 per cent a year from these with no immediate tax charge. Income tax is deferred.
- Purchase annuities – a special type of annuity bought with non-pension assets. Your lump sum counts as non-pension. This will give a guaranteed return, a large portion of which can be counted as return of capital so is free of income tax. This may be an attractive option for those aged seventy or more. See the next chapter for more information on purchase annuities.

It is possible to make your own decisions on these investments, but individual financial advice is recommended. It makes sense to think through all the options before deciding how much of a tax-free lump sum to take. Once you have retired you cannot change your mind.

Producing income from other investments at retirement

Depending on how you have been saving for retirement, your pensions are likely to form only part of your retirement kitty. You may have a string of other investments that can be used to support you. These investments are not directly affected by whether you are in work or not. There is no compulsion to cash things in or move them around when you retire.

Most savers, though, will want to give the rest of their savings portfolio a thorough review. In particular, they will have to assess whether they need to switch the emphasis from growth to income. If you are using a higher-risk strategy such as income drawdown or phased retirement for your main pension fund, you might also want to shift some of your other assets into lower-risk investments to act as a kind of insurance policy.

In summary:

- Do not leave claiming your pensions to the last minute. Give yourself three to six months to sort through the paperwork.
- You have to claim your state pension and decide how you will have it paid.
- Company pensions may pay benefits at different ages. If you have more than one, you will need to decide when you are going to retire.
- You will have to decide how to convert your personal pension funds into an income.

- Annuities, drawdown and phased retirement are your three options for this.
- Use your open-market option and shop around for the best income.
- Most savers will end up buying an annuity.
- Decide how you are going to make the best use out of a tax-free lump sum.

CHAPTER 10 Managing income in retirement

Read this chapter if:

- You have already retired, or started to draw an income from pensions and savings.
- You want to know more about how to manage your income through retirement
- You want to know about meeting the costs of long-term care.
- You want to know how to help a friend or relative who has already retired.

Once you have decided to stop working, and so have ceased earning, the challenge of retirement planning is to husband what you have got. A lucky few may win a big cash prize in the lottery, or through Premium Bonds. But you cannot count on this. The name of the game is to make the best use of the assets and resources already in the kitty.

Don't stop planning

When you have reached retirement, it might be tempting to stuff all your bank books, investment paperwork and Isa valuations to the back of a drawer and forget this dreary money stuff. Tempting, but a mistake.

Hopefully, you will be looking forward to a long retirement. You can never know what the future holds, but you might have twenty-five or thirty years of healthy life ahead of you. The best way to make sure that your retirement kitty stretches smoothly over these years is to keep a cautious eye on spending, saving, income and other investments. This doesn't mean counting every penny. Relax and enjoy yourself because that is what retirement is for. But at least once a year it is advisable make the time to sit down and see how much of your retirement pot is left, and work out how quickly you are going through it. If you have to complete an annual tax form, maybe do the sums alongside this.

If you are married or with a partner, try to make this a joint process. Frequently one partner handles the financial affairs in isolation. If they die first, the other is left floundering.

This annual review is not rocket science. It is a matter of asking yourself basic questions, which you are probably already thinking about anyway. These include:

- How much income have you received this year? Is it what you expected? Has it increased from previous years? Is it likely to increase again next year? Have you got deferred pension to collect?
- How much have you spent over the past twelve months? Again, how does it compare with last year and is it what you expected? If it is more than you had planned for, where did the extra costs come from?
- How are your savings holding up? Are you having to dip into them to make ends meet? Or are they actually increasing in value? If so, do you want to increase the income you are taking from them?
- Do you have any major expenses on the horizon? Does the car need replacing, or the roof need fixing? Is it time for that trip to

see grandchildren in Australia? If so, how will you pay for this? Do you need to budget over several years?

- Do you have any one-off extra money coming your way? This might include a maturing investment, such as an endowment, or perhaps an inheritance.

This process should ensure that you have an accurate picture of how well you are positioned. Hopefully, your income is rising and keeping pace with any increased costs, and you can afford to do the things you had planned to do. If you do predict problems ahead, or you are already struggling, there are ways to try to make your existing assets sweat (see 'Boosting your income', page 183).

The good news: your income will increase

Once you are retired, your income should keep on rising. Different chunks of pension income will increase in different ways.

State pensions

The state pension will increase each year. How rapidly it grows is in the hands of the politicians. Officially, the basic state pension is index-linked. It rises in line with inflation. But when inflation is low, this can trigger very small rises. For example, the basic pension was increased by only 75p a week in April 2000. This caused huge pensioner protests. Partly as a result, the basic pension was boosted by more than inflation in April 2001 and will again be increased by more than inflation in 2002. Such extra rises are welcome, but there is no guarantee they will be repeated.

Your Serps pension will rise each year in line with inflation.

Company pensions

If you are drawing a company pension, this too should keep on increasing in value. How it grows will depend on the type of pension you have and the particular rules of your pension scheme.

With final salary pensions it is up to each scheme to set rules on how pensions in payment increase, within Inland Revenue limits. A few schemes do not give any increases. The vast majority do pay increases, sometimes generous ones. There are lots of different methods used to calculate annual pay rises. Some schemes will increase at the higher of a pre-set rate or inflation, e.g. your pension may rise by 3 per cent each year or inflation if it is higher. Other schemes link to inflation. Others follow limited price indexation, that is the lower of inflation or 5 per cent a year.

The increases are set out in scheme rules and cannot be changed arbitrarily. In addition, where investment performance is good, final salary pensions can make occasional discretionary increases in pensions: for example, upping the value by 2 per cent on top of a usual annual rise. Discretionary increases cannot be used to take your pension higher than the maximum levels set by the Inland Revenue.

Any pension that has been earned by you and your scheme contracting out of Serps has to be increased in line with a government formula. This is called Guaranteed Minimum Pension. All GMP that you earned based on employment before April 1997 has to be increased in line with RPI, that is in line with inflation.

Money-purchase company schemes may provide annual increases for all or for part of your pension after you retire. Again, the value of the increase will depend on exactly how the scheme was structured, what sort of annuity, if any, was purchased by the scheme when you retired and what the scheme rules say about annual increases. The 1995 Pensions Act made it law that money-purchase schemes should provide *at least* limited price indexation on funds earned in the pension since April 1997. As time goes by this will apply to a greater proportion of the pension paid to those who retire.

Company money-purchase pension earned through contracting out is also treated on a special basis. The so-called protected rights from your pension must increase in value by:

- the lower of RPI (inflation) or 5 per cent a year, for pension accumulated after April 5 1997;
- the lower of RPI or 3 per cent a year, for pension accumulated before April 6 1997.

Many company pension schemes run pensioners' associations for the retired members of their schemes. This is effectively a club for former workers. Some associations run social programmes and provide services to members, such as legal and financial advice.

Even if these aspects of the association do not appeal, getting involved is still important because it gives you the chance to have a say in the way the pension is run. Pension schemes now have to have at least one trustee who is nominated and voted for by members. Some have more. Associations may nominate their own candidates to ensure that the interests of retired members are not forgotten, although trustees have a legal duty to act in the best interests of all members.

Personal pensions

Personal pension earned through contracting out is treated in the same way as for a money-purchase company pension. The protected rights from your pension must increase in value by:

- the lower of RPI (inflation) or 5 per cent a year, for pension accumulated after April 5 1997;
- the lower of RPI or 3 per cent a year, for pension accumulated before April 6 1997.

Whether your other income from a personal pension keeps rising depends on what you did when you retired. If you used the fund to buy a level annuity, which would have paid the highest income when you retired, then you cannot expect any increase in this income. It will stay the same until the day you die. If inflation races ahead, the spending power of this pension will decline rapidly.

If you opted for an escalating annuity, then you can expect to see increases in your income. How it increases depends on the type of escalation you choose (see page 168). It may increase by a set amount each year; for example, 3 per cent, or it may go up in line with inflation. Alternatively, if you have an investment annuity the income will fluctuate, rising dramatically some years and then staying level or possibly falling the next.

Those who used some or all of their pension to go into income drawdown or phased retirement schemes will have more control over how they manage their income from year to year (see below).

Linking pensions to inflation carries its own risks. If earnings increase more rapidly than inflation, as they did for most of the 1980s and 1990s, then pensioners' standard of living can fall behind that of those in work.

Other income

How your other income rises, or falls, depends on where it is invested, what happens to general interest rates and how stock markets perform.

Many of those who have retired like to lock at least a portion of their savings into products which give them some predictable income, such as a guaranteed income bond. This isolates them from the effect of fluctuating interest rates.

With-profit bonds are another popular investment. Savers hope that over the medium term, at least five years, they will see a gradual rise in income from the bond.

But if you are hoping for twenty or more years of retirement, it is likely that you will have kept some of your money invested in funds or products linked to equities. Again, these funds need to be monitored and you have to decide when and if to cash in on any gains. This can be a tax-efficient way of taking some income, if you are willing to put up with an income that might fluctuate (see below).

All these investments and financial products are discussed more fully in the next chapter.

The bad news: costs are likely to rise too

Unfortunately, the cost of living in retirement is likely to keep on increasing too. Pensioners are not immune from general rises in prices. And some things that older people spend more on than the average household, such as medical expenses, tend to increase in price faster than general inflation.

Your spending needs are likely to change gradually over the years of retirement. Pensioners who have recently retired tend to be more active and more vigorous. They tend to spend more. They travel more, have more leisure pursuits and keep busy. All this takes cash.

Then, in later years, you naturally slow down and spend more time at home. Spending will then dip. In the last years of life costs may rise again as help at home or nursing care fees become an issue.

It is quite proper to plan to spend more in the early years of retirement, provided you are aware that you might then have to cut back later – and that you keep enough in reserve for the potential costs of looking after yourself if your health eventually fails.

Boosting your income

If you feel that your income is falling short of what you need, there are ways you may be able to increase it.

Firstly, check whether you can reduce the amount of tax you pay on your income. If you can trim the tax bill, you can make your income go further.

Can you make more use of tax-efficient investments? These include:

- Individual savings accounts (Isas) – each person can invest up to £7000 each tax year. The income produced is free of tax and so is any capital growth. A couple can together invest up to £14,000 a year. Have you sheltered all the money you can in an Isa?

- National Savings products – several of these pay income free of tax, including the fixed-interest savings certificates, index-linked savings certificates and Premium Bonds. Though interest rates may seem low, they may compare well with what a higher-rate taxpayer would get from an ordinary investment after tax.
- Investment bonds – higher-rate taxpayers can draw up to 5 per cent a year from these with no immediate tax charge. Income tax is deferred.
- Purchase annuities – a special type of annuity bought with non-pension assets. This will give a guaranteed return, a large portion of which can be counted as return of capital so is free of income tax. This is may be an attractive option for those aged seventy or more (see box 10.1 for more details).
- It may also be tax efficient gradually to cash in investments. Selling a small portion each year allows you to use the annual capital gains tax allowances. In this way, money you make from selling investments is not counted as income for tax purposes.

You can find out more about Isas, National Savings and investment bonds in Chapter 11. Independent financial advisers can also help with tax planning.

If you are a couple in retirement, also consider juggling assets so that you can each maximise your annual tax allowances. This is particularly important if only one of the couple is getting a pension income.

Personal tax allowances are more generous for older people. In tax year 2001/02, a couple who are both aged over sixty-five can each have £5990 a year of income before they have to pay any income tax. Those aged over seventy-five are allowed £6260 a year before they pay tax. Are you making the most of your allowances?

Secondly, make sure that you are not carrying needless debt. It is unwise to have savings stashed in a bank earning interest, when you have an overdraft, credit card bill or loan which is charging interest at a higher rate. The interest you earn on the savings will be less than you pay on the debt. Be prepared to dip into savings to clear the debt, then try not to overspend again.

Thirdly, you might want to think about eating into savings to boost income. Many of those in retirement are reluctant to eat into cash or other reserves. They fear they might run out of money or have nothing to pass on to family. Caution is certainly prudent. But you can take prudence too far. If you have saved to support yourself in retirement, then that is surely what your assets should be used for. There is little point going without essentials and hoarding thousands of pounds in the bank. It may be possible to stretch your savings further than you think. Box 10.2 explains more about drawing down part of your savings in a controlled fashion.

State benefits and allowances may also be a source of extra income. Chapter 3 explains in detail what is available at the moment. Only those on lower incomes qualify at present. If the new pension credit kicks in as planned in 2003, then more and more people will gradually qualify for modest increases to their income.

Homeowners might be able to boost their income by releasing some of the value tied up in their property. Dramatic increases in house prices over the past two decades mean that some retired people are living in and own properties worth six-figure sums, yet are struggling to make ends meet.

Moving house and trading down to a smaller property is one way to release value. Many, though, are reluctant to leave homes they love. Several financial products are available to help you take an income from your home, without selling it or leaving it. These are discussed in the next chapter on page 222.

As a last resort, it may also be possible to boost income through returning to work. This will not suit every retired person. It may be hard to find a suitable job and an employer who is willing to take you on. Your health may not be robust enough. The costs of travelling etc. may make the return on your efforts poor. There are, however, a growing number of jobs which can be done part-time from home. What is more, you will continue to get pension and other income (except for some benefits), regardless of whether you work or not and – once you have passed state retirement age – will not have to pay National Insurance. So do not dismiss the idea of work out of hand. It may be preferable to other alternatives.

Box 10.1: Purchase annuities

Purchase annuities, also called immediate life annuities, can be an extremely tax-efficient way of producing a guaranteed income in retirement. Like the pension annuities mentioned in Chapter 9, they involve you exchanging a cash lump sum for a guaranteed income. Once the annuity is purchased, you lose control over the lump sum and cannot pass it on to anyone else.

However, income from purchase annuities is taxed very differently to that from pension annuities. Part of the income is treated as a return of the capital you invested. This portion is called the capital content. The capital content is not taxed. The idea behind the capital content is that if you live to average life expectancy, you will get your original money back.

Like other annuities, the rate of income you will get depends on your age and sex. Men will receive a higher income than women and older people more than younger people. Age also has an effect on the capital content: the older you are, the higher it is. This can make a purchase life annuity extremely attractive for older pensioners.

You can select the usual variety of annuity options, including increasing income, money for a partner after your death and a guaranteed period of payment. There is also a special option called capital protection. This means that if you die before your original capital is returned, the remainder due is paid to your estate as a lump sum. If you opt for added features, the income you will start with is reduced.

The table below shows some examples of how much after-tax income a purchase life annuity might produce. This is for guidance only. Annuity rates fluctuate daily.

Details of annuitant	Gross annual income in year one from £10,000 investment	Capital content (portion of income free from tax)	Income after tax for a 22 per cent taxpayer
Male, 70, level income	£968	£695	£908
Male, 75, level income	£1130	£871	£1073
Male, 80, level income	£1334	£1096	£1282
Female, 70, level income	£907	£594	£838
Female, 75, level income	£1078	£753	£1006
Female, 80, level income	£1312	£970	£1237
Male, 70, income rising 5 per cent	£666	£435	£615
Male, 75, income rising 5 per cent	£834	£603	£783
Male, 80, income rising 5 per cent	£1051	£830	£1002
Female, 70, income rising 5 per cent	£612	£329	£550
Female, 75, income rising 5 per cent	£788	£465	£717
Female, 80, income rising 5 per cent	£1034	£664	£953
Joint life, male 65, female 65, level income	£711	£413	£645
Joint life, male 70, female 65, level income	£835	£538	£770
Joint life, male 75, female 70, level income	£1012	£629	£928

Source: *Financial Mail*/Annuity Direct. All figures to the nearest pound.

Box 10.2: Living off your savings

People are rightly cautious of nibbling into their accumulated savings. They will take the income from these savings, but feel uncomfortable about dipping into the actual capital pot. We all know that if you keep on eating into your savings, the money will eventually run out. But how long will this process take? The answer can be surprisingly long – if you are careful about how you take the money.

In fact, a cautious and controlled run-down of your savings can be a very wise and tax-efficient way to provide an income in retirement. While the income from your savings will be taxed, any capital you take out and use to support yourself will not. It is like getting a chunk of tax-free income each year.

The table below shows one example of running down savings.

Daisy, seventy-one, has £50,000 in a deposit account. The account pays annual interest at 5 per cent, which is then taxed. This gives Daisy interest of £2000 a year after tax. But she needs £3000 of income from savings to make ends meet. And she expects prices to rise by roughly 5 per cent a year. This means she expects she will need a slightly bigger income each year, and will have to take more from capital. How long can she stretch her capital for? As table 10.2 shows, she runs out of money in the seventeenth year, when she is aged eighty-seven.

If Daisy needed even more income, the money would last for a shorter period. If she wanted an after-tax income of £5000 a year, also increasing by 5 per cent a year, her money would run out towards the end of the tenth year.

If Daisy were willing to take only a level £3000 each year, and see her spending power diminish as inflation raises prices, she could go for twenty-eight years before exhausting her cash.

Put in a higher, more optimistic, interest rate and the

equation changes again. If interest were 7 per cent a year, then Daisy (who is taking £3000 a year, with rising income) would not run short of funds until year nineteen.

What does all this show? Simply, that eating into savings is not an absolute no-no. If you come from long-lived stock and expect a lengthy retirement, maybe you prefer the certainty of using the savings to buy an income through a purchase annuity. Conversely, a man who is eighty might feel absolutely justified in starting to draw down savings if he can see that this process is sustainable for fifteen or twenty years into the future.

Table 10.2: Living off your savings

	Capital at start of year	Gross interest	Interest after tax	Capital taken	Total income	Capital at year end
Year 1	50000	2500	2000	1000	3000	49000
Year 2	49000	2450	1960	1190	3150	47810
Year 3	47810	2391	1912	1395	3308	46415
Year 4	46415	2321	1857	1616	3473	44799
Year 5	44799	2240	1792	1855	3647	42944
Year 6	42944	2147	1718	2111	3829	40833
Year 7	40833	2042	1633	2387	4020	38446
Year 8	38446	1922	1538	2683	4221	35763
Year 9	35763	1788	1431	3002	4432	32761
Year 10	32761	1638	1310	3344	4654	29417
Year 11	29417	1471	1177	3710	4887	25707
Year 12	25707	1285	1028	4103	5131	21604
Year 13	21604	1080	864	4523	5388	17081
Year 14	17081	854	683	4974	5657	12107
Year 15	12107	605	484	5456	5940	6652

Year 16	6652	333	266	5971	6237	681
Year 17	681	34	27	6521	6549	-5840

Source: *Financial Mail*. Note: this projection assumes tax and interest rates are constant and that money is taken from account at the end of each year, not the start. In reality, interest rates will vary and tax rules may change.

Managing income drawdown or phased retirement

If you have chosen to put some or all of your pension into income drawdown or phased retirement, these funds will need monitoring on a regular basis.

In an income drawdown product your money remains invested, with the bulk likely to be in equity funds. The value of these funds will hopefully continue to grow, allowing you to take a regular income, while preserving the value of the capital. You can choose how much income to take each year, within limits laid down by the Inland Revenue.

As well as thinking about how much income to take, you may have a close month-to-month involvement in how your funds are invested. Drawdown products can be run on a hands-on basis, where you discuss how your funds are invested with investment managers and/or stockbrokers. Together you decide where and how to invest the money. Drawdown schemes can also be hands-off, where you leave the decisions up to someone else. Finally, there are completely self-invested drawdown schemes. Here you make all the decisions.

The final issue to think about if you have funds in income drawdown is whether or not to convert part or all of your fund into an annuity. This will involve monitoring annuity rates, plus assessing what the general investment outlook is. All the time you have to make a judgement on whether the money is better off remaining invested rather than converted to an annuity. You have to convert the entire fund by the time you are seventy-five, though these rules may change.

By law, drawdown products have to be reviewed at least every three years. This is to ensure that you are not taking too much income from the scheme. But advisers usually recommend informal annual reviews.

Similar issues face someone who has chosen the phased retirement option. Here, a pension is split into a thousand separate segments. Segments are cashed in throughout retirement, producing a mixture of tax-free cash and annuity income. Alternatively, a segment or segments can be switched into income drawdown.

This sort of plan really does need to be actively managed. Each year a decision has to be taken about how many segments to cash in; about how much tax-free cash to take and about what kind of annuities to buy. Additionally, the investment performance of the funds which remain to be cashed also needs to be closely monitored.

Both drawdown and phased retirement are discussed in more detail in Chapter 22.

The potential impact of ill health on your finances

It is impossible to discuss managing your income in retirement without considering the impact of ill health.

An inevitable side effect of getting older is that you are more likely to need medical care and are more prone to illnesses. It is prudent at least to consider how being ill might affect your finances.

Minor illness and short spells in hospital are not much fun. But essential medical care on the NHS is still free – and relatively prompt for accident and emergency cases, or acute conditions.

However, you will have to wait for up to eighteen months for so-called non-essential cases, such as hip replacements, cataract operations or varicose vein treatment. These conditions can cause huge discomfort. Those with private medical insurance may be able to get prompt attention. For the rest it is a question of waiting in pain or digging into savings to be treated privately. Pay-as-you-go health care is a fast-growing area. Table 10.3 shows a list of approximate prices for common private treatments.

Where you have to stay in hospital for a longer period, your state pension will be reduced. If you are hospitalised for six weeks or more, your pension will be cut by 40 per cent. If your hospital stay persists beyond fifty-two weeks the pension is reduced again, normally to 20 per cent of the standard basic-rate pension.

Table 10.3: The costs of common self-pay medical treatments

Procedure	Price range*
Cataract removal	£1800–2400
Heart bypass	£9500–12,500
Hernia treatment	£1000–1500
Hip replacement	£6000–7800
Hysterectomy	£2300–4300
Knee replacement	£5700–8400
Prostate treatment	£2000–3400
Varicose vein (single)	£1000–1500

* Price depends on location, hospital and surgeon chosen.

Paying for long-term care

The biggest costs of ill health, however, hit those who are in need of long-term care. Care can include either help around the home, to assist with basic tasks like bathing and dressing, or a move to full-time residential care.

Around one in ten of those in Britain aged sixty-five or over are unable to manage some aspects of their personal care without nursing assistance and one in seven need some assistance with mobility.[1] Help the Aged estimates that around 540,000 adults currently need some form of care. Three-quarters of them receive it in their own homes.

It is a commonly held belief that the state will pay. In fact, the amount of help that you can expect from local authorities or from central government is limited.

What are the costs of care?

Care costs can be a staggering drain on your resources. The British Nursing Association reckons the average cost of care provided in your home is £11.43 an hour. But there are wide regional variations, with London and the south-east of England the most expensive. Care for two hours a day – enough to get you up and give you a shower – costs £130–200 per week, or £6800 to £10,500 a year.

Residential care costs are also high. The average cost of full-time care in a nursing home is £19,084 a year.[2] Again, this varies from region to region and depends on whether you want basic or superior quality accommodation. In London you would pay on average more than £25,000 a year. Care in the north-east costs on average just under £17,000 a year.

What will the state pay?

Treatment within NHS hospitals remains free. Outside this, costs escalate quickly. The Community Care Act of 1990 makes each local authority responsible for long-term care (LTC) provided outside hospital. If you are assessed as needing care, either within your home or residential care, your income and other assets will be assessed to decide how much you should pay.

A distinction is made between help at home and residential care. Dealing with help at home first:

- Where you have assets worth £18,500 or more, you will get no help from the state.
- If your assets are worth between £10,000 and £18,500 you may get some partial help. It is assumed these savings produce an income at the rate of £1 per week per £250 of savings.

- If assets are below £10,000 you may get your bills paid, if you are assessed as having a low enough income.

The assessment is a fiendishly complex process and it is hard to generalise what level of income qualifies for help. To give one example, a single person aged sixty-five, who qualified for a disability benefit such as attendance allowance and had the full basic pension plus an occupational pension of £80 a week, might have to pay £2.50 a week for care. If the same person had an occupational pension of £400 a week, they could be billed up to £200 a week for care costs.

Your home should not count as an asset if you receive care at home.

Controversially, local authorities can choose to take account of a partner's or spouse's income or savings that the person who needs care 'has reliable access to'. This could, for example, include income from an occupational or personal pension paid to your partner or spouse.

For residential care the rules are slightly different. If you have to move into residential care, your home is excluded from the list of assets means-tested for the first three months. If a spouse or dependent relative shares the house with you, then it continues to be excluded. Otherwise it is added to the list. Beyond this, similar capital limits to above apply:

- Where you have assets worth £18,500 or more, you will get no help from the state.
- If your assets are worth between £10,000 and £18,500 you may get some partial help. It is assumed these savings produce an income at the rate of £1 per week per £250 of savings.
- If assets are below £10,000 and you cannot meet care bills from your income, you will potentially have to give up all your income to the local authority who will put it towards the cost of care. You get 'pocket money' of £15.45 a week to meet personal expenses.

Local authorities are free to set higher capital limits, which would let you keep more assets and still get help. But few do.

Politicians in Scotland have signalled they are willing to be more generous in paying for care, footing the bill for both personal needs and nursing for those who live north of the border. Details were still to be announced at the time of writing, with payments starting in April 2002.

Homeowners, whose house is their main asset and who live alone, may be able to get an interest-free loan from their local authority to pay for care costs. The loan is secured by a charge on their home. This avoids the emotional trauma of having to sell the home while they are still alive. But the loan has to be repaid and will start racking up interest after the recipient dies. So the sale of the property is simply deferred unless the family has other assets to pay the debt.

Since October 2001, nursing costs for those who need long-term care are paid by the government. Nursing care is strictly defined as medical assistance that needs to be provided by a registered nurse. It will not normally include help such as bathing or dressing. For the average person in a residential nursing home, free nursing care cuts the care bill by £3,500 a year.

Local authorities will investigate all claims for care costs. They take a dim view of those who have transferred assets to a partner or given them away to family to scrape through the means test.

How can you plug the gap between the cost of care and what the state will pay?

Most people who need care have no option but to run down savings, and many are forced to sell their homes. Between 35,000 and 40,000 homes each year are sold to pay care costs. The loan scheme outlined above will delay but not eliminate these sales.

If you are faced with care costs there are a number of ways you can plan so that you will not run out of cash to pay or will not be forced to move to an alternative, cheaper care home.

Consider buying a purchase life annuity out of the proceeds of the sale of your home or from other assets. That will give a guaranteed income for life. Alternatively, an immediate care insurance plan may help. Some plans provide an income through an annuity. Others take your lump sum and invest it. A mixture of growth from the investment and capital is used to pay for your care costs. This will stretch your capital further if stock market growth is good and may even preserve a good slab of it for others when you die.

The alternative is to plan for care costs well in advance. You can buy long-term care insurance. Like other insurance, it only pays out if you need to make a claim. Claims are judged on whether or not you can do certain activities of daily living, e.g. washing, feeding and moving from room to room. You can pay for this insurance with either a lump sum premium, or through monthly payments. The younger you are when you buy the cover, the cheaper it is.

The costs of care insurance in advance are much lower than meeting the full costs of care. But if you pay in advance and do not need the insurance because you are in good health up to the end of your life, then you get nothing for your premiums. They have bought you only peace of mind.

Companies offering pre-funded long-term care policies include BUPA, PPP Lifetime, Norwich Union, Scottish Provident and Scottish Widows. Age Concern also offers a policy in partnership with Norwich Union.

In summary:

- It pays to keep on top of your money after you have retired.
- Your income in retirement will keep on rising, but so will costs.
- If you are running short, you may be able to rearrange finances to boost income.
- Those with income drawdown or phased retirement plans need to manage these carefully.
- Be mindful of the potential costs of long-term care. How would you pay?

Notes

1 Government General Household Survey, 1996.

2 Laing & Buisson, 1999.

CHAPTER 11

Alternatives to pensions

Read this chapter if:

- You want to find out about other ways to save for retirement aside from pensions.
- You want to know more about alternative ways of producing income with your funds when you retire.

Pensions are likely to be an important part of most savers' retirement plans. But they are not the only option. There are many other ways to save, all of which have advantages and disadvantages when set against pensions. Finding the right mix of savings and investments is a matter of personal choice. Among other things, this choice depends on:

- your income and the amount you are able to save;
- whether you are a taxpayer and if so, whether you pay top-rate tax;
- your attitude to investment risk;
- how much involvement you want to have in your savings – are you a hands-on or a hands-off person?

- whether you have dependants, and how concerned you are about passing assets to them or to other individuals after your death.

This chapter will explain the alternatives to saving through a pension and how, in practice, a selection of different investments suits the majority of retirement savers.

The pros and cons of a pension

Throughout this chapter, ways to save will be compared with pensions. So to start with, the table below acts as a quick reminder of the pros and cons of paying into a pension.

Main advantages of a pension	Main disadvantages of a pension
Tax-favoured: money paid in free of income tax and can grow free of tax	Limits on how much you can save (though most rarely hit the limits)
A tax-free lump sum, typically 15–25 per cent of the fund, is paid on retirement	The rest of your pension income is taxed as earnings
Company schemes provide extra benefits such as life insurance or income if you have a long-term illness or have to retire early through ill health	Lack of flexibility. You can only draw the money at certain times
	Compulsory annuity purchase by age 75 for personal pensions and some company schemes

The key disadvantage of pensions is the lack of flexibility. This is the price pension savers must pay for generous tax concessions. Inland Revenue rules govern everything about a pension: how you save into a pension, where the money can be invested, when you can retire and what you have to do with your savings when you retire.

Making alternative savings alongside your pension brings added flexibility. You control how much and when you save, and then how and when you cash in on these savings.

Growth and income

There are essentially two types of investment: those producing capital growth and those which pay an income based on a sum invested. When you are saving for retirement, capital growth is all important. You want to turn the money you save into the biggest fund that you possibly can. After you stop working and start to live off your savings, income is key. You want to find the most efficient ways of turning your funds into a sustainable income.

The division between growth and income is not entirely black and white. Some kinds of investment can give both growth and income; property, for example, can provide a rental income and grow in value at the same time. Another way to achieve growth is to buy an income-producing investment and not take the income, but instead leave it to roll up. For example, sticking £10,000 in a savings account paying 6 per cent interest after tax and leaving it for three years will see that £10,000 grow into £11,910.16.

Conversely, an alternative way to get an income is to keep your money invested in growth assets and then sell a slice each year, hoping that continued growth means the total value of your capital is preserved. Managed correctly, this can be a tax-efficient way to take an income.

In general, however, you will look to save in certain ways for growth and then move into other investments for income.

Box 11.1: Risk versus reward

Fitness trainers are fond of shouting 'No pain, no gain!' at their sweaty students. A similar rule applies in investment. You must be prepared to take some risks to secure the highest returns. It is important to be aware of this relationship between risk and reward when you are considering different types of investment.

A useful rule of thumb is that the higher the risk in an investment, the higher the potential profit or loss you may make on it. It is a bit like the odds a bookie will quote on a horse race: you win less if the favourite romps home because it is the more certain outcome. But if you stick your neck out and successfully back a long shot, a less likely outcome, you get a much bigger prize.

It is possible to grade investments along a risk scale of one to ten. One represents no risk; your capital is absolutely secure and you will get it back no matter what. The higher the number, the greater the danger of loss, but the greater the chance of profit. The investments discussed in this section are ranked below, along with a few more specialist options.

Each of us needs to consider the level of risk that we are comfortable with. There is no point investing in high-risk assets if you cannot afford to lose a penny of your capital. Attitude to risk may change over time. For example, when you are saving hard with twenty years to go to retirement, you might be more willing to take a chance because even if there are temporary losses, there is still time for the investments to bounce back into profit. However, as retirement approaches you become more cautious and move into lower-risk investments.

A rough and ready risk grading

Risk level	Type of investments*
One	National Savings products
Two	Deposit investments with UK authorised banks and building societies

	Government bonds/gilts
Three	Deposit investments with offshore banks
	Guaranteed income bonds
Four	Collective funds investing in fixed-interest securities
Five	With-profit funds
	Collective funds investing in higher-yielding corporate bonds
	Income bonds where capital is at risk
	Cash squirrelled under your mattress
Six	Collective funds investing in UK equities
	Most investment bonds
Seven	Property
	Collective funds investing in overseas equities
	Specialist collective funds, e.g. technology, smaller companies
	Employee share schemes
Eight	Individual shares on the UK stock market
Nine	Individual shares on overseas stock markets
Ten	Futures, options and derivative contracts

*International investments have a higher grading because of the added risks of exchange rate fluctuations.

Alternatives at a glance

There is a huge choice of ways to save. Not every possible alternative will be covered in this section. Specialist options, such as venture capital trusts, require individual advice and appeal to only a tiny fraction of savers. But the areas discussed cover the key choices relevant to 95 per cent of readers 95 per cent of the time. The choices include:

Savings type	Good for income	Good for growth
Deposit accounts	✔	✔✘
National Savings	✔	✔✘
Isas	✔	✔
Collective funds – unit trusts, investment trusts and open-ended investment companies	✔	✔
Endowments	✘	✔
Corporate bond funds	✔	✔✘
Investment bonds, including with-profit bonds	✔	✘
Directly held shares	✔✘	✔
Property	✔	✔

Where an investment is rated ✔✘ this shows that it is possible to use that investment for that purpose, but that there may be better alternatives.

Deposit accounts

These are the first step towards saving. Most households have at least one deposit-based savings account with a bank or building society. The account pays interest, daily, monthly, quarterly or annually, on the average sum deposited with the bank. Interest can be drawn out or added to the account to grow with the rest of the money.

Deposit saving is flexible. Money can be paid in at any time. There are sometimes conditions imposed on withdrawals; higher-interest accounts may require a set number of days' notice. But essentially, the money is there to be used at any time.

Interest rates may be variable, that is they move up and down in line with the pressures of international money markets. Alternatively, savers can opt for the security of fixed rates. These are set and cannot change for a specified period, for example, one year or three years.

Deposit saving is safe and secure. Banks can go bust, but this is extremely rare in the UK. Even then, deposit protection schemes ensure you get something back. Savers get refunded a maximum of 90 per cent of deposits up to £20,000, if an authorised bank goes bust.

The bigger danger to your savings of deposit accounts is that the money you have put away loses value against increasing prices or earnings. Though inflation is low in the UK at the time of writing, there have been periods in the past twenty years when the interest you have earned from the bank is less than the rate of inflation. In recent years, earnings have moved ahead faster than prices.

Deposit accounts are not tax-efficient. Unless the deposit is part of an Isa (see below) or a Tessa (no longer on sale), the account is taxed. Interest is automatically taxed as income at 20 per cent and higher-rate taxpayers will need to pay extra. Non-taxpayers can reclaim the tax deducted by the bank.

Historically, it is unwise to rely on deposit accounts for long-term growth. Take the example of £1000 saved into the average bank or building society deposit account over the fifteen years to the beginning of July 2001. If this money was left untouched and the interest added to the account each month, the balance would now be £2007.[1] The same £1000 spread across a basket of UK shares – both winners and losers – would have grown in value to £5414 over the same fifteen-year period.[2]

So stashing £200 a month into a deposit account as your retirement saving is unlikely to produce the best income when you retire. Nevertheless, deposit accounts have a vital part to play as a first step to saving and as a source of ready cash in emergencies. They can also be a way of producing a regular income when you have retired.

National Savings

These are a series of deposit-based savings, made not with commercial banks or building societies, but with a government agency. National Savings has the key advantage of being backed by government guarantee. It is the safest investment you can buy. Your money is 100 per cent secure. Unfortunately, the interest rates paid are not always attractive. National Savings used to be a key part of many people's savings plans, but its appeal has waned in recent years.

National Savings accounts are primarily aimed at income investors, although its tax-free savings certificates are designed to appeal to those who want low-risk growth. At the time of writing, the main National Savings products include:

- Investment account – a deposit account, paying variable rates of interest. The more you save, the higher the rate. Historically, the account has not been as competitive as the best deals on the high street.
- Tax-free savings certificates – a fixed-term investment for either two or five years. There are two versions, one is fixed interest, paying a set return on maturity. The other is index-linked. This pays a variable rate of interest on maturity, which is guaranteed to be better than inflation. All returns are free of income tax. But there are penalties for cashing in early. The products are sometimes attractive for higher-rate taxpayers. You can invest up to £10,000 in each issue of certificates.
- Pensioners Bonds – these are fixed-interest investments, sold only to men and women aged sixty or over. They pay a set sum over a set time period of one, two or five years. Interest can be taken monthly and is paid gross of tax. This does not mean it is tax-free, simply that non-taxpayers do not have to go through the trouble of reclaiming tax. You can invest up to £1 million in these bonds.
- Income Bonds – these pay a variable rate of interest. Up to £1 million can be invested and they can be cashed in by giving three months' notice.
- Premium Bonds – a tax-free prize draw, made by the famous Ernie computer. Each £1 invested buys you the chance to play in a monthly prize draw. There is always one £1 million prize, plus thousands of smaller prizes ranging in value from £50 to £100,000. You can buy up to £20,000 of bonds, giving you 20,000 chances to win each month. Statistically, this should

produce an average annual return of around 3.75 per cent free of tax.

Interest rates on the products are changing all the time. For up-to-date information check at your local post office, telephone 0845 964 5000 between 8 a.m. and 8 p.m. on weekdays or look at the website www.nationalsavings.co.uk.

Individual Savings Accounts (Isas)

The Isa is not a type of investment itself, but a wrapper or shell which can be put around a series of other investments. Putting something into an Isa wrapper means you will not have to pay capital gains tax on any growth in the value of the investment and any income you take from it will be free of income tax. Investments which can be sheltered from tax in an Isa include cash deposits, shares, holdings in unit trusts or oeics and investments in life insurance funds.

Isas were launched in April 1999. At the time, the Chancellor pledged that they would be available for at least ten years and that the tax benefits would last for at least ten years. Even if no new Isas are sold after the ten years are up in 2009, it is unlikely that those already in force would lose their tax privileges. Certainly any government doing this would be unpopular with the millions of voters who have invested through Isas.

The key attraction of an Isa is its tax-favoured status. It allows you to grow an investment over a number of years, without any worries about capital gains tax. Then, at the right moment, you can switch the Isa into an income-producing investment and draw that income free of tax.

Each adult aged eighteen or over can invest up to £7000 per tax year into an Isa. This may dip to £5000 a year after April 2006. On current limits, over five years a couple could shelter up to £70,000 from tax through Isas. Once you have invested, Isa money can be switched between funds and between like kinds of investment without losing its tax-free status. But when you sell an Isa altogether the tax privileges go. You cannot pass on an Isa's tax breaks after your death. The assets it contained will form part of your estate.

Money invested in an Isa can be split a number of ways. Either the whole sum, up to £7000, can go into stocks and shares; that is equities and company or government bonds. Alternatively the money can be split: up to £3000 can go into a deposit account (a cash Isa), up to £3000 into stocks and shares (an equities Isa) and up to £1000 into an insurance fund (an insurance Isa).

Your Isa can be a maxi-Isa, that is all the money invested through one financial company. Or you can buy a series of mini-Isas; for example, buying your cash Isa from one company and an insurance Isa elsewhere.

Money paid into the equity component of an Isa can be used to buy collective funds (see below) or can be invested directly into shares, through a self-select Isa.

If you are aiming for growth, then Isa funds should be invested mainly in equities or insurance with-profit funds. For income, switch Isa investments into bond funds or invest in the cash component of the Isa. However, on current rules, money invested into the equity component of an Isa cannot be switched into cash and vice versa.

Isas are frequently compared with pensions because they are the two mainstream tax-favoured investments. Essentially, with a pension you get the tax break up front. Money goes in free of tax. But the income is then taxed when you start drawing down a pension. With an Isa, the tax break comes later. Money invested comes from your income and so is taxed up front, but when you start taking money out of the Isa there is no tax to pay.

So which is more attractive? Box 11.2 compares the potential value of saving through a pension and saving through an equity Isa.

Whatever the sums, Isas have one key advantage over pensions. They are far more flexible. You choose when to take an income and how that income will be structured. Isas can also be taken out in addition to annual limits on pension contributions. Isas definitely have a place alongside pensions in retirement planning. Many people who want to boost their retirement income are splitting their resources and paying some into a pension, some into an equity Isa.

Box 11.2: Isa saving versus pension saving

Is it worth saving in a pension? Or is an Isa better value? A simple enough question, but worryingly difficult to answer.

The big catch with saving into a personal pension, money-purchase company pension and most AVC schemes is that the majority of your fund is eventually used to buy an annuity. And annuity rates have been falling steadily for the past decade, reducing the amount of income your pension fund can provide. See Chapter 22 for more information on annuities.

This fall in annuity rates has prompted many savers to hedge their bets and use alternative means of saving, such as an Isa, instead of their pension. Are they wise to do so?

Take the case of Ben who has just turned forty and is planning retirement at the age of sixty. Ben wants to save an extra £200 a month from his take-home pay towards retirement. He has no company pension. He can invest this into a personal pension, knowing that his contribution will be subsidised by the government thanks to income tax relief at his highest marginal rate. Assuming 22 per cent basic rate tax, Ben's £200 net contribution is grossed up to £256.41 a month.

Using standard industry formula,* this contribution is projected to produce a pension fund worth £119,000 on retirement. Of this Ben could take a maximum of £29,750 as a tax-free lump sum and the rest would go into an annuity. Using a typical annuity rate available in July 2001,† this would provide Ben with an annual income, which is taxed, of £7074 at sixty. This income is guaranteed and will not fall.

If Ben were a 40 per cent top-rate taxpayer, his monthly contribution for a net cost of £200 would be £333.33. This is projected to grow into a pension fund worth £156,000 at retirement. Ben would get a maximum of £39,000 tax-free and an annual income before tax of £9273 when he retires. Again, this income is guaranteed for life.

What might Ben get if he invests in an Isa instead? Using the standard 7 per cent growth projection and 1 per cent annual charge, £200 a month invested into an equity Isa for twenty years is forecast to produce a fund worth £95,540. Switching all this Isa fund into an income investment, say into a corporate bond fund yielding 8 per cent, would produce a tax-free annual income of £7643.

So which is the better outcome? At first sight, the Isa looks to outdo a pension for a basic-rate taxpayer. Ben is comparing a potential income from the pension route of £7074 before tax – around £5517 after tax – against £7643 a year tax-free from the Isa.

Even if Ben is a higher-rate taxpayer, and so has bigger pension contributions, the Isa looks to have an edge. His gross income on retirement is £9273 a year. If he pays basic-rate tax after retirement, this works out as £7233 a year after tax; if he has enough income to retire as a top-rate taxpayer it dips to only £5564 a year. Both incomes are less than the projected Isa income.

Furthermore, in both cases Ben retains full ownership of the Isa and can pass it on as part of his estate, whereas the capital is gone once the pension fund is used to buy an annuity.

However, with the pension route Ben also has a tax-free lump sum to consider. This can be used to increase his income or to offset day-to-day costs, such as clearing any debt when he retires. For example, if the whole of Ben's fund is used to buy an annuity, the annual gross income jumps to £9432 a year (£7357 after tax) or £12,365 a year (£9645 after tax) if he has built a bigger fund with top-rate tax relief.

And it may be possible to use the lump sum to generate a higher income by investing it in a different way; for example, making a lump sum investment into an Isa, if such things can still be purchased when Ben retires.

It is also worth emphasising that by going down the pension route and buying annuities, Ben is setting himself up for guaranteed income. Whereas if he goes down the Isa route, the amount of income his fund produces may vary over the years of his retirement.

Don't forget, too, that if you are saving into a pension through your employment, payments you make may be matched by an employer. This might switch the balance completely in favour of the pension option.

One final thought. This example assumes that you are going to buy an annuity. The rules currently say you must do this by the age of seventy-five. It is likely that this requirement may be relaxed in the next few years. This may alter the equation once more.

To summarise, it looks as if basic-rate taxpayers can produce almost as much income in retirement by investing through Isas as through money-purchase pensions. This income may be variable, but with an Isa the saver retains control of the money. They can retire when they like and can pass it on as part of their estate.

Pensions still appear to be the best way to produce income in retirement for top-rate taxpayers. The Isa cannot compete with the high up-front tax relief a pension saver gets. But going down this route means losing control of how you cash in your funds and – ultimately – ownership of your funds. For what it is worth, the author is hedging his bets and using both pensions and Isas to save.

WARNING

These examples make assumptions about future investment growth, future tax rates and future annuity rates. They are the best guesses that can be made today. But the actual picture may look very different in twenty years.

* Growth of 7 per cent a year, annual management charge 1 per cent a year.

† The Annuity Bureau, male aged sixty, single-life, level annuity.

Collective funds: unit trusts, oeics, investment trusts and ETFs

Teaming up with others shares the risks and the costs of investing. This is the principle which lies behind collective funds. These funds take the money from thousands of savers and pool it together to buy assets. This means that each investor gets to spread their cash between a diverse selection of holdings, reducing risk. They can also share the cost of paying for expert management, which will hopefully ensure their money grows at a good rate.

Collective funds can invest in a range of assets, including shares, property, government bonds and corporate bonds.

There are three main types of fund: unit trust, investment trust and open-ended investment company, also called oeic. All share common features. They are liquid investments that can easily be traded. They can be held by individuals, either within or outside an Isa. Each has a slightly different structure and each has its own series of charges.

A fourth type of fund, called an Exchange Traded Fund or ETF, was launched into the UK during 2000. It is very popular in the US and may become more mainstream in the UK.

Box 11.3 compares the main features of the different types of collective funds.

Each fund has a specific investment goal or remit. This can be a geographic area, a type of industry or a type of asset. For example, a unit trust may specialise in only UK big company shares; it may buy just smaller companies in the US; it may buy only the shares of technology companies; or it may invest only in Asian corporate bonds. Funds can also be active, picking and choosing their shares, or may be passive. Passive funds, also called tracker funds, mirror the performance of an investment index and slavishly follow it up and down.

Savers pick the kind of fund which suits their investment goals, timescale and appetite for risk. Past performance of these funds varies tremendously; some growth funds can show huge gains one year followed by massive losses the next. Others are managed to take far fewer risks, aiming for slower but steady growth, or to give a regular and sustainable income.

Investors can buy into collective funds either through independent financial advisers, direct from the product provider or through one of the growing number of discount broking services or on-line fund supermarkets. The latter two will not provide any advice, but usually offer discounted charges.

You can invest a lump sum, or choose to pay a series of monthly contributions, starting a regular savings plan. You can hold a collective fund for as long or as short a time as you like. Dealing charges mean it may not be prudent to switch every week, but sensible investors will certainly tweak their holdings every year or two.

Where a collective fund is held within an Isa, the underlying performance of the fund is not affected. It will grow or fall just the same. The Isa simply means that any growth or income you receive is free of tax. However, charges for investments held in Isas may differ slightly from those held outside.

For more details on unit trusts and open-ended investment companies contact the Association of Unit Trusts and Investment Funds. Call on 020 8207 1361 or log into www.investmentfunds.org.uk.

For more details on investment trusts contact the Association of Investment Trust Companies. Call 0800 085 8520 or log into www.itsonline.co.uk.

Box 11.3: A quick guide to collective funds

Unit trusts

Still the most popular collective fund. Unit trusts are controlled by fund management companies who create new units on demand and back these with investments in underlying shares or other assets. There is an initial charge to buy, which can be as high as 5 or 6 per cent (expressed through different prices to buy and sell), plus annual management fees of up to 1.5 per cent. The price of the trust is revised daily and applies to all deals in the next twenty-four hours.

Open-ended investment companies (Oeics)

An evolution of the unit trust. Around one in three of all unit trusts have now converted in oeics, which are structured as a company, complete with AGM and board of directors. Investors buy shares not units. New shares are created as needed and then cancelled again when investors sell. Oeics have a single buying and selling price, updated once every twenty-four hours. Initial charges and annual management fees are on average slightly lower than for unit trusts.

Investment trusts

The oldest UK collective funds, these are listed companies whose only assets are investments such as shares, cash or bonds. Investors buy shares in an investment trust and can deal throughout Stock Exchange hours. Prices can vary by the minute. Unlike unit trusts or oeics, investment trusts can 'gear up' and borrow against their assets. This can boost returns or losses. Charges are generally much lower than unit trusts because no commission is paid to advisers, but stamp duty applies to purchases. Shares can trade above (at a premium) or below (at a discount) net asset value, adding to investor risk.

Exchange traded funds

Very new. Will either remain a niche product or everyone will end up using them. Like the investment trust, shares can be bought or sold whenever the stock market is open. But ETFs are open-ended and new shares can be created when demand exists, meaning that shares should always trade at or near the net asset value of underlying assets. Very low charges make these funds competitive but they are only available to track indices. They are not actively managed.

Endowments

Once the king of saving, the crown of the endowment has slipped dramatically in recent years. Endowments are a packaged product. They combine life and other insurance, plus investment, in a single entity. Part of the monthly premium you pay goes towards the cost of the insurance, the bulk is invested to grow. Endowments have a set lifespan, usually at least ten years, often twenty-five years and sometimes longer.

Endowments became part of everyday life when they were linked with homebuying. The endowment provides enough insurance to repay a mortgage should you die or suffer from a serious illness. Meanwhile the investment grows and hopefully when the endowment matures it delivers a lump sum big enough to clear the mortgage with extra cash to spare. Almost all these long-term policies which matured during the 1990s did just that, providing handsome dividends to homebuyers. Prospects for the future are less rosy..

Endowments do not have to be tied into a mortgage. They can be a stand-alone savings product. And they can be structured with minimum life insurance, so that effectively 99 per cent of what you pay in goes towards investment.

The problem with endowments is they lack flexibility against other types of investment, such as collective funds. Endowments give best value to the saver when they are held to maturity. Those who stop paying and surrender their endowment early get a poor return, sometimes less than they have paid in. Charges can appear high against some collective funds, although there is a modern breed of endowments which are now much more competitive.

The structure and value of money invested in endowments can also be unclear to investors. This is particularly the case with those endowments which invest in insurance company with-profit funds. Here, the final value of the endowment may be unclear until just before maturity. It may depend heavily on what terminal bonus the insurer declares. Bonus rates vary over time and maturity values can move up or down by 10–15 per cent in a year.

Endowments have had a particularly bad press in recent years over fears that a significant proportion, perhaps as high as one in five of those currently in force, may not produce enough to repay mortgages. This is because the investment climate has changed and future growth is expected to be lower than the growth rate which was forecast when the endowments were sold.

Is there a role for endowments going forward? Yes. The issue of lower growth applies to other kinds of investments too; it is not purely an endowment problem. Some investors like the steady and cautious approach of investing through a with-profit endowment. Endowments can also have a place in retirement planning. They can be set up so that they mature at a specified point in the future; for example, when you turn sixty-five. They are not to everyone's taste, but they should not be dismissed out of hand as a potential growth investment.

Investment bonds, including with-profit bonds

Investment bonds come in all shapes and sizes. They are another way to package an investment in cash, shares, government bonds, corporate bonds or a mix of all of these. Bonds can be set up to provide a monthly, quarterly or annual income. Or they can be designed as a medium-term growth investment.

Bonds are not aimed at those who want to add a little to their savings each month. Investments in are made as lump sums up front.

There are two very different types of investment bonds, which are issued by life insurance companies. Guaranteed bonds, also known as income bonds, are akin to investing in a deposit account. They run for a fixed term, anything from one to ten years, and usually pay a fixed rate of return over this time. For example, a bond may offer 7 per cent a year for the next five years. The saver's original capital is returned at maturity.

Money cannot be added or taken away with this kind of investment once it has been started. The income may be paid out monthly, or annually. Or it can be left to roll up and taken in one lump at the end, often called a growth option. The funds the bonds invest in are taxed. This means basic-rate taxpayers are not taxed on the income. Higher-rate taxpayers need to pay the difference between basic and top rates of tax.

Guaranteed or income bonds will appeal to investors who want to secure a known income for a set period. Once you put your money into this kind of bond, you know you will get the income promised, even if general interest rates fall in the meantime. Such bonds are often attractive to those at or near retirement. They may also appeal to an investor seeking growth, who opts to let the interest roll up. It is a very low-risk growth vehicle, though returns may well be lower than other forms of investment.

Banks and building societies also issue similar products, confusingly also called investment bonds. These too provide a fixed return over a fixed time period.

Savers can achieve higher incomes by opting for versions of these bonds where the capital is not guaranteed. Instead, the amount of capital you get back at the end is linked to the performance of a nominated stock market. If the market fails to grow as expected, you may only get back a portion of the original investment. Typically, a risky bond will pay 2 or 3 per cent a year more income than a no-risk bond.

The other main type of bond is the traditional investment bond. This includes the popular with-profit bond. These bonds do much the same as unit trusts and oeics. They allow a saver to invest a lump sum in one of a range of investment funds. Money invested buys units in the chosen fund. The fund may invest in a specific area, such as US shares, or be a more general managed fund. Some funds are more suited to growth, others provide an income. Savers can usually switch between funds offered by the same company.

Charges on the bonds tend to be slightly higher than for collective funds and the investment fund itself has to pay capital gains tax. This means returns are generally lower against a similar unit trust or investment trust. Income from the bond is automatically taxed at basic-rate income tax.

Unlike collective funds, savers are tied to investment bonds for a minimum period, usually five years. There may be penalty charges and loss of capital if you cash in the bond before this.

But there are some advantages in this kind of bond. They allow savers to access insurance company with-profit funds. These funds split savers' money across a wide range of equities, bonds, property and cash, and aim to provide smooth and steady growth over the medium to longer term.

These bonds are popular with income investors, who select a desired level of annual income and hope that the fund will grow enough each year to leave their capital intact.

Higher-rate taxpayers can also benefit from investment bonds. They are permitted to take up to 5 per cent of the original capital each year as income, with no immediate extra tax charged. The extra tax on this 'income' is deferred until the bond is cashed in.

Again, this kind of investment bond can be an attractive way of turning existing savings or cash lump sums into an income during retirement. They are generally not the most tax-efficient way to build a retirement kitty.

Directly held shares

Investing in shares directly is more risky than buying them through collective funds – and usually more fun too.

The art of investing through shares is a huge topic. Indeed, it is the subject of a separate *Financial Mail* book. So what follows can only be the briefest of introductions.

By historic measures, shares have the potential to make you more money than any other kind of investment. The stock market as a whole has delivered sound long-term growth throughout recent years; the FTSE All Share index, which measures every listed share in the UK, grew in value by an average of 18.47 per cent each year from 1973 to 2000.[3] Some individual shares have allowed investors to make ten, fifty or a hundred times their money over much shorter time periods.

But buying individual shares can also be a route to big losses; hundreds of companies have failed over the years, leaving their shareholders with worthless investments. Other once great names have hit hard times, prompting big falls in their share price. So stock picking, the practice of selecting individual shares to invest in, is not a game for the faint-hearted.

The basic principles are easy to grasp. You want to buy a share which you think has the potential to rise in price. This may be because the market has undervalued the share. A share's price may also rise because the company, or the industry that company is part of, has the potential to grow. Having invested, you then hold the share while you wait for the price to increase. When it reaches a level that you feel is overpriced and vulnerable to fall, it is time to sell. You make a profit on the deal and go on to the next one. While you hold the shares you may receive dividends, income from the company. You can either spend the dividends or reinvest them.

It sounds simple in theory. But in practice calling the low points and high points of individual shares, or even of the market as a whole, can be fiendishly tricky.

Share investors want to build a portfolio of different holdings, rather than plunging all their money into one stock. A portfolio gives diversification and reduces risk. Even if one share goes badly wrong, money invested in the other companies is protected.

The advantage of shares over a managed pension investment is that you are in control. You decide when to buy and sell, when to take profits and when to switch from growth shares to ones paying a high income. However, when markets are plunging and the value of your shares is falling, it may not feel as if you are in control!

Your investment in shares will be taxed. Income tax must be paid on dividends, and profits you make may be subject to capital gains tax at your highest income tax rate if they exceed the annual capital gains allowance (£7500 in tax year 2001/02). You can avoid tax by sheltering your shares in a self-select Isa, provided you are not using the Isa allowance for other purposes.

To invest in shares you need a stockbroker. Brokers are the only bodies which can buy and sell through the Stock Exchange. There are three levels of service.

Discretionary management, also called portfolio management, is the most expensive. Here you hand control to the stockbroker. They choose what to buy and what to sell and when, although working within guidelines you set. This really only makes sense for those who are willing to invest substantial lump sums, typically £50,000 upwards, which can be used to build a reasonable portfolio. Management fees may be anything from 1 per cent to 3 per cent a year of the total you have invested.

With an advisory service the stockbroker guides your decisions. You can talk to the stockbroker for advice and guidance and they may call you with tips or when the prices of shares you hold are moving rapidly. But ultimately you decide what to buy and sell. The broker will charge from 1 per cent to 1.75 per cent of the value of each deal you do.

The most basic service is execution-only. You decide what to buy or sell, when and at what price. A broker will simply follow your bidding. You will not get phone calls, even if your shares are all in free fall. You are on your own. Dealing costs can be as low as 0.5 per cent for bigger transactions.

All the main banks offer stockbroking services. There are national chains of specialist brokers as well as established regional stockbrokers in most of the UK's main cities. Alternatively, for the lowest-cost dealing-only service, try one of the twenty or so Internet stockbrokers.

In addition to the stockbroker's dealing costs, you will have to pay the government tax of stamp duty on all shares you buy. This is priced at 0.5 per cent of the value of the deal.

As well as finding a stockbroker, you also need to think about an investment strategy. How much will you invest? What targets will you set yourself? Do you expect to be a frequent trader, that is, someone who buys and sells regularly, exploiting short-term price movements? Or are you a long-term investor who selects a share and is willing to hold it for years? Frequent traders can make, or lose, money most quickly, but they have much higher transaction costs.

For the novice investor, joining or forming an investment club can be a way to dip your toes into the share-dealing waters. Investment clubs are groups of friends who band together to invest in shares. They each pay a modest sum each month, typically £20 to £50. This is pooled and used to invest in shares. The club collectively decides what to buy and sell. Profits – or losses – are divided equally between the club members.

Proshare is the trade body promoting share ownership in the UK. It provides literature and runs educational seminars. It also gives advice on setting up investment clubs. Call on 020 7394 5200 or log into www.proshare.org.uk.

Employee share schemes

If you are lucky, you may have the chance to participate in an employee share scheme to obtain shares in the company that you work for.

Share schemes approved by the Inland Revenue have tax benefits for staff. It is usually a good idea to take part in these schemes, if you can find the money to contribute. They provide another savings pot, which is distinct from your pension but which is tax-favoured.

There are several different schemes. But they share a common theme. The employee is encouraged to buy shares in their employer. Incentives include cut-price shares, free shares and tax breaks on any profits made on the venture. The ultimate value of the perk depends on how well the company performs and on the value the shares reach.

The downside of employee share schemes is that they only let you buy shares in one company. Those who stay with an employer for a long period can find they build very large holdings of shares in that firm, which can be risky if the share price suddenly drops. However, the tax benefits of the schemes help to balance these risks. The most common two schemes are:

- Save as you earn (also called SAYE or Sharesave): here you agree to save a fixed sum from your monthly pay for a set period, usually three or five years. The money is paid into a special bank account on your behalf. At the end of this period you have the option of buying shares at a predetermined price. If the market price of the shares is higher than this, you buy and make an instant paper profit, free of income tax. You may have to pay capital gains tax on the profit if you sell your shares in one go and go above your annual capital gains allowance. Employees sometimes stagger their sales over different tax years to avoid a hefty bill. If the market price is lower than the option price you do not buy the shares and instead keep the money.

- All-employee share plan: each year you have the chance to buy shares in your company from untaxed pay. Your employer can match the shares you buy and give you free ones too. Provided you hold on to the shares for at least five years, you can sell them free of any tax. But you are allowed to hold on to the shares for as long as you want.

Older schemes, such as approved profit share schemes, are being phased out.

Proshare can also provide you with more details about the different kinds of employee share schemes. Contact details are as above. Alternatively, the Inland Revenue produces booklets for employees. IR97 covers save as you earn share schemes and IR177 covers the all employee share plan. These are also available on line at www.inlandrevenue.gov.uk.

Property

If you are buying your own home, then you are already investing in property. Buying a house can form a valuable part of many families' retirement plans. Once the mortgage is paid off, the home is an asset to cherish. Owning your own home will cut down on the day-to-day cost of living in retirement: you do not have to pay rent. Alternatively, the house can be a way of saving. Many people move to smaller homes when they retire or shortly after. Typically, the existing home is sold for more than the cost of the new one and the extra cash released goes to help fund retirement.

It is also possible to tap into some of the capital in your own home without moving. A range of equity release and home income plans allow homeowners to derive an income from their homes, either by arranging a new mortgage on it or by selling a portion of the property. There are three main types of scheme in use:

- The home income plan: a portion of the property is remortgaged at a fixed interest rate. The proceeds are used to buy an annuity which both pays the mortgage and provides an additional monthly income. When the owner dies, the annuity income ceases and the mortgage is repaid from the proceeds of selling the home. The fall in annuity rates and end of mortgage interest tax relief mean that these are now only attractive for a minority of older investors.
- The home reversion plan: the owner sells a chunk of their home outright, say 50 per cent, usually for a cash lump sum. The money is then free to be spent or invested as they choose. They live in the property rent free for the rest of their life, or lives in the case of a couple. When the homeowner dies, the house is sold. Their estate gets the proceeds from the portion of the home they own.
- Equity release loan: the homeowner is granted a loan secured again their property. The loan attracts interest, but it is not charged. Instead, interest rolls up. When the owner dies and the property becomes free, the original loan must be repaid, along with accumulated interest. Usually the house is sold to provide enough money. The loan is safeguarded so that even if the value of property is not enough to cover the total due, there are no further charges on the owner's estate.

All schemes should be flexible enough to allow you to move home; for example, to go into sheltered housing or to cope if the owner has to go into long-term care.

Entering into one of these schemes will reduce the value of the inheritance you can pass on to family. But it can be a way of benefiting from rising property values without selling your home. The trade association Safe Home Income Plans (SHIP) can provide more information about the companies offering these schemes and how they work (see contact information).

Buying your own home is simply the tip of a property investment iceberg. There are other ways in which you can play the property market for gain. Buying some, or all, of a property which is then let out gives investors the chance of both income and an increase on their capital.

You need some capital to get on to the property ladder. The easiest way to start is through a buy-to-let mortgage. This allows you to borrow up to 80 per cent of the purchase cost of a house or flat, which you then rent out. The expected rent has to be enough to comfortably cover the running costs of the house, repairs, periods where you have no tenants and, of course, the mortgage repayments. Anything left is your rental profit. However, the bigger returns can come from any appreciation in the value of the property. Even though you have put up perhaps only one-fifth of the capital needed to buy the property, you will get 100 per cent of any gain in value.

Profits on your investment will be taxed. Rental income counts as your income and is taxed, although you can offset costs such as repairs and mortgage against this. And any profits made from the sale of the property will be subject to capital gains tax – only gains on your main residence are tax-free.

This kind of investment will not appeal to all. You have to be hands-on to find the right properties and manage them well. You can pay a letting agent to deal with tenants on a day-to-day basis, but this will cost you 12–15 per cent of your rental income. And there are big risks. What if you cannot find a tenant for a few months? How will you pay the mortgage? Also, property markets are notoriously fickle. If values fall and you have to sell, you are the one who bears the loss. To be sure of capital growth you may need to hold a property for ten or more years.

Nevertheless, a few dedicated investors have made significant sums out of running portfolios of rental property. Once they manage to repay mortgages, the incomes can be substantial. Property has the key advantage over pension investment in that you call the shots: you decide when to buy and sell, and what to do with your profits.

Those with substantial capital sums, typically £30,000 to £50,000, may be able to join syndicates which buy, redevelop and then let commercial property. Again, this is a high-risk, high-return investment.

The Association of Residential Letting Agents can provide some basic fact sheets on buy-to-let investments. Call 01494 431680 for details.

In summary:

- There is a wide range of alternatives to saving through a pension.
- Most savers use a mixture of pensions and other options to build their retirement fund.
- Having a diverse range of savings will allow you more flexibility over how and when you retire.
- There are additional options to save or defer tax.
- Not all kinds of saving will suit all kinds of investors. You must be comfortable with what you are doing.

Notes

1 UK £2500 + savings account average to 2 July 2001, net interest reinvested.

2 FTSE All Share index to 2 July 2001, net dividends reinvested.

3 Standard & Poor's Micropal, FTSE All Share index, 1 January 1973 to 31 December 2000.

CHAPTER 12

Seeking help – financial and pensions advisers

Read this chapter if:

- You want to know more about advisers who can help with retirement planning.
- You want help in choosing an adviser.
- You want help in finding an adviser.

It is a twisty path to a prosperous retirement. There are many rules and regulations to follow; a wide choice of savings opportunities and few simple answers. Even a comprehensive guide such as this book cannot answer all the questions. There will be times when you might benefit from having an expert on hand to help. You will need a financial adviser.

Financial advice has a mixed reputation. There are some very skilled and talented advisers, who have undoubtedly helped their clients to a far more prosperous future. Equally, there have been – and unfortunately still are – advisers who are more concerned about enriching themselves, rather than their clients. Advisers in general are still trying to shrug off blows to their reputation, such as past pension mis-selling. It is no wonder that many potential savers are sceptical of advice.

This chapter will help you to understand what kinds of advisers are out there and how you can sort the wheat from the chaff.

Even if you are doubtful of advice, there is one important reason why it is worth considering using an adviser. Where you make decisions on your own, without consulting an expert, you have no recourse if your plans go badly wrong; for example, you realise that you are trapped in a scheme which does not let you retire when you wanted to. You made that decision on your own. However, if you use an adviser and things go awry, you may have recourse against that adviser.

Regulation

Anyone who wants to advise the public on certain financial products, including investments and pensions, has to be regulated by the Financial Services Authority. The FSA monitors both individuals and their employing firms to try to ensure both are keeping to the rules.

The regulations specify how an adviser should work with a customer, what information that customer should receive and what action an adviser has to take before they can sell a financial product to that person. Regulated financial products include unit trusts, investment Isas, personal and stakeholder pensions, endowments and other whole-of-life insurance products.

For more details on what products are regulated and how, contact the FSA customer helpline on 0845 606 1234 or log on to its excellent consumer website www.fsa.gov.uk/consumer.

The Financial Services Authority also keeps a central register of all firms in the UK who are or have been authorised for investment business. You can check with this register to ensure that someone you are thinking of doing business with is a legitimate organisation. Again, call 0845 606 1234 or enquire on-line at www.thecentralregister.co.uk.

Before an adviser can work unsupervised with the public they must pass certain qualifications. These are designed to give the adviser a base level of knowledge.

The most common qualification is the Financial Planning Certificate (FPC), examined by the Chartered Insurance Institute. More than 110,000 people in the UK have passed this three-part exam. Alternatives include the Certificate for Financial Advisers (CeFA), awarded by the Chartered Institute of Bankers, and the Investment Advice Certificate (IAC) from the Securities Institute. More than 20,000 people have taken these.

A whole tree of financial learning lies beyond these basic qualifications. Advisers can voluntarily take extra exams and/or join professional organisations, which commit them to further study. So far, relatively few have done so. Just over one in twenty advisers holds a higher qualification.

Advisers who want to work on pension transfers have to do a higher exam called G60, part of the Advanced Financial Planning Certificate.

Box 12.1 lists some of the qualifications that financial advisers can hold and their abbreviations. Look out for the letters on an adviser's business card or ask what exams they have done. Do not be overly impressed by someone who proudly displays their FPC certificate in a frame behind their desk; it is nothing special, simply their ticket to do business.

Qualifications are not the only way to judge a good adviser. Experience, skill at judging clients' needs, common sense and an aptitude for people are all important. Some well-qualified advisers sometimes struggle to translate book learning into real-life situations. However, further qualifications and membership of professional bodies that demand continuous study to stay up to date are a mark in an adviser's favour. They demonstrate a commitment to customers and suggest that a person is making a career out of advice, rather than just being a slick seller who wants to make a fast buck.

Box 12.1: Decoding financial advisers' qualifications

Advisers can put a vast range of letters after their name, representing the different qualifications they take. The list below decodes some of the most common qualifications. It splits them into basic, intermediate and elite so that you can tell what level in their profession someone has reached.

Basic qualifications (minimum required by the regulator)

CeFA – Certificate for Financial Advisers
CIP – Certificate in Investment Planning
FPC – Financial Planning Certificate
IAC – Investment Advice Certificate
MLIA(Dip) – Member of the Life Insurance Association

Intermediate qualifications

ACII – Associate of the Chartered Insurance Institute
AFPC — Advanced Financial Planning Certificate
AIFP – Associate of the Institute of Financial Planning
ALIA(Dip) – Associate of the Life Insurance Association
ASFA – Associate of the Society of Financial Advisers
DFSM – Diploma in Financial Services Management
FLIA(Dip) – Fellow of the Life Insurance Association
MSFA – Member of the Society of Financial Advisers
MSI – Member of the Securities Institute
PIC – Professional Investment Certificate

Elite qualifications

FCII – Fellow of the Chartered Insurance Institute
FIFP – Fellow of the Institute of Financial Planning
FIA/FFA – Fellow of the Institute/Faculty of Actuaries
FSFA – Fellow of the Society of Financial Advisers
FSI – Fellow of the Securities Institute

What kinds of advisers are there?

Advisers come in different varieties. There are three types at the moment, with the prospect of a fourth on the horizon. The main categories of financial advisers are:

- Direct sales people – these advisers are directly employed by the organisation which provides a financial product or products. They have to be qualified advisers, but can only sell you products offered by their employer. This is the type of adviser you are most likely to encounter if you wander into a high-street bank or one of the bigger building societies looking for help, or call up a big-name insurer direct.
- Tied agents – these advisers work for themselves or for a firm, selling a limited range of products. They agree to tie to one organisation and sell only the products of that firm. They may be able to link to a second or third firm where their main tied company does not operate in that part of the market. For example, they may have a main tie covering life insurance, pensions and investments, and subsidiary ties for income replacement insurance and private medical insurance. Again, tied agents have to be qualified but can only advise on and sell you the products of the organisations they are tied to.
- Independent financial advisers – these advisers, commonly known as IFAs, are free to advise on products from across the market. They can pick and choose from the best providers for pensions, different companies for Isas and other firms for life or health insurance. In theory an IFA can review the whole market before recommending a product to you. In practice, most have their regular favourites for particular types of business, a list which changes gradually from year to year.

There is a fourth type of adviser poised to shake up the market. At the time of writing, the government was starting to relax the rules that say advisers have to be either tied or independent. It thinks there is room for a new category of adviser: one with multiple ties. That is, the adviser might sign up to sell on behalf of five or six different pension companies and do deals with ten different investment houses. Initially, such multi-ties would only be permitted on supposedly simple products, such as stakeholder pensions. In time, the rules might be relaxed further.

IFAs do not like the idea. They fear it will lead to more confusion and will muddy the position of truly independent advice.

For advice on more complex products, such as executive pensions, self-invested personal pensions or income drawdown schemes, an independent adviser is essential. Likewise, those who are about to retire and need to shop around for an annuity are strongly advised to use an independent adviser to give them the widest possible choice.

How will you pay for advice?

Initial consultations with an adviser are usually free of charge. After that you will pay for the adviser's time, even if you don't realise you are doing so.

There are two ways to pay for advice: commission and fees.

Commission remains the most common way to pay. The saver pays their money directly to a financial provider; for example, to a pension company. That pension firm in turn pays the adviser a slice of the money back as a commission. Advisers can earn a lump sum of commission up front, often called initial commission, plus a smaller slice paid each year that you stay invested, called renewal or trail commission. On regular savings products the up-front commission can be much bigger than your first few monthly payments. This is because the product provider is paying for the advice up front and will claw back this money from you as part of its charges over the life of the product.

Advisers can also vary the amount of commission they take up front, sacrificing some in exchange for a bigger renewal commission each year.

The level of commission varies from product to product and

from adviser to adviser. Some advisers will get more generous terms than others because they give a lot of business to a particular company. Typical commissions on a range of products are shown in table 12.1.

Table 12.1: Typical adviser commissions

Type of financial product	Initial commission	Annual commission
Unit trust or oeic	3 per cent of initial investment	0.5 per cent of fund value
Endowment	25–45 per cent of first year's premiums depending on term of policy	2%
Old-style personal pension	25–50 per cent of first year's premiums depending on term of policy	2%
With-profit investment bond	5 per cent	None

An adviser has to tell you how much commission they, or more usually their firm, will earn from each piece of business. This needs to be disclosed in pounds and pence before you commit to an investment. This is not what the individual adviser gets paid; the commission has to cover items like office costs, administration, fees to the regulators and professional indemnity insurance for the adviser.

The main advantage of choosing to pay through commission is that it can avoid the need to find cash to pay up front. It may cost an adviser £500 worth of their time to set you up with a personal pension into which you pay £100 a month. Rather than facing a bill for £600 in your first month, the commission option spreads this cost to you over a much longer period. However, the adviser is likely to get more than £500 over the life of the pension.

Commission has two potential disadvantages: firstly, there is the possibility that an adviser has been influenced in their choice of advice by the amount of commission that they can earn. They suggest what is best for them not what is best for you. Some investment options, such as National Savings and most investment trusts, pay no commission at all so do not generate revenue for an adviser. Even if commission bias is not the case, another disadvantage of commission is that clients with bigger sums to invest can end up paying sky-high prices.

Take the case of a client who has asked for advice on investing a lump sum for income. The adviser recommends splitting it between two income-producing unit trusts from two different firms. Where the lump sum is £20,000, the adviser might earn commission worth an initial £600, plus £100 a year thereafter. But if the lump sum is £100,000 and the advice the same, the adviser will earn £3000 up front and £500 a year, for essentially the same amount of work.

There are ways around this problem. Many advisers agree to rebate, or pay back to the client, a portion of the commission on larger investments. In the £100,000 case outlined above, the adviser might agree to refund £2500 or more of the initial commission because they expect a healthy sum each year anyway.

Another option is to move away from commission altogether and pay fees to your adviser instead. Advisers who charge fees operate in a similar manner to accountants, lawyers or private doctors. They set an hourly rate, which covers both their own pay plus all the office costs. Clients are charged for the number of hours of work that their particular case generates. Some clients also agree to pay an annual retainer to buy ongoing advice and help at the end of the phone.

If you choose to pay fees, you will get an estimate of the likely fee your case will generate. The adviser will tell you their hourly rate and estimate the number of hours it will take to handle your business.

Where the adviser's recommendations generate commission this is refunded to the client. Often the refund is handled by boosting the value of the money invested or increasing the benefits a policy provides. Depending on how the adviser works, the renewal commission paid over later years may or may not be refunded too. It may be kept by the adviser and used to pay for ongoing advice.

Fans of fee-paying advice claim that it removes any incentive for an adviser to select products that pay a high commission. The customer knows that they are getting the advice that is best for them. Fees may also better suit those savers who have got larger sums to invest, or high-value pension funds to transfer. On the biggest deals such as putting the pensions of high-earning executives into income drawdown, commissions could run to £30,000 or £40,000. Fees for the same case might total £10,000.

There are two disadvantages of fees, both relating to tax. Firstly, fees are usually subject to VAT. Where you are quoted a rate, check whether this is inclusive or exclusive of VAT, currently 17.5 per cent. Secondly, the fees are paid out of your normal taxed income. In the case of pensions this can make advice more expensive than commission.

Take the case of a top-rate taxpayer who is saving through a personal pension. The adviser wants £510 to cover his work and is relaxed about whether he gets it as a fee or as a commission. As a fee, he will add VAT to this, which rounds the total up to £600. The client then has to pay this out of taxed income, which means the fee has cost him £1000 out of his untaxed gross income.

If the same sum were being taken as commission, it would come from the client's pension contributions, which are made free of tax. The cost to the client could be only £510 of pre-tax income.

There is a halfway house between fees and commission which may appeal. Here, the adviser charges notional fees. These fees are worked out on an hourly scale as before. But instead of the client paying fees direct, they are paid for out of commission. Any surplus commission is earmarked in your name and used to cover the costs of future advice, or is refunded to the investor.

Where an adviser is being paid an ongoing commission from your business, they should be earning it. Expect them to be in touch regularly, with reviews of how your funds are doing and suggestions for what your next step might be. Hearing nothing from an adviser for more than a year to eighteen months could be the signal to go elsewhere. When you switch to a new adviser, the regular commission from previous investments can often be switched over too.

How you can find an adviser

Often the best route to an adviser is through personal recommendation. Ask friends and colleagues whom they use, how long they have been dealing with them and see whose name keeps cropping up. Your employer may be willing to introduce you to an adviser, though staff are frequently coy about dealing with someone who also talks to their boss. Many trade unions also have relationships with advisers. They may offer preferential terms to union members.

Alternatively you can try to find an adviser for yourself. There are two main organisations that will put you in contact with a local independent financial adviser. IFA Promotion runs a free telephone helpline on 0800 085 3250. This will give you the name and address of three local advisers, along with details of how they charge and what their main areas of business are. It can provide a list of only female advisers too, for anyone who prefers to take advice from a woman. Alternatively, try its website on www.unbiased.org.uk.

The Society of Financial Advisers (SOFA) has its own register of advisers. Called the Find an Adviser Service, it will only put you in touch with advisers who have taken further qualifications and completed extra study. Call 020 7417 4419 or log on to www.sofa.org. Both organisations also provide general information leaflets about advisers and how they work.

The relationship with an adviser should be viewed as a long-term one. So it makes sense to invest some time and effort in selecting the right one. As a rule of thumb see at least three people for an initial interview.

You need to feel comfortable with an adviser on both a personal and a professional level. Don't be afraid to ask a potential adviser hard questions. But remember it is a two-way relationship;

to do their job properly, the adviser will need you to be honest with them too. Do not hold back information or be embarrassed about disclosing details such as debts or divorce settlements. You can only be advised properly if someone has a full picture of your financial situation.

Box 12.2 suggests questions you might want to ask when you meet an adviser for the first time.

Box 12.2: Key questions to ask a potential adviser

- How long have you been an adviser?
- What qualifications do you have?
- Are you studying for any more qualifications?
- How long has your company been in business?
- How long have you been with the company?
- What were you doing before that?
- How many clients do you have?
- What are your areas of specialised skill?
- Are there other advisers in your company who can help me if I need advice outside your areas of specialised skill?
- What happens if you leave or retire?
- How do you charge for your services?

Specialists

The vast majority of financial advisers can help you across the broad range of retirement-planning issues – pensions, investments, insurance and other savings. There can be times, however, when you need something beyond the ordinary. In these cases you may want to consider taking specialist advice. It is often possible to do this in conjunction with your regular adviser. Areas where specialist advice could be wise include:

- transfers between two occupational pensions;
- buying an annuity: consider going to one of the specialist annuity advisers (see Chapter 22);
- putting a pension fund into income drawdown or phased retirement (again see Chapter 22).

You and your regular adviser may also need to call on the help of other professionals from time to time, especially if your financial affairs are more complicated than average. You may need to consult an accountant for tax planning and a solicitor for legal issues such as will writing, the formation of trusts and other estate planning. You may also need to call on the services of a consulting actuary if you are negotiating a high-value pension transfer. These professionals will all charge by the hour.

PART Three
Retirement Challenges

CHAPTER 13
Early retirement

Read this chapter if:

- You plan to retire early.
- You want to know whether this is a realistic goal.
- You want to maximise your chances of early retirement.

Early retirement is a key goal for many, many of us. We want to stop work as soon as is realistically possible and try to enjoy the opportunities of an active retirement while we are still fit and healthy.

There can be pressing reasons for quitting early; for example, to coincide your retirement with that of a husband or wife so that you can both enjoy time together. Or to be with other members of the family; for instance, to help out in caring for grandchildren.

But amassing the funds and the pension rights to be able to afford to quit early is one of the key challenges of retirement planning. This is a challenge which is set to become tougher, rather than easier, over the years to come.

This chapter explains the main barriers to retiring early and how you might be able to overcome them.

Early retirement – so common it is expected

Over the past two decades, early retirement has become much more common. Changing economic and social factors have led to vast numbers of people retiring earlier. More than half of men aged sixty are no longer registered as part of the labour force; they have in one way or another retired – more than five years before the official state retirement age. This upswing in early retirement has had the effect of changing people's expectations about retirement. Most of those now working who are in their thirties and forties confidently expect to retire early. Many now assume it is a right.

Yet early retirement is not a right and is far from guaranteed. It is possible, indeed likely, that economic and social factors are going to swing round over the next two decades and push workers towards later and later retirement dates.

Why has there been an early retirement boom and why can't it go on?

Two main factors have enabled more people to retire earlier. Firstly, the economic climate over the past quarter of a century has been generally favourable. Stock markets have grown well, house prices have moved ahead in real terms. Inflation has been largely contained. This has left growing numbers of people able to afford to stop working sooner than they had expected.

At the same time, employers have been willing to subsidise early retirement as a way to help trim staff numbers. They have used surplus assets in their company pension schemes – largely built up through better than expected investment growth – to boost the pensions of people who retire early and so, in some cases, avoid making compulsory redundancies.

But the demographics of the labour market are changing. There are forecast to be fewer workers in years ahead as the wave of post-war baby boomers starts to retire. Employers will increasingly want to hang on to the staff they have got. They will be less willing to incentivise early retirement and ready to penalise those who do go early by reducing their pensions.

At the same time, economists forecast a period of lower inflation and lower stock market growth ahead. Money saved through pension funds and other investments is likely to grow more slowly. The amount of income that annuities provide has fallen dramatically in the last few years, reflecting this changed economic environment. Lower annuities mean pension funds can buy lower incomes. This makes early retirement a more expensive proposition.

The government has already responded to some of these pressures. It had to equalise male and female state retirement ages on sex equality grounds. Rather than bringing the male age down to sixty, it is increasing the female age to sixty-five. It is possible that state retirement age may rise again later in this century, especially if average lifespans keep increasing. Company pensions too have equalised retirement ages, often at the higher male age, not a lower female age. There are now proposals being aired to start increasing the minimum age at which people are allowed to draw personal and company pensions (see below). Again, this is aimed to keep more people in the workforce.

These political, social and economic changes will not make early retirement impossible. But they will mean that if you are serious about wanting to quit ahead of the normal retirement age, you will have to start planning and saving well in advance, and keep absolutely on top of the situation.

Can you afford it?

The key issue around early retirement, even where rules permit it, is can you afford to go early?

Early retirement catches workers in a two-way squeeze. You have fewer years in employment to save, then you have to spread your money over an extended retirement. Retiring early means either accepting a lower standard of living in retirement, or saving a much higher proportion of your income while working in order to achieve the income you might have had if you had stayed working to normal retirement age.

Box 13.1 shows an illustration of how much more you might have to save to retire early.

The closer you are to the prospect of early retirement, the better able you are to judge whether or not savings are on target to make it possible. Projections about growth and inflation over the next five years are likely to be much more accurate than those made twenty or thirty years into the future. Unfortunately, the closer you get to retirement, the harder it is to put yourself back on track if you do need to save more. There are only a few years left over which to spread the costs of extra saving.

Final salary company pensions reward you with a bigger pension for each year of employment with that organisation. If you retire early the pension will be based on fewer years of service, so it will be smaller than if you stay on until normal retirement age. There may also be extra penalties imposed for taking your pension early (see below).

Those who are saving into money-purchase pensions face a different challenge in retiring early. This includes both members of a company money-purchase pension and those who invest money into a personal or stakeholder pension. Here problems occur because you have to use the bulk of your funds at retirement to secure an income for life by purchasing an annuity. The younger you are, the lower the annuity rate will be. The combination of smaller fund and lower annuity rate means that even a few years of extra saving make a big difference to the final pension income.

Take the example of Andrew, aged sixty. He is trying to balance early retirement today against retirement at sixty-five. He has a personal pension fund of £267,000. If he retires today and takes the maximum tax-free lump sum, he will have £200,000 left to buy an annuity with. At today's annuity rates this fund might buy him an inflation-proof income of £11,276 a year.[1] If we assume inflation averages 2.5 per cent a year, this income would increase to £12,758 a year by the time Andrew turns sixty-five.

Suppose he carries on working and is able to save an additional £8000 each year into his pension. If investments grow at an average of 7 per cent a year, at age sixty-five his fund would be worth

£423,707. This would give him a maximum £105,927 as a tax-free lump sum and a remaining fund of £314,313 a year. At today's annuity rates a sixty-five-year-old with this remaining fund could secure an inflation-proof income of £21,244 a year.[2] So by working an extra five years, Andrew has boosted his potential income in retirement by 65 per cent or just over £8486 a year. Can he really afford to retire at sixty?

Box 13.1: The costs of early retirement

Sophie is thirty. She works as an IT consultant, earning £40,000 a year. She has so far made no special savings for retirement, although she is paying a mortgage on a house. She fancies the idea of stopping work when she is in her fifties and estimates she would need an income of about £25,000 a year, in today's money. She asks a financial adviser for a projection of how much she would need to save into a personal pension to achieve this. The adviser produces four projections for her. These are shown in the table below.

Sophie's target retirement age	Monthly saving required (gross of tax)	Estimated annual income, expressed in today's money *	Cost of saving as a percentage of her gross income today
50	£1250	£25,013	37.5 per cent
55	£941	£25,016	28.2 per cent
60	£729	£25,027	21.9 per cent
65	£574	£25,024	17.2 per cent

This shows that the cost of retiring at fifty-five is more than one third greater than the cost of staying on in work to sixty-five. Quitting at fifty is even more expensive.

Even if Sophie could afford to set aside these amounts, almost all the numbers produced require her to save more than the annual Inland Revenue limits for a person of her age. These cap pension contributions at 17.5 per cent a year of earnings. She could, of course, use non-pension savings such as an Isa or an endowment to save extra. As she gets older she is allowed to increase payments into a pension.

But set against this, Sophie's earnings may well increase over time too. Her expectations of retirement may then rise and she would look for a higher income when she retires. So she may already have left it too late to secure a comfortable retirement at fifty and will have to save very hard to manage it by fifty-five.

* Source: Hargreaves Lansdown. Assumptions used: investment growth of 7 per cent a year, contributions are level, annual charge on the pension of 1 per cent, inflation 2.5 per cent and annuity rate 6 per cent.

It may be possible to defer taking an annuity by opting for income drawdown or phased retirement with some of your pension fund. However, this is a more risky strategy which may not appeal to all savers. See Chapter 9 for an introduction to annuities, drawdown and phased retirement. Chapter 22 has more in-depth information.

If you are thinking about whether or not you can afford early retirement, remember to consider beyond the first year or two. You may calculate that by taking a level annuity, which will pay the highest income in the first year, you can afford to retire early. Is this just wishful thinking? Early retirement almost inevitably means longer retirement. Would you really be able to cope if your income remained the same for twenty-five or thirty years of retirement? Allowing for the costs of buying a rising income may mean you have to delay retiring for a few more years.

Scaling back pensions on early retirement

Final salary pension schemes may reduce the value of a pension paid on early retirement. This is because the employer's pension fund is likely to have to pay a pension for longer than was originally budgeted for. If someone quits five years ahead of the normal retirement age then, all other things being equal, they will receive an income for five years longer. To balance the books, most schemes will scale back the pension by a set amount for each year that you retire before normal retirement age. A typical reduction might be 6 per cent a year; a generous scheme might only reduce by 4 per cent a year.

Alternatively, some employers are more flexible. Their pension schemes might allow you to retire without penalty at any age between sixty and sixty-five.

Box 13.2 shows the impact on income that early retirement can have to someone on a final salary pension.

Box 13.2: How early retirement can reduce a final salary pension

Sylvia, fifty-eight, is thinking about taking early retirement. She works as a jewellery buyer for a big store group on a total package of £38,000 a year. She has twenty-three years of service. Her employer runs a final salary pension scheme. Each year of service entitles her to one-sixtieth of her final salary as a pension. The scheme's normal retirement age is sixty-two.

How will early retirement affect her income and tax-free lump sum?

Suppose she works until normal retirement age at sixty-two. Her salary by then might be £42,770, assuming an average 3 per cent increase each year. She would have twenty-seven years of service. Her maximum pension would then be 27 x $\frac{1}{60}$ x £42,770 = £19,246 a year. Alternatively, she can take a tax-free lump sum of £43,304 and a reduced annual pension of £15,638 a year.

If Sylvia retires today, her pension will be based on a lower salary and less service. She will be entitled to 23 x $\frac{1}{60}$ x £38,000 = £14,567 a year. Alternatively, she can take £32,776 as a tax-free lump sum and have a reduced annual pension of £11,836 a year. Once Sylvia starts drawing her pension it will rise in line with inflation. Assuming inflation of 2.5 per cent a year, by the age of sixty-two her maximum pension is worth £16,079 – around £3200 a year less than she would have got by carrying on working to sixty-two.

However, what if Sylvia's employer scales back pension on early retirement because it has to pay the money for more years? This is very common.

Let us assume the scheme reduces pension by 5 per cent for each year ahead of normal retirement age you retire. In this case, Sylvia is quitting four years early, so the total reduction is four x 5 per cent or 20 per cent. Now her maximum annual pension would be £11,654 a year. Or she could take a lump sum of £26,221 and a reduced pension of £9469 a year.

After allowing for inflation-linked increases, by the time Sylvia reaches sixty-two, her maximum pension is worth £12,863 a year. This is £6383 a year less than if she had stayed in work to normal retirement age.

Retiring four years early has cut Sylvia's annual pension by almost a third.

Is early retirement permitted?

Even if you think you have enough stashed in the retirement kitty to quit work early, it may not be possible to go when you want to. The Inland Revenue sets out strict limits over the ages at which people can retire and start to draw benefit from a company or personal pension scheme. The limits it lays down are the earliest permitted; employers are free to set higher ages or more restrictive terms. And a personal pension may have contractual terms and conditions which penalise you if you start taking an income earlier than the age that you nominated when the pension was first started.

The Inland Revenue limits for retirement vary with different types of pension. They are:

- Occupational pensions – normal retirement age for schemes can be set between sixty and seventy-five. Early retirement is permitted from the age of fifty.
- Personal pensions, including group personal pensions, self-invested personal pensions and stakeholder pensions – benefits can be taken at any time from fifty up to the age of seventy-five. You can 'retire' and take an income from a personal pension regardless of whether you continue in employment or not.
- Retirement annuity plans – income can be taken from the age of sixty. It may be possible to transfer funds to a personal pension plan to then retire earlier.
- Self-administered small schemes – a scheme can set a normal retirement age between sixty and seventy-five, but early retirement is possible from fifty.

Remember, these ages are a Revenue minimum. A particular pension may impose more restrictive terms.

Those who work in some types of job may be allowed to retire earlier than the standard rules. This mainly applies to professional sportsmen and women or entertainers, where they cannot carry on to normal retirement age. Box 13.3 sets out some qualifying occupations.

It may also be possible to retire earlier than these minimum ages where you are in poor health. Chapter 15 discusses in detail the options for retiring early if accident or illness means that you are no longer fit to work.

Where someone has had a varied career with different employers, they may have two or more different pots of company pension entitlement. These may be linked to schemes with different retirement ages and with different early-retirement rules.

The limits set out above are enshrined in law. However, there are pressures to increase the minimum ages as a way of keeping more older people as part of the workforce. A Cabinet Office report published in 2000 proposed raising the minimum retirement age for all pensions to fifty-five, taking effect on a gradual basis between 2010 and 2020. This would mean anyone born between April 1960 and April 1965 would have a different date for earliest retirement. Anyone born after April 1965 could not benefit from a pension until the age of fifty-five. At the time of writing this remained a proposal and had not been put into any legislation.

As part of the same initiative, the Inland Revenue has also agreed in principle to relax the rules around how someone draws a company pension. At the moment you cannot take a partial pension from your employer and still keep on working as a member of the pension scheme. You have to be either working or retired. The plan is to change this, which would aid partial retirement or down-shifting (see below). No date has been set for the changes.

Box 13.3: Occupations where especially early retirement is permitted

Occupation	*Earliest retirement age*
Athlete	35
Badminton player	35
Boxer	35
Cricketer	40
Cyclist	35
Dancer	35
Diver	40
Footballer	35
Golfer	40
Jockey (flat racing)	45
Jockey (National Hunt)	35
Model	35
Motorcycle racer (track or motocross)	40
Motor-racing driver	40

Royal Marine reservist (non-commissioned)	45
Rugby player (League or Union)	35
Skier	30
Speedway rider	40
Squash player	35
Table tennis player	35
Tennis player	35
Trapeze artist	40
Wrestler	35

Note: Only pension savings based on income directly earned in this profession count. So a professional cyclist who also ran a cycling shop would be able to take a pension based on income from cycling, but normal rules would apply to any pension based on an income from the shop.

Likewise, a cricketer could use income from playing or prize money to fund a pension that he could take early. But coaching income would be treated under the normal rules.

Contracted-out earnings

It is not possible to draw anything from a state pension until you reach the normal state retirement age, that is sixty-five for a man or between sixty and sixty-five for a woman, depending on when she was born. This restriction applies to both the basic state pension and to additional pensions such as Serps or the new State Second Pension. If you have been contracted out of Serps into a personal pension or an employer's pension, then restrictions will apply to when you can take the proportion of your pension that contracting out has provided. Restrictions will also apply to contracting out of the State Second Pension when it is introduced in April 2002.

When you contract out, National Insurance rebates are paid into a fund or pension scheme on your behalf. Where contracted-out rebates have gone into a personal pension, they form what is known as a protected rights fund. This cannot be taken before the age of sixty (the same age applies for both men and women, despite differences in the state retirement age). If you retire before then, the fund must remain invested, hopefully growing in value. When the pension is taken, it must be used to provide an income in a specified way.

The same rules for protected rights apply where rebates have been paid into a money-purchase occupational pension scheme. Again, no benefit from this can be drawn until the age of sixty.

Where contracted-out rebates have been paid into a final salary pension, early retirement may still be possible using the contracted-out portion of your pension. However, this will need to be revalued because it is being taken early, which could reduce other benefits the pension can pay. For example, it could reduce the tax-free lump sum. Occasionally, where the contracted-out payments form a large portion of your entitlement, it may not be possible to draw a pension from the scheme until nearer normal retirement age.

If an employee has been contracted-out of Serps for a long period and has earned at or above the National Insurance upper earnings limit for much of that time, it is possible that the contracted-out pension could be worth around £100 a week – more if the money has been invested in a strongly growing fund. The ability not to take this pension until sixty may be a serious drawback in early-retirement plans.

For more detail on the mechanics of contracting out, see Chapter 21.

State pensions and early retirement

It has already been mentioned above that you cannot retire early and claim a state pension. These are not paid until the official state retirement age.

Early retirement can also reduce the value of the state pension you might collect when you reach sixty-five (or an earlier age for some women). As Chapter 3 explained, the basic state pension depends on someone having paid National Insurance contributions for enough years of their working life. A man needs forty-four years of contributing to collect the maximum pension, for example (see table 3.2). Retiring early makes it more likely that you will not have racked up sufficient years to qualify for the maximum pension.

Does this matter? The basic pension itself is not huge by comparison with average earnings. For some wealthy retired people it will be almost irrelevant. But it is an important part of income for others in retirement, not least because it will provide a rising income with a certainty that the government will pay.

If you are uncertain about what state pension you might be entitled to you can ask for a forecast from the Benefits Agency (see page 35).

Retiring early may also reduce the value of any additional state pension you can claim because you will have fewer years of earnings to be assessed on.

Ways round the retirement rules

It is possible to work round the limits on minimum retirement ages. You can hand in your notice and stop working at any age, subject to the notice conditions of any employment contract. If you have enough non-pension savings and investments to support you until it becomes possible to claim a pension income then you can effectively retire as early as you like.

If you were a member of a company pension scheme and you quit in this way, you would become a deferred pensioner. Your entitlement to a pension would be preserved. But you would not be drawing any income. Money invested in a personal pension would also remain your own and could grow over the years. Once you reach the permitted retirement ages, you simply turn on the tap and draw down these assets.

To retire safely this early, you need to be confident that you have sufficient other assets both to keep you in a desired standard of living until the pension is available and to act as an emergency fund. If you run out of savings too soon you may struggle for income or be forced to try to find other work.

So it is wise for those who are committed to early retirement to use a variety of methods of saving to build up their kitty. Paying everything into a pension limits your options.

How can you maximise your chances of being able to retire early?

There are some golden rules to follow if you have your heart set on early retirement. These are:

- Start saving early – the earlier you start saving for retirement, the more chance you have of being in a position where you can afford to retire early.
- Save as much as you can – to achieve early retirement a significant portion of your income will need to be going towards your retirement kitty. You are likely to have to be prepared to make sacrifices on current spending.
- Use your allowances – there are generous limits on how much an employee or self-employed person can save towards their pension. Be prepared to pay in up to these limits. Use AVC or FSAVC schemes if necessary (see below).
- Save outside the pension – this will give you more flexibility in when and how you can retire. It also allows you to increase your overall level of saving. Alternatives to pensions include Isas, endowments, savings plans, unit trusts, investment trusts, property and shares. Chapter 11 has more details on all these.
- Get into the habit of using a portion of any pay rise to boost saving – this will ensure that your saving keeps pace with a rising income and with your rising expectations about the standard of living you will have during retirement.

- Do not fritter away bonuses and windfalls – if you are paid annual bonuses, or get a windfall such as a demutualisation pay-out or an inheritance, do not blow the lot. Be willing to commit a slice of it to your retirement fund.

Using AVCs and FSAVCs

Members of a company pension scheme can choose to make voluntary extra payments into their pension. These are called additional voluntary contributions (AVCs). An in-house AVC scheme is connected to the main company pension and designed to pay benefits integrated with that pension. There are also independent AVC schemes which can run in parallel with your company pension. These are called free-standing AVCs or FSAVCs.

One of the main uses of AVC schemes is to boost the value of an employer's pension to make early retirement a possibility. Members of a company pension can use an AVC or FSAVC to increase their tax-efficient pension savings up to a maximum of 15 per cent of earnings in any one year. This 15 per cent cap includes anything the employee pays into their main company pension, but not the money paid in by the employer.

Where an employee is saving into a final salary pension, their AVC payments may:

- buy added years of pension service, or
- buy a fixed annual pension on top of their normal pension, or
- be invested into a money-purchase fund and hopefully grow to fund an additional pension.

If the employee is a member of a money-purchase pension scheme, their AVC will be an extra money-purchase investment, but possibly invested in a different fund from the main scheme.

AVCs can aid early retirement because they increase the overall size of the pension pot. This helps employees to afford to retire early. The impact of AVC funds may also counteract the effect of other penalties imposed for early retirement. Box 13.4 shows an example of how this can work.

Historically, benefits from an in-house AVC had to be taken at the same time as the employee retired from the main pension scheme. The Inland Revenue rules were changed in 1999 permitting AVC benefits to be taken at any age between fifty and seventy-five, providing the employer's pension scheme rules allow this. In fact, few employers have bothered to change their rules, so most AVCs have to be taken at the same time as normal retirement age.

FSAVCs can be set up to pay out at any retirement age between fifty and seventy-five. This can help those who are in company pensions with rigid and unfavourable rules about early retirement. They can set up an FSAVC to pay out when they want to retire. The income from this can then help sustain them up to the stage when the main pension scheme allows them to take an income.

Imagine, for example, a man who wanted to retire at fifty-seven, but whose company pension penalised those who quit before the official retirement age of sixty-two. He could set up an FSAVC designed to mature at fifty-seven and pay into this on top of his contributions to the main pension scheme. He would resign at fifty-seven, but remain a deferred member of his company's pension scheme. The FSAVC would provide him with an income for five years, before he was able to retire without penalty from the main pension scheme and take a full pension.

Chapter 20 has more detail on the AVC rules.

For many of those who are in a company scheme, a stakeholder pension might be a more appropriate top-up savings scheme than AVCs. It is more flexible about when you can retire and allows tax-free cash.

Box 13.4: How AVCs can aid early retirement

Example 1: Sylvia, fifty-eight, wants to retire early. Her circumstances are outlined in box 13.2. This shows that her retirement pension for leaving work at fifty-eight is worth an initial £14,657 a year, but is scaled back to £11,654 a year because she takes the money early.

Suppose she had paid additional voluntary contributions to the company pension scheme. These AVC payments go towards buying Sylvia 'added years', which have the effect of increasing her pensionable service. Her payments have bought five added years, on top of her twenty-three years of employment with the firm.

Her early retirement pension is now calculated as 28 x 1⁄60 x £38,000 x 0.8 = £14,186 a year. The increase in pension through the added years of service has almost counteracted the effect of the early-retirement penalty.

Her AVC contributions have bought Sylvia enough extra pension to be able to afford to retire at fifty-eight.

Example 2: Suppose Sylvia had instead saved into a free-standing AVC scheme run by an independent pensions company. She has saved hard and has managed to build a fund worth £87,000.

If she retires at fifty-eight, her company pension will still be reduced to £11,654 a year. But she can use her FSAVC fund to secure an inflation-linked annuity income of £4302 a year. This means her total pension income is £15,956 a year. Again, Sylvia can afford to retire early thanks to her extra voluntary savings.

Partial retirement

An increasingly popular alternative to early retirement is partial retirement, also called downshifting. Where someone cannot afford, or does not want, to retire for good, they move from full-time into part-time work. They gradually wind down.

Employers too are becoming receptive to partial retirement. It helps them to hang on to key staff and experienced workers for longer, while at the same time creating more opportunities for younger workers coming through the business.

Partial retirement helps make the move from a work life to a leisure life a more gradual process. Reducing hours in the main employment will reduce income. But, depending on your circumstances, it may be possible to take an income from a personal pension or from a pension from previous employment to make up for some of the lost earnings.

Alternatively, it might suit you better to retire from the main pension scheme, possibly taking a tax-free lump sum, but to defer taking any pension income. The tax-free lump sum can help plug the gap between your part-time earnings and your former salary. Meanwhile the value of the main pension income should increase for each year it is deferred.

Those in a final salary scheme should be careful before agreeing to any cut in hours or salary. They need to make sure that their pension on retirement is based on their pay for previous full-time employment, not the reduced rate for part-time work.

In summary:

- Early retirement is common today.
- It will become harder and more expensive in the future.
- Retiring a few years earlier can reduce dramatically the value of a pension.
- There are limits on the age at which you can take a pension.
- There are much stricter limits on when a state pension can be collected.
- Saving outside a pension will give you more choice over when you retire.
- To maximise the chances of early retirement, save early and hard.
- AVCs and FSAVCs will help you maximise your pension contributions.
- Partial retirement may be a more realistic option.

Notes

1 The Annuity Bureau, July 2001. Man aged sixty buying an RPI-linked annuity. Annuity rates change daily.

2 The Annuity Bureau, July 2001. Man aged sixty-five buying an RPI-linked annuity.

CHAPTER 14 Divorce

Read this chapter if:

- You are in the process of a divorce.
- You already have been divorced.
- You are divorced but plan to remarry.
- You want to know about rebuilding savings after a divorce.

Divorce is now commonplace. Around 170,000 marriages each year end in divorce. Aside from the huge emotional upheaval involved in splitting apart couples and families, divorce can have significant implications on both partners' retirement plans.

A couple's retirement fund is made up of a mix of assets and entitlements, such as pensions, savings, property and investments. An equitable divorce will see this fund split in two. Changes in legislation over the past decade have ensured that all assets in the retirement kitty are taken into consideration, including pension funds or entitlements to future state and company pensions. This has transformed the way divorce settlements are arranged; it ensures that lower-earning or non-working spouses, usually women, get the chance of a much higher income in retirement than they would have got under old-style divorce settlements. And it means the higher earner, typically the man, may have to start again with fresh retirement saving.

This chapter explains the laws on divorce and pensions, and what this means for both parties.

Basic principles

Divorce settlements are structured to ensure that a couple's assets are split evenly and fairly between the two. Many assets are jointly owned; for example, a home or savings. Carving up these is straightforward. But other assets may belong to only one of the couple. When middle-aged people divorce, pension rights are frequently the largest asset which is not owned jointly.

Where only one of the couple has been working, or one has been a much higher earner than the other, there will be great differences in value between these pension rights. So divorce settlements have to find ways to account for these individual assets and balance out the whole.

There are three methods that can be used to apportion pension rights and so create a truly equitable settlement. These are: offsetting, earmarking and pension sharing. Each has advantages and disadvantages for both sides. Which one is used will depend on a couple's other assets, their individual preferences and the counsel of their legal and financial advisers.

Offsetting

Offsetting is the longest-established method of dealing with retirement funds in divorce. It is still widely used, though it has been superseded by later arrangements.

Historically, it was impossible to carve up a pension. The pension fund, or the entitlement to a future income from accumulated pension rights, remained the property of the spouse who had earned it. The idea behind an offset is for the spouse with the bigger pension rights to accept a smaller share of the other family assets to balance out their more valuable pension.

Take the example of a couple who jointly own a house worth £180,000. They also jointly have savings and investments worth £50,000. In addition, the husband is a member of a well-funded company pension scheme. This is valued at £160,000. So total assets are £390,000. Shared equally, this means giving each partner £195,000. Under an offset arrangement, the wife might take the whole house and £15,000 of the savings. Her husband would keep the pension and take £35,000 of savings.

The main advantage of such an arrangement is that it is simple. It allows the couple to have a clean break and to have no further contact with each other. However, it can also lead to problems.

- The man is left with his pension intact, but with nowhere to live. Moreover, his assets are tied up until retirement. He cannot sell his pension to release cash to buy a house or move away. While his retirement may well be prosperous, the years until then are uncertain.
- The woman retains a property, but has a very small retirement pot left. Her assets are tied up in the property. If she is near retirement she will probably have to sell the house to release funds to support herself. Alternatively, if she has some years to go to retirement, she may have to find work and start saving so that she has enough other income to keep the house after retirement.

In order to give more flexibility in splitting pension rights, the alternative of earmarking was introduced in 1996.

Earmarking

Earmarking, also known as attachment or deferred maintenance, can be applied by the divorce courts in cases where a couple have failed to reach an alternative settlement. Under the Pensions Act 1995, the courts now have a duty to take account of pension rights in drawing up a financial settlement.

The principle behind earmarking is simple. Where one spouse has superior pension rights to the other, a portion of their entitlement is reserved or earmarked for their ex-spouse. This earmarked pension is then paid to the ex-spouse when the owner of the pension retires.

The process normally works as follows. The courts ask for the pension to be valued. For a money-purchase pension or personal pension this will be a transfer value. For a final salary pension the scheme will have to calculate a cash equivalent value as if an employee were changing jobs.

The valuation is based on the full value of the pension, including those pension benefits which were earned before the marriage took place. This means that those who marry later in life and then divorce could see a big dent made in their fund. In Scotland the law differs. Here the valuation is only for that part of the pension which has been earned since marriage and up to the earlier of the date of the petition for divorce or when a couple stopped living together.

A pension scheme or pension provider must give this valuation within three months. The court will then give the ex-spouse an order which can be served on their former partner's employer or pension provider. Orders can be issued covering one or more pensions. The order may direct that:

- a portion of a person's pension benefits – for example, one-quarter or one-half – must be paid to their ex-spouse from the date the pension starts to be drawn;
- some or all of the tax-free cash produced at retirement must go to the ex-spouse. The court can also insist that tax-free cash is taken;
- some of any lump sum payments made if the pension holder dies before retirement may be directed to the ex-spouse.

The order will follow that portion of the pension if it is transferred to another scheme.

If the person benefiting from the order remarries, the order automatically lapses. That means they will get nothing from the pension, regardless of their financial position after their new marriage. This applies even if the pension is already being paid.

Depending on the exact terms of an earmarking order, a couple are more likely to take even shares of non-pension assets. However, there are some drawbacks with earmarking. These include:

- Although the beneficiary of the earmarking, usually a woman, has a financial interest in a pension, they have no control over it. Their ex-spouse decides where it is invested and when to retire. A vindictive ex-husband or ex-wife could deliberately run down the value of this portion of their pension, especially if it were a relatively modest fund. And the date they retire may not suit the former spouse, who might want money earlier or later.
- Benefits paid to the ex-spouse will cease when the pension holder dies. In some cases the ex-spouse may get nothing at all if their former partner dies before retiring.
- The pension is taxed according to the holder's circumstances. This means that an ex-spouse who pays basic-rate tax nevertheless gets a slice of pension income which has been taxed at the top rate. There is no way to reclaim the difference.
- Earmarking contradicts the idea of a clean-break divorce. The financial affairs of husband and wife are still linked.
- Serps pension is not covered by earmarking.

To work round these objections a third option has been introduced – pension sharing.

Pension sharing

Sharing or splitting a pension was introduced in December 2000. It means that the courts are now able to order an immediate division of someone's pension rights. This measure can be applied to occupational pensions, personal pensions, retirement annuities and Serps pension benefits.

With a pension split, the court again calls for a cash valuation to be put on a person's funds or entitlement to future pension. The court then decrees that a percentage of this fund belongs to the ex-spouse from the date of the divorce. The split does not have to be 50:50. The exact measure will depend on how the other assets are being divided up between husband and wife.

To make the order work, the pension holder is given a pension debit and their ex-spouse a pension credit.

Where the pension being split is a money-purchase fund, the original holder would see their fund reduced and their ex-spouse would effectively be credited with a new fund in their name.

For a final salary scheme, the split is more complicated. The ex-spouse's pension credit is calculated by taking their proportion of the pension entitlement on the day before the sharing order takes effect and then revaluing this to the date of normal retirement.

For a Serps pension, the ex-spouse simply becomes entitled to a percentage of their former partner's pension earned up to that date. They get this when they reach normal state retirement age.

In many cases the ex-spouse is then free to transfer their pension credit to an alternative pension scheme. Some occupational pensions will force these credits to be transferred to make administration more simple. Other occupational pensions, particularly those unfunded schemes in the public sector, will not be able to afford big lump sum transfers, so the ex-spouse becomes a member of the pension in their own right.

Pension splitting can also be applied to pensions that are already being drawn. Here the annual income is simply carved up according to the percentages set out by the court.

The advantage of pension sharing is that it gives the beneficiary control over their portion of a pension fund. In most circumstances they will be able to transfer it, either into an existing pension of their own or into a new one. They decide how it is invested and they can decide when to retire, within the legal limits and any rules set by their new pension scheme. And they do not forfeit these funds if they remarry or if their former spouse dies.

There are still some flaws in the scheme. Where the fund being split is a final salary scheme, the valuation of the pension will be calculated using the salary at the date of divorce. But the actual pension paid to their former spouse will be based on the salary when they retire, which could be much higher. The ex-spouse gets no part of this increase.

Nevertheless, pension splitting is expected to be used in at least one-third of divorces and gives another alternative for sharing out pension rights.

State pensions and divorce

If you divorce before state pension age, you can use your former husband's or wife's National Insurance contribution record to claim your own basic state pension. This will be advantageous if a former spouse has more years of qualifying contributions than you do. Likewise, if divorce takes place after pension age it is possible to retain this higher pension based on your former partner's NI contributions. These rights to claim against a former spouse's pension are lost on remarriage.

Additional pension such as Serps is not normally affected by divorce. It stays with the person who earned entitlement to it, unless there has been a pension-splitting order granted by the courts.

Divorce advisers

If you are engaged in a divorce, you need good advice on your side. As well as a divorce solicitor, consider appointing your own financial adviser. Pension splitting and pension earmarking is still a relatively new area, and only a small number of law firms have the in-house expertise in valuing funds and decoding pension jargon. Adding your own financial adviser to the team can help. For more information on financial advisers read Chapter 12. The Law Society runs a service to put you in touch with local solicitors who have expertise in particular areas of the law. Call 0870 606 6575 or log on to www.solicitorsonline.com.

Life after the divorce

Once the divorce is done and dusted, retirement plans will need to be rebuilt and reassessed. Exactly what happens next will depend on the circumstances of the divorce.

If there is already another partner on the scene and remarriage is on the horizon, the new bride or groom may bring with them savings, pension funds or pension entitlements of their own. The new couple can then start building a joint plan. Be aware, however, that marrying again will mean that any entitlement to a share of a former spouse's pension made under an earmarking agreement will cease. You may also lose entitlement to state pension claimed against a former spouse.

Where someone is settling down to life as a single person, retirement plans may have to be completely rewritten. As was discussed in Chapter 2, the expenditure of a single person in retirement is likely to be more than half that of a couple. And if the pension kitty has been depleted by an earmarking or pension-splitting agreement, you may need to consider saving at a much higher rate than before to make up for lost ground.

Non-working divorcees can now use some of the assets from a divorce to kick-start a pension of their own. Under the contribution rules introduced in April 2001 they can pay up to £3600 a year into a pension even if they have no earnings of their own.

If you are starting retirement planning for the first time after a divorce, read Chapters 2 and 4 for a good introduction of the general principles.

In summary:

- Divorce will see the entire retirement kitty split in two.
- Pension assets have to be counted as part of a settlement.
- There are three ways in which the pension can be dealt with. Two give you a clean break, the other does not.
- Separate rules cover the state pension.
- Remarriage can void your entitlement to deferred maintenance and earmarked pensions.
- Be prepared to start from scratch in your retirement planning once the dust has settled.

CHAPTER 15
Ill health

Read this chapter if:

- You want to know more about what happens when ill health forces you to stop working early.
- You want to know what support you will get from the state.
- You want to know about ill health retirement from company and private pensions.

An accident, a sudden illness such as a heart attack, or a long-term illness can put your retirement plans in jeopardy. Where recovery is swift and complete, you may be able to return to work, having missed only a few months. Where the condition is permanent, you may only manage to work part-time or have to cease work altogether.

This chapter assesses your options if long-term illness forces a permanent change of circumstances upon you.

There can be obvious and immediate problems. Income is likely to drop and your opportunities for future saving may be reduced. But there may also be opportunities; ill health retirement can turn into a surprising and welcome career change.

Early days

In the first few weeks of an illness employees will get support from their employer. At the very least they will qualify for statutory sick pay; the vast majority for a much higher income.

The self-employed are in a different position. If they have not made any provision for ill health insurance, they may be forced to start running down savings or claim state benefits straight away.

But if the illness continues beyond a certain point, employers' sick pay will run out too. Statutory sick pay runs for twenty-eight weeks. Many firms will keep some form of sick pay running longer, perhaps for a year. When the sick pay stops, employees face some difficult decisions. Early retirement on the grounds of ill health can be a common choice, rather than just sacking someone.

State help

If you are forced to give up work early because of ill health, the state will provide only modest assistance. You cannot claim any state pensions until you reach the official retirement ages – sixty-five for a man, between sixty and sixty-five for a woman, depending on when she was born. Instead, you may qualify for one of two benefits which are paid to the long-term sick until retirement age. These are Incapacity Benefit and Income Support.

Incapacity Benefit

This is targeted specifically at those who cannot work through ill health. To qualify you must have paid National Insurance contributions in one of the two tax years before you stop working.

In addition, you undergo a personal capability assessment. This is effectively a test of how ill you are. It will determine whether or not you are capable of any work and whether retraining or specialist equipment might help you find alternative work. To get the benefit you have to be largely incapable of any employment. You will be regularly re-assessed.

Incapacity Benefit is paid at three rates. The short-term basic rate, paid between one and twenty-eight weeks of your illness, is £50.90 a week. Only those who do not get statutory sick pay from an employer qualify for this. After twenty-eight weeks of illness the rate increases to £60.20 a week. After fifty-two weeks it rises to the long-term standard rate of £67.50 a week. The benefit is taxed.

There may be extra payments made. If you were under thirty-five when your illness started, add £14.20 a week. If you were aged between thirty-five and forty-five add £7.10 a week. Supplements are also paid if you are responsible for looking after dependent adults aged sixty and over, or dependent children.

But Incapacity Benefit is clawed back if you have income from a company pension. For each £1 of extra income over £85 per week, you lose 50p of the benefit. Someone who qualified for the standard-rate benefit but had an ill health pension income of £220 a week or more would get nothing.

If you are paid Incapacity Benefit, you will be also be paid National Insurance credits, which build you entitlement towards the basic state pension. You will not earn credit towards Serps. But, from April 2002, you will earn credits under the State Second Pension, which will be worth the equivalent of earning £9500 a year.

Income Support

This is a means-tested catch-all benefit designed to give the most basic of incomes to those who do not get money from anywhere else.

Anyone with savings of more than £8000 gets nothing. Savings of £3000 or more will reduce the amount that you can qualify for. A partner's income will be taken into account.

The value of the benefit depends on age and family circumstances. For example, in tax year 2001/02, a couple with one child aged under sixteen gets a basic £114.70 a week. Other benefits, such as the Working Families Tax Credit, and Housing Benefit may boost the value of weekly payments.

For more information about these state benefits contact your local DSS office or log on to www.dwp.gov.uk.

Ill health retirement from an occupational pension

The definitions of ill health are interpreted very widely when it comes to taking early retirement from an employer-run pension scheme.

In pension terms, ill health does not mean that you are too sick to do any job. It is defined in the Inland Revenue's pension rules as a mental or physical condition which prevents an employee from doing their normal job, or which substantially reduces their earning power. So you can be retired sick from a company pension scheme even if you would not qualify for state help under the Incapacity Benefit rules. Many public-sector pension schemes, such as those for the police and fire services, retire large numbers of their staff early on ill health grounds. Many of those retired early then go on to do second jobs and make new careers for themselves.

Claims for early retirement need to be supported by medical evidence. Administrators or trustees of the pension may ask for an independent assessment or second opinion. They are protecting other scheme members against the possibility of bogus claims.

The amount of income you will get depends on what type of pension you have and how your scheme is set up. In general, ill health retirement from the different types of pension works as follows.

Ill health retirement from occupational final salary pensions

Where you are a member of a final salary scheme, Inland Revenue rules permit you to take early retirement on the grounds of ill health at any age. The maximum pension allowable is calculated using the years of service you would have accumulated if you had worked until normal retirement age, but based on the salary you earn when you retire.

However, some final salary schemes are less generous than this. They do not have to offer the maximum permitted benefits. Some schemes may scale back the ill health pension, reducing it by a percentage for each year you quit ahead of the normal retirement age. At worst, the conditions for ill health retirement are the same as those for other early retirement.

It will still be possible to take a tax-free lump sum if you retire through ill health. Again, this would be smaller than the sum you could have had if you carried on working to retirement, because it will be calculated on salary now, rather than what your salary would be in the future. Taking the lump sum will reduce the size of the annual pension.

Benefits from any AVC and FSAVC schemes you are paying into alongside the company scheme can also be taken early if you retire through poor health.

Once an ill health pension is in payment, it will increase in line with all the other pensions being paid by that company scheme.

Box 15.1 shows two contrasting examples of how final salary schemes can treat ill health retirement.

Where you are medically certified as having a very short period to live, usually less than a year, the whole pension can be paid out as a lump sum. The portion of this payment over and above the normal maximum tax-free lump sum is taxed at 20 per cent. This option often dramatically improves the amount of income available for survivors and dependants after your death. Act quickly if you think that you or someone in your family might qualify for such a lump sum payment. The payment can only be made while the ill person is alive and the paperwork can take several weeks to process. If you die before the forms go through, this may be treated as death in service (see Chapter 16).

There is usually little point in deferring a pension if you are forced to retire through illness and can afford to live off other savings for a while. Even though you will get an increased income when you take the deferred pension, you will have lost the years of income until then. Most of those who are retiring in ill health would rather take the cash while they can use it, in case their condition deteriorates further.

Box 15.1: Ill health retirement from a final salary pension scheme

John is aged fifty-five. He is an electrical engineer earning £32,000 a year. He has suffered a serious heart attack and has been forced to take early retirement on the grounds of ill health.

John's firm operates a final salary scheme, which credits staff with one-sixtieth of final salary for each year of service. John started with the company when he was thirty-two. The scheme's normal retirement age is sixty-two.

Under the rules of the pension, John can retire early through illness with no reduction in his pension. His service is extended as if he had worked to the normal retirement age of sixty-two, and benefits are calculated as follows:

- Thirty years of service (twenty-three real and seven added) give an immediate annual pension of thirty-sixtieths or half of John's salary. This is worth £16,000.
- Alternatively, he can take a tax-free lump sum of up to ninety-eightieths of final salary, which is £36,000, and a reduced annual pension.

Now suppose John's employer had chosen to structure its pension scheme differently. Instead, pension paid on early retirement for any reason is scaled back to reflect the fact that the pension has to be paid for longer. It trims back the value of an early-retirement pension by 4 per cent for each year before normal retirement date that the pension has to be paid.

In this case, because John is retiring through illness, he would still have his pensionable service increased. But the overall value of the pension would then be trimmed back. So his pension is calculated as follows:

- Thirty years of service (twenty-three real and seven added), to give a notional maximum annual pension of half of salary or £16,000.

- This is reduced by 28 per cent (seven years multiplied by 4 per cent) to produce a maximum annual pension of £11,520.

He still fares better than if he were voluntarily retiring early, but his pension scheme is not as generous as the Revenue rules allow it to be.

Ill health retirement from occupational money-purchase pensions

The situation governing ill health retirement from an occupational money-purchase pension is similar to that discussed above for a final salary scheme. Again, the Inland Revenue rules permit you to take early retirement on the grounds of ill health at any age. Normally early retirement is not sanctioned until after the age of fifty. The maximum pension allowable and maximum tax-free lump sum are again calculated assuming that an employee would have carried on working until normal retirement age but based on current salary.

However, the size of the pension available from a money-purchase scheme will depend on how big a fund has been accumulated in your name and what sort of annuity that will buy for a person of your age. It will also depend on exactly what the scheme rules are and what they say about how you retire. Some schemes, for example, do not allow tax-free cash for ill health early retirement.

Early retirement through ill health can work both for and against you in the annuity market. Annuities are priced on life expectancy. The longer you are expected to survive, the lower the income a fund of a given value will provide. In the case of someone retiring at forty-five, where the condition is debilitating but not life-threatening and so a long retirement is possible, the annuity income may be very low indeed.

However, where the illness is recognised as shortening your expected lifespan, you may qualify for an impaired-life annuity. This buys a higher level of income than would be normal for someone of your age.

Some employers get round the annuity problem by purchasing

income replacement insurance on behalf of their staff. This runs alongside the pension and the insurance provides an income until normal retirement age in the event of ill health. Your pension fund stays invested and it may even be possible to make additional contributions, depending on your income and the scheme's rules. Other benefits built into the pension, such as life insurance, can also be retained. Then, at normal retirement age, an annuity is purchased for future income. As you are older, you get a better rate and therefore a higher income from your pension fund.

The disadvantage of keeping the fund invested like this is that any tax-free cash also has to be put off until normal retirement age.

The other option on early retirement through ill health may be to put your fund into income drawdown. In general this will only be practical with large funds, though it may appeal to those whose illness is such that they feel they have a relatively short life expectancy. If you die while the fund is in drawdown, the bulk of the fund can be passed on to others minus a tax charge. Once an annuity is purchased, the capital has gone. Chapter 9 introduces the main features of annuities and drawdown, and they are explained in full detail in Chapter 22.

As before, where you are medically certified as having a very short period to live, usually less than a year, the whole of your fund can be paid out as a lump sum benefit. The portion of this payment over and above the normal maximum tax-free lump sum is taxed at 20 per cent.

Ill health retirement from personal pensions

Personal pensions are generally more flexible than occupational ones. Even without any evidence of ill health, it is usually possible to start taking income from the age of fifty. You can do this and continue to work, either full- or part-time.

It is possible to draw money from personal pensions earlier than at fifty on the grounds of ill health. You will have to prove to the pension company that through mental or physical ill health you are unable to carry on with your normal occupation or another of a similar nature for which you are trained and which you are able to do. You will need doctors' reports, medical evidence and may have to undergo a second examination to certify your ill health.

Where the funds in a personal pension come from contracting out of Serps or the State Second Pension, that element of the fund cannot be used to provide an income any earlier than sixty – even if you are in ill health.

If the illness is not deemed life-threatening, it may be better to hold off taking a pension until a later stage. This is because the older you are, the bigger the annuity income you can buy. However, depending on the nature of your condition, you might want to take as much out of the pension as you can while you still are able to benefit from the money.

If you had the foresight to invest in waiver-of-premium insurance then you also will want to try to delay taking your pension. Waiver of premium will pay your regular monthly premiums into the pension if you are unable to do so because you cannot work through illness. This means that your pension fund can continue to grow. These monthly payments will continue until the age you had originally intended to retire. At that point the pension fund can be used to provide an ongoing income.

If, however, you have no other savings to live off, then ill health retirement may be the only option. You will be able to take up to a quarter of the pension as a tax-free lump sum and then can either buy an annuity or go into phased retirement or income drawdown with the rest.

Other insurance benefits

Your options, if you stop working through illness, will also depend on what other savings, income and insurance you have. Some types of insurance can provide vital extra cash if illness strikes. Aside from waiver of premium, discussed above, you may also be able to claim on:

Income replacement insurance

Income replacement insurance, also called permanent health insurance, is designed to pay a regular monthly income if you cannot work through illness. It will pay this as long as you remain too ill to work, up to the age at which you originally planned to retire. There is a deferred period at the start when the insurance does not pay. This ranges from one to twenty-four months, depending on what option was selected when the policy was purchased. Payments from this insurance are free of income tax.

Critical illness insurance

This will pay a tax-free lump sum to you if you are diagnosed with one of a list of specified illnesses. Each insurer has slightly different lists, but virtually all policies cover common conditions such as heart attack, stroke or cancer. The lump sum is yours to do with as you like. It can pay for modifications to your home, be invested for additional income or be used to fund a holiday. There is no need to pay the insurance back if you make a full recovery.

Terminal illness benefits

Some life insurance policies offer a terminal illness option. This pays out the lump sum of the life insurance if you are diagnosed with a terminal condition that is likely to cause your death within a year. Effectively, it gives you money while you are still alive and can use it, rather than paying it to others after your death. Your condition may need to be assessed by additional doctors but once paid, the money is yours. It does not need to be returned if you survive beyond the year.

Accident sickness and unemployment insurance

This is frequently sold alongside loans, credit cards and mortgages. The insurance pays the monthly interest payments if you are unable to work because of an accident or ill health. The cover may only run for a limited period – for example, two years – but it can buy vital breathing space where debts are not mounting up.

The Association of British Insurers produces fact sheets on

these different types of cover. Call 020 7600 3333 or log on to www.abi.org.uk.

Other implications of ill health

Where the ill person is married or has a partner, their illness can prompt a wholesale reorganisation of retirement plans for both. Insurance payments and ill health pensions can provide a reasonable standard of living, but are unlikely to match the original income that someone was on target to achieve in retirement. This means the healthy partner may need to take a greater responsibility for both earning for today and saving for the future. Any plans which they themselves had for early retirement may have to be reassessed and they may need to increase contributions into their own pensions or savings plans if they now have to assume the role of the main provider.

Alternatively, the illness of a partner or relative can be such that you yourself are forced to give up work to care for them. Unfortunately, the pension regulations do not recognise 'compassionate early retirement', so if you are too young to take early retirement it will not be possible to draw on your own accumulated pension benefits to help make ends meet when you are caring for another.

Qualifying careers do continue to build entitlement to the basic state pension and will also be credited towards the State Second Pension from April 2002. They will be treated as having earned £9500 a year, even if they have no earned income.

In summary:

- Ill health is a significant challenge to retirement planning.
- The state provides only modest assistance.
- Pension schemes will let you retire early, but with reduced income.

- Separate insurance schemes can provide vital extra income.
- The ill health of one partner is likely to mean a change of plans for the other.

CHAPTER 16 Dying before retirement

Read this chapter if:

- You want to find out more about what happens to your funds if you die before retirement.
- You want to find out how to provide an income for dependants such as children.
- You want to find out about state help.

It is cruel fortune when someone plans and saves hard for retirement, only to be robbed of the chance of enjoying their efforts by dying before they give up work. An untimely death before retirement age will not mean all this savings effort counts for nothing; it is likely that dependants such as a spouse or children will be able to share in some of the retirement kitty that was supposed to provide for the deceased. But an early death may mean not all the money comes back to family and, in some cases, it may cause financial hardship for those left behind.

This chapter explains what happens when someone dies before they retire and how their retirement funds are split up.

Help from the state

The state provides some limited help for widows and widowers. State benefits for these groups were radically overhauled in April 2001. The intention of the changes is to try to treat both sexes equally. Prior to this, widows had access to a range of benefits, but widowers got practically no state help.

The effect has been to open up some benefits to men, but to reduce the overall level of assistance that women can expect on the death of their husbands. The new rules apply to all those whose spouses die after 5 April 2001. Those already receiving benefits under the old system can continue to collect them. The cohabiting partner of someone who dies has no rights to these benefits, even if they have been living together for years and have children.

Under the new system, there are three main benefits:

- The Bereavement Payment – this is a tax-free lump sum of £2000. It is payable to a married person on the death of their spouse, providing that the recipient has not yet reached state pension age. The payment also depends on the National Insurance contribution record of the person who died. This payment replaces the Widow's Payment, which was worth £1000.
- The Widowed Parents Allowance – this is paid to widowed parents who have one or more children who receive Child Benefit. It is worth a basic £72.50 per week. It replaces a previous allowance that was only available to mothers. The payment is not means-tested, so you can get it regardless of other income, but it will be taxed. The allowance is dependent upon the National Insurance contribution record of the person who died. They have to have paid for at least one whole tax year and for 90 per cent of their working life for a spouse to be entitled to the full benefit. Fewer contributions will mean the payment is scaled back. Fathers who were widowed before April 2001 can also start to claim this.
- The Bereavement Allowance – this is paid to widows and widowers with no dependent children and who are aged forty-five or over. It is worth a maximum of £72.50 a week for those

over fifty-five. Those aged between forty-five and fifty-four get a portion of this, starting at only £21.75 a week for a forty-five-year-old. The benefit is not means tested but is taxed. It is only paid for fifty-two weeks. Again, Bereavement Allowance depends on the person who died having paid sufficient National Insurance contributions, using the same formula as for Widowed Parents Allowance.

While the reforms mean that widowed men get some state help, they have also disadvantaged women. The main impact of the change is that state pensions can no longer be paid before someone reaches retirement age. Prior to the reform, a woman who was aged forty-five or over when her husband died could get a scaled-down pension based on her late husband's entitlement to state pension and Serps pension. This was paid until she reached sixty and the official state pension kicked in.

Under the new arrangements, when someone dies before they retire, their spouse has to wait until they reach official state retirement age to claim a pension. This pension will be based on the better of their own National Insurance contribution record or their late spouse's NI contribution record for the period they were married and on any Serps pension that has been accumulated by both. However, the rules for inheriting Serps pensions have also just been reformed (see box 16.1 for details).

Box 16.1: Confusion over inherited Serps

When someone dies before normal retirement age it is possible for a spouse to inherit some, or all, of the Serps pension that they had earned entitlement to.

Changes originally announced in 1986 were intended to reduce this inheritance. Rather than inheriting all a person's pension rights, a bereaved spouse would get half. This change was due to take effect for all deaths after April 2000. But successive governments failed to communicate the rule change. After a massive outcry from pensioners and near pensioners who had no chance to make alternative arrangements, a compromise measure has been introduced. This means that your rights to inherit Serps will depend on when a husband or wife dies.

The actual pension is not paid until the spouse who is claiming inherited rights reaches state pension age. Even though it is not paid, the value is uprated each year in line with pensions in payment.

The table below shows how much of a former spouse's Serps pension a widow or widower is entitled to if their partner dies before reaching pension age.

Date of spouse's death	percentage of Serps pension passing to widow/widower
5/10/2002 or earlier	100
6/10/2002 to 5/10/2004	90
6/10/2004 to 5/10/2006	80
6/10/2006 to 5/10/2008	70
6/10/2008 to 5/10/2010	60
6/10/2010 or later	50

Occupational pensions

The vast majority of company and public-sector pension schemes provide structured benefits for spouses and other dependants if an employee dies before they have retired. Exactly how these benefits are paid depends on the type of pension scheme and what rules it has drawn up. Typically, dependants can expect a lump sum payment plus a regular income.

When you join a company pension scheme, you will be asked to complete an 'expression of wish' or 'next of kin' form. This tells the pension scheme trustees who you want to benefit from your funds in the event of your early death. It does not bind them, but they are usually guided by this. These forms should be updated if your circumstances change; for example, on marriage, divorce or following the birth of a child.

Where no expression-of-wish form is completed, the trustees have to investigate your family circumstances to find out who should benefit.

How dependants benefit from your funds will depend on the type of occupational pension or pensions you have. However, benefits are not affected by any other income or employment. So a woman who is working in a high-earning job, for example, can still expect to receive an income based on her husband's pension if he dies suddenly.

Employers vary in how they treat unmarried couples and partners of the same sex. Some company pension schemes now extend some or all spouses' benefits to both groups. Others ignore them. If benefits are extended, the partner may need to show that the relationship has been long-standing and that they were financially dependent upon the person who died.

Death in service and final salary occupational pensions

Final salary schemes usually make a tax-free lump sum payment if an employee dies before retiring, also called death in service. This payment is usually between one and four times your salary at the time of death. Four times salary is the maximum permitted by the Inland Revenue. Salary may be your basic pay, or it may include an allowance for extras like bonuses and overtime. Each scheme will have different rules.

This lump sum is usually paid direct to the scheme trustees, so it does not form part of the deceased employee's estate and will not attract any inheritance tax. The trustees in turn pay this money to dependants and those nominated on an expression-of-wish form. Lump sum benefits can be split between more than one person or even put in trust for children.

The maximum lump sum limit of four times salary also has to take account of any lump sums paid on death by deferred pensions from previous employment, unless your current pension pays a lump sum of no more than twice salary. So if a current pension is generous and offers the maximum, other lump sum payments from other company pensions are not possible. For those who joined their pension scheme after June 1989 there is also a ceiling to the value of the lump sum. For tax year 2001/02 this is £381,600, so it catches only those earning more than £95,400 a year.

On top of this lump sum there is usually also a return of any money the employee has paid into the scheme themselves. Compulsory contributions made by an employee are returned, sometimes with interest, sometimes without. For someone who has paid in 5 per cent of salary for twenty or more years, this can itself add up to a significant sum.

Contributions into an AVC or FSAVC may be returned too. But these schemes can also be used to provide extra death benefits (see below), in which case the contributions are not necessarily paid back.

In addition to the lump sum, spouses and other dependants can expect a regular income for life from the pension. This is typically calculated as a percentage of the pension that an employee would have expected to receive if they had carried on working until normal retirement age, but earning the salary they were being paid on death.

Most commonly, a final salary scheme will pay a spouse 50 per cent of the pension her husband or his wife would have received. Sometimes it may be a lesser figure. The maximum it can pay is two-thirds of what the deceased person would have got. The pension is payable for the rest of the spouse's life and will increase each year in line with other pensions being paid by the scheme. This pension is subject to a maximum cash limit (£63,600 in tax year 2001/02).

Where a pension scheme has been contracted out of Serps or the State Second Pension, additional rules apply to safeguard the pension that has been accumulated through contracting out. Broadly, a spouse must get at least half the guaranteed minimum pension to which the employee was entitled. See Chapter 21 for more information on contracting out.

Some occupational pension schemes will stop the annual pension if a spouse remarries or, very occasionally, if they are found to be cohabiting with someone. Others allow the payment to continue. Again, each scheme has its own rules.

Sometimes the value of the spouse's pension will be slightly reduced if the recipient is much younger than their former husband or wife. This is because they can be expected to live far longer and therefore receive a pension for longer than if they were of a similar age to their late spouse. For example, a scheme might reduce the spouse's pension by 2 per cent for each year by which the spouse is more than ten years younger than the original employee.

There may be additional pensions paid if an employee had dependent children. Who qualifies as a dependant child will be defined in a pension scheme's rules. Common definitions include children aged under eighteen or children still in full-time education. Their pension again is expressed as a percentage of what the employee might have received and typically would be 20 or 25 per cent for each child.

Total dependent pensions cannot add up to more than 100 per cent of the original expected pension if that person had not died. So if someone had a large family with three or four young children, the child pensions might have to be scaled back to keep the total payments within the 100 per cent limit.

Box 16.2 gives an example of how survivors' pensions are calculated.

Where someone is entitled to deferred pension from previous employment and dies before collecting it, there is likely to be an extra spouse's pension and dependants' pension available from this. This can be collected too, providing that it does not take a spouse over the two-thirds of salary limit for the maximum pension someone would have had from all their pension schemes had they continued working until retirement.

Box 16.2: How much pension might a widow or widower get?

Tony, forty-six, works as a service engineer for a power company. He earns £27,000 a year. He dies from a massive heart attack. He leaves a wife, Debbie, and children Sarah and Luke aged fifteen and thirteen. What will his family get from this company pension?

Tony's employer runs a final salary pension scheme with a normal retirement age of sixty-five. Each year of service builds pension at one-sixtieth of final salary. Tony joined the pension scheme when he was thirty-three.

The family will get a lump sum payment. Tony's employer pays three times salary on death. This is £27,000 x 3 = £81,000. On top of this, money that Tony has paid into the pension himself (5 per cent of salary for thirteen years) is returned. With interest this adds up to another £16,300.

The family gets a total lump sum payment of £97,300.

Debbie, forty-five, will get a spouse's pension. This is valued at half the pension Tony might have expected if he had worked to normal retirement, calculated on today's salary.

If Tony had worked to sixty-five he would have had thirty-two years of service. On today's salary his annual pension would have been 32 x 1/60 x £27,000 = £14,400.

Debbie's pension is half this = £7200 a year. This is guaranteed to increase at 3 per cent a year. This income will be taxed.

Sarah and Luke will also each qualify for a pension income. Under the scheme rules, dependent children get a pension until they are eighteen. They will each get 25 per cent of Tony's projected pension; that is, £14,400 x 25 per cent = £3600 a year.

If Tony had had four children, each child would only get 12.5 per cent of his pension, or £1800 per year. Otherwise the total paid to dependants would be more than the projected value of the pension if Tony had not died.

Death in service and company money-purchase pensions

A similar set of rules applies where a member of a money-purchase company pension scheme dies, though there are some key differences.

There is usually a lump sum death in service payment. This is subject to the same overall limit of four times salary and the same absolute earnings cap that was outlined above. This payment will typically be insured by the pension scheme or funded directly by the employer. This means it will not come out of the pension fund that the employee's and employer's contributions were building up. However, if a pension scheme chooses to pay only two or three times salary as a death benefit, it can be topped up to the maximum of four times salary by dipping into the fund.

On top of the lump sum there will be other benefits paid, depending on the value of the employee's fund and how the pension fund has been structured.

Suppose that a person's fund is valued at £100,000 when they die. The trustees of the fund and/or the pension holder's spouse have to decide how to take this fund. A widow or widower might choose to opt for the certainty of an annuity. The size of the pension produced will depend on the age and sex of the spouse and on prevailing annuity rates at the time. The younger they are, the less they will get. Table 9.1 on page 166 gives some examples of what annuity income £100,000 might buy.

Alternatively, a widow or widower might choose to keep the fund invested and draw an annual income from it under the income drawdown rules. This would give him or her the chance of potentially growing the income over the years if the value of investments increased too. This is a more risky strategy but might give a higher income in the long term.

Where a money-purchase pension scheme is contracted out from Serps, part of the employee's fund will be classed as protected-rights. This part of the fund must be used to provide a pension on a basis specified by the government when the employee retires. If they die before retirement, their widow or widower must be paid a protected-rights pension of half the value the employee could have got. They cannot use this protected-rights portion of the fund to do anything else.

Saving through an AVC

Further choices may have to be made where an employee who dies has used additional voluntary contributions (AVCs) or free-standing AVCs (FSAVCs) to boost the value of a company pension.

Where the AVC scheme is integrated with a company final salary scheme and buys added years of service, the situation is straightforward. The extra contributions the employee has made increase their length of service with the employer. This boosts the value of the pension paid to a widower or widow. For example, box 16.2 sets out the circumstances of Tony, who dies while a member of a final salary scheme. If he had been paying into AVCs which bought added years of service, his length of service might have been increased by 10 per cent and the final dependants' pensions by 10 per cent too.

Where an AVC is separate from a main scheme and is invested to grow into a stand-alone fund, the situation is more complex. The AVC fund can be used to boost the value of the lump sum payment to a spouse, provided the total payment from all sources does not exceed four times salary plus any refund of member contributions. The same applies to an FSAVC, which will always be separate from the main scheme.

Alternatively, money in an AVC or FSAVC can be used to augment the pension paid to a spouse or other dependants. The entire value of an AVC can be used in this way, providing it does not mean that total annual payments to the spouse are more than two-thirds of what a member could have expected to receive had they lived to normal retirement age.

Take the case of Sandra, for example. She was a member of a final salary pension scheme who dies before retirement. She was earning £32,500 a year. Her main pension pays a lump sum of three times salary for death in service – a total of £97,500. Sandra has also been saving hard into the company's AVC scheme and has a fund worth £50,000. A slice of this can be used to increase the lump sum payment to her family by another £32,500, making it the maximum four times salary of £130,000. This leaves £17,500, which can be used to provide a modest increase in the annual widower's pension being paid to her husband.

Personal pensions

What happens when someone with a personal pension fund dies varies according to the type of fund they have and what arrangements, if any, they made when they started the pension.

It is possible to nominate a spouse and/or other dependants who could receive an income from a fund if the fund holder dies before retirement. This income will be largely determined by the value of the fund that has been accumulated and the ages of those who are to benefit. The fund will be used to buy annuities on behalf of these dependants.

More usually, the value of the pension fund on the date a person dies is paid as a tax free lump sum. This lump sum may be paid direct to nominated beneficiaries, to the pension holder's legal representative (normally the executor of their will) or to another person if the pension trustees feel this is appropriate.

Having the whole fund returned will give dependants more flexibility over how they use the money. This might be particularly advantageous if the spouse receiving the money is relatively young and would get only a modest annuity income.

Where some of the personal pension consists of money transferred from an occupational pension, only one-quarter of this section of the fund can be paid as a lump sum. The rest must be used to buy an annuity.

Special rules apply to those personal pension funds which have been accumulated by contracting out of Serps. Here a spouse's pension must be paid if the spouse is aged over forty-five, so taking the fund as a lump sum is not possible. This spouse's pension must increase in line with inflation up to either 3 or 5 per cent a year. If a pension fund is mixed, that is, it contains both contracted-out payments and extra contributions from the pension holder, the whole fund has to be taken as a pension and cannot be paid out as a lump sum. Chapter 21 covers contracting out in more detail.

Personal pensions can also be used to buy tax-efficient life insurance, which will provide a lump sum if the holder dies before retirement. This cover is something you need to sign up for when you start the pension. Up to 5 per cent of your pension contribution can go towards paying the insurance premium. If someone dies, the lump sum life insurance payment is tax-free.

Other savings and investments

Savings and investments made outside a pension are largely unaffected by the saver's death. They will form part of that person's estate and can be passed on to members of the family or to other people as outlined in the deceased's will. If they have died without a will, the assets will be split up according to the laws of intestacy – be aware, this does not automatically mean that a wife or husband gets everything. Under these laws children too are provided for and, where there are none, other relatives are in line for a share. So it is imperative to make a will if you want to have full control over what happens to your wealth if you die.

Any life insurance policies and endowments arranged on the life of the deceased should pay out. This will provide additional capital on top of lump sums from pensions or employment.

Tax-favoured investments, such as Isas, Peps or any Tessas still running, die with a person. Although the assets themselves are untouched and remain to form part of the deceased's estate, future income from these investments and any future capital growth will be taxed.

What happens next depends largely on the personal circumstances and the preferences of a spouse or partner who is left behind.

If they do not work and are close to normal retirement age

anyway, the surviving spouse may effectively retire. They will be able to invest lump sums for additional income and use this to supplement any survivor's pension they get. The total value of these retirement benefits may be only marginally less than their partner would have expected to get if they had survived to retirement. For further guidance on managing an income in retirement see Chapter 10.

Alternatively, where the widow or widower is relatively young and many years away from normal retirement age, it is likely that they will have to continue working or even start work for the first time. Though lump sums from insurance and pension funds may help clear the mortgage, pay off other debts and leave a healthy surplus in the bank, the annual income from any widow's or widower's pension is likely to be much less than the income they and their family were used to. This is because a husband or wife who dies young will only have had the opportunity to build up a modest number of years of service in a pension scheme or a few years of payments into a personal pension.

In summary:

- State benefits for death before retirement are modest, though men as well as women now qualify for some help.
- Dying before retirement does not mean pension assets are wasted.
- All types of pension return some benefit to any dependant or other individual nominated by the deceased.
- Company pension schemes can provide generous tax-free lump sum payments, plus an annual income for a spouse and children.
- Personal pension funds can be passed in their entirety to another person.
- There are restrictions on what to do with pensions earned by contracting out of Serps.

CHAPTER 17 Problem pensions

Read this chapter if:

- You have a pension which seems to be worthless.
- You fear that you have been mis-sold a pension.
- You are worried that a company pension might not be able to fulfil its promises to you.

The pensions industry in the UK is far from perfect. Although the quality of personal pensions on offer today and the level of advice given to those who buy them has improved, problems still occur.

More importantly, pension contracts have a long life. It can take years for a problem to develop or for a saver to become aware that all is not well. There are still hundreds of thousands of older-style personal pensions in force, sold in the 1980s or early 1990s, which have the potential to trip up someone who is planning for retirement.

Company pensions, too, have their troubles. Employees can find that their pension is not worth what they thought it would be, especially if their employer has been struggling financially.

This chapter highlights some of the common pension problems and suggests, where possible, what you can do to keep trouble to a minimum.

What is a problem pension?

Problem pensions split into two types: where there is a problem because someone, somewhere, has broken the rules or fluffed the paperwork, or where there is a problem because a combination of poor investment, insufficient contributions and high charges means the pension will produce a modest income or even none at all.

In both cases the situation poses a problem for the saver. Your level of income in retirement may not be as high as you were hoping for or were entitled to. However, only in the first case, where rules have been broken, might any outside help be available to get your savings back on track (see below).

Sluggish pensions: when growth is low and charges are high

The income that you get from any money-purchase pension, either a personal pension or one arranged through an employer, will depend on three things: how well the pension is invested, what charges are levied on the fund and what is happening with annuity rates when you retire. If your pension has not grown well, because of poor or unlucky investment, or if annuity rates are low when you retire, the income may well be a disappointment. Likewise, high charges can hold back the value of a pension, especially when it is coupled with sluggish growth.

This dependency on investment and annuity markets is one reason why it is vital for savers to monitor the performance of their funds on a regular basis. If you see that a fund is lagging behind, there is the chance to move the money and hunt out better growth.

Regular reviews of how the investments are performing and of how much you are saving will help to avoid sudden disappointment at retirement. Chapter 6 explains pension reviews in more detail.

It is also possible for savers to find themselves with worthless pensions. This often occurs when someone has paid into a personal pension for only a few years and then has stopped making contributions. They may have stopped because they moved to a new job with a company pension, because they hit financial problems or because they became disenchanted with the pension.

When you stop paying into a personal pension, the money invested there remains your own. It can be left to grow and can be drawn on retirement. However, if initial contributions are modest, the running charges on such a paid-up pension can be so high as to eat into the fund. In some cases this can reduce the fund to nothing.

This is particularly the case where a pension had high front-end charges, as was common among those sold ten or fifteen years ago. Here, a large proportion of the money invested in the first two years was used for up-front fees and commissions, and only a small proportion was invested for the saver. Had contributions continued to normal retirement age, the return might well have been reasonable. If, however, payments into the pension ceased, the fund left might be very small.

If you have one of these historic, or paid-up, personal pensions, it is important to monitor it closely. Ask what are the ongoing charges on the fund. Are there any monthly policy fees charged? Is this fund actually increasing in value or are the charges eating it away? In such cases a transfer out of the fund into a better-performing pension might be the best option, although you cannot recover losses already sustained, such as charges paid up front.

If it is already too late and the pension has a nil transfer value, unfortunately there is little recourse against the pension company. It has applied the rules of its contract, even if these are weighted against the individual who stops paying.

However, some savers may have a case against the adviser who sold them a pension. Proving that you were badly advised to take out that pension may be difficult. A clear-cut case of poor advice would be that an adviser knew that your circumstances were likely to change soon, e.g. that a woman was expecting a baby and was going to have to give up work, yet still signed you up to a pension which offered poor value if contributions ceased early.

Box 17.1 explains more about pursuing cases against pension advisers or pension companies.

Such worthless pensions are far less likely under the new stakeholder regime. Here personal pension charges are strictly limited and payments in can be stopped or started at will without any penalty.

Box 17.1: Making a complaint

Customers of all organisations have rights to complain. Customers of regulated financial services companies have more rights than most.

As well as the usual process of complaining direct to the company or going to law through the courts, customers can opt to use the industry's own established and regulated complaints procedure. This includes an independent arbitration service, the Financial Ombudsman Service. Going to the Ombudsman can be a swifter and certainly cheaper option than using the courts.

In the first instance, a complaint should be directed to the organisation that sold you a pension. This could be a bank or insurer or a firm of financial advisers. There are special procedures if the organisation that sold you a product has gone out of business and no longer exists (see below). It is always best to make your complaint in writing and in a professional and businesslike manner. State the facts of your case simply and if possible give the dates when something happened.

Each company will have its own internal complaint procedures. They will have to look into your complaint and get back to you with a response. Where a company is regulated by the Financial Services Authority, it will have to make an initial response to your complaint within four weeks and has a maximum of eight weeks to make a final response. This might be enough to settle a complaint.

If you are still unhappy, or for any reason the company has not responded within eight weeks, you can take your complaint to the Financial Ombudsman Service (FOS). This is an independent service, funded directly by a levy on the financial services sector. It investigates complaints against banks, building societies, insurance companies, stockbrokers and investment advisers. It does not cost you anything to ask for your complaint to be examined by the Ombudsman.

The FOS is genuinely independent. Many of its staff have a legal, rather than a financial services background. Where it makes a ruling, this is binding on the company. So if it finds in favour of the consumer, the company has to do what the Ombudsman tells it. If you do not like the settlement that is being offered, you still have the right to go to court. The service can make awards worth up to £100,000.

The Ombudsman service is also able to take a rounded view of a complaint. As well as looking at the strict wording of a pension contract or policy, it can consider what is best practice elsewhere in the industry. This gives it wider discretion than a court of law.

Private individuals can use the FOS service. So can small businesses, with an annual turnover of less than £1 million.

Going to law is a last resort. It can be a long, drawn-out process. It can be expensive. You will have to pay a solicitor and possibly a barrister. And if you lose, you could face a big bill for the company's legal costs. Bear in mind that if the Ombudsman has decided that your claim is not valid, it is highly probable that a judge presented with the same facts will come to the same conclusion.

The small claims court is an option if the total value of your claim is less than £5000. It is swifter and cheaper, because you do not have to hire a solicitor. But few pension cases are likely to be worth less than £5000.

If you cannot track down the firm that sold you a pension or it appears to have gone out of business, contact the pensions unit of the FSA. Where companies have gone out of business a special fund, called the Investors Compensation Scheme, exists to pay valid claims against a defunct company.

The Financial Services Authority publishes a booklet called *The FSA guide to making a complaint*. This lists your options in more detail. For a free copy call the FSA on 0800 917 3311. Alternatively, you can download the booklet from www.fsa.gov.uk.

To contact the Financial Ombudsman Service call 020 7964 1000, or log on to www.financial-ombudsman.org.uk. Alternatively, write to:

The Financial Ombudsman Service
South Quay Plaza
183 Marsh Wall
London E14 9SR

Pension mis-selling

There are some clear-cut cases where individuals in the pensions industry have broken the rules. One example of this was pension mis-selling.

The phrase mis-selling is now bandied about to encompass all kinds of problems, ranging from poor-performing pensions to sharp practice or breaking the law. But pension mis-selling has a clear meaning in the eyes of financial regulators. It refers to those individuals who were:

- sold a personal pension when they could have joined a company pension instead;
- advised to opt out of their company pension and buy a personal pension;
- advised to opt out of their company pension and to transfer money already accumulated in it to a new personal pension.

Someone who followed this advice could potentially have been left worse off. Those in company schemes often have their pension contribution subsidised by the employer and running costs are usually less. Plus there can be extra benefits, such as life insurance, which are not always provided with a personal pension. In the majority of cases if you have the option of joining a company pension it makes sense to do so.

By the mid-1990s it became clear that many hundreds of thousands of savers had potentially been mis-sold a pension. Salesmen had ignored the rules. So financial regulators, who have since merged into one body called the Financial Services Authority, announced a review of pension selling. This review covers sales of pensions made in the period between 29 April 1988, when the Financial Services Act of 1986 came into force, and 30 June 1994, when the regulators issued new guidelines to companies.

The review compels pension companies and financial advisers to investigate their sales. If evidence of mis-selling is found, the pension seller has to pay money to leave a saver no worse off than they would have been had they stayed in or joined their employer's pension. The total bill for the mis-selling review, including the administration costs, is expected to run to around £14 billion. Box 17.2 explains more about the pension review.

It is now too late for someone who started a personal pension during the period 29 April 1988 to 30 June 1994 to demand to have their case checked as part of the official review process. The last deadline for claims was 31 March 2000. Some companies may still accept additional cases and add them to the review, but they do not have to. However, it may still be possible for you to lodge a claim for mis-selling using the normal industry complaints process outlined in box 17.1. This will also apply to those who feel they have been mis-sold a personal pension since June 1994.

Box 17.2: The pension mis-selling review

The pension review is run by the Financial Services Authority. Pension providers, banks, and financial advisers have to follow strict rules in how they contact savers, investigate their cases and then pay any compensation due.

The process of reviewing sales was split into two phases. The first phase was priority cases, that is those who were close to retirement or who had already retired. Companies had to hunt out and individually check all these priority cases. Just over 717,000 people have had their pension sale checked and so far compensation worth £3.6 billion has been offered to 406,000* of them.

Younger savers were the target of the second phase of the review. Advisers and pension companies had to write to over 2 million people inviting them to have their pension sale reviewed. More than a million responded to this process, with over 880,000 turning out to have a case that was appropriate for review.

At the time of writing, around 448,000 phase-two cases have been completed, with 365,000 offers of compensation made worth £2.7 billion. The whole review process is due to be complete by June 2002.

The aim of the process is to try to put individuals in the same financial position as if they had never left an employer's pension scheme or if they had joined one instead of taking a personal pension. Where possible the pension provider will pay money to buy an employee back into their employer's pension. Where this is not possible – for example, if you have moved jobs – the pension company will instead pay extra money into your personal pension. It may also have to pay to replace additional benefits like life insurance. Only rarely will cash be paid directly to you.

The company conducting your review may write to you to request further information. This might be needed to help calculate the extent of a loss, or to help the company work out the costs of putting things right. They must write to you every six months to keep you informed of the progress to date.

If, when a case has been reviewed, the pension company or adviser finds that:

- you were given advice which followed the rules at the time, or
- you have not suffered a loss, or
- you were given advice which broke the rules but which has not caused a loss (for example, the pension fund you were invested in has performed very, very well),

no further action is necessary.

If the review does identify a loss because mis-selling has taken place, the company must put things right. You will be sent either a formal offer of redress, or a letter of intent. Letters of intent are used where it is not yet clear how matters will be put right; for example, if an employer is undecided about whether or not to let you back into a company pension scheme.

You can have the offer checked by an independent expert, at cost to yourself, and have the right to complain if you think it unfair.

Full information about the pension review process is provided by the Financial Services Authority. Call either its consumer helpline on 0800 917 3311 or 0845 606 1234, or log on to www.fsa.gov.org.

* All figures FSA, July 2001.

A second mis-selling review: free-standing AVCs

Additional voluntary contributions are a way for savers to top up their occupational pension. You can make these payments, called

AVCs, into an in-house scheme that is linked to your employer's main pension scheme. Or you can choose to pay into a free-standing scheme, an FSAVC. This is run by an independent pension company and is completely separate from the main pension. You can carry on paying into an FSAVC when you move jobs and arrange for it to pay benefits at a different date from your pension scheme's normal retirement age.

In 1999 the FSA became concerned about the standards of advice being given to those savers who were making AVCs. In particular, the regulator was worried that savers were being encouraged to invest in FSAVCs when AVC schemes attached to the main company pension were likely to offer better value. An in-house scheme might be better for a saver if:

- the employer was willing to match an employee's contributions into the scheme;
- the employer was willing to subsidise AVC benefits in other ways, such as granting guaranteed annuities or added years of service;
- running costs for the scheme were far less than for an FSAVC.

Early in 2000, the FSA decided that companies would have to launch a second formal review of pensions selling, this time covering AVC sales. The review covers sales made between 29 April 1988 and 15 August 1999. Companies have to write to savers who in certain circumstances invested in an FSAVC when there was a superior in-house scheme available. Savers were being asked if they want to have their cases reviewed.

All claims for review had to be sent to the company which sold you the pension before 30 June 2001. Reviews have to be completed by 30 June 2002. If you missed the deadline to submit a claim for the official review, it may still be possible to claim through the normal channels set out in box 17.1.

Where a saver has been given incorrect advice and has been mis-sold an FSAVC, the pension company or adviser has to pay to put things right. They either have to buy the saver back into the employer's scheme or, if this is not possible, boost the value of the free-standing scheme to match.

This review is on a much smaller scale than the first pensions review. Around one million FSAVC schemes were sold during the period under review. It is thought that less than 10 per cent of these sales will be mis-sales. It is estimated that the total compensation bill could be £95 million to £200 million.

For more details on the FSAVC review contact the Financial Services Authority helpline on 0845 606 1234.

Box 17.3: Guaranteed trouble at Equitable Life

One of the most recent shocks to the pensions industry was the effective collapse of Equitable Life. The insurer was once seen as a leader in providing personal pensions and top-ups to company pension schemes. Equitable closed its doors to new business in December 2000. Its financial plans had been savaged when it lost a complex court case in the House of Lords earlier in the year.

Equitable's troubles stemmed from pensions it sold between 1956 and 1988. These pensions came with annuity guarantees (see Chapter 9). This entitled the saver to convert their pension fund into an income for life at a pre-set rate. Throughout the 1970s and 1980s these guarantees were effectively worthless – the annuity rate on the open market was higher, so no one wanted to take up the guaranteed option. But as annuity rates started falling in the 1990s, the guarantees became increasingly more valuable. At the time of writing, the guaranteed income from a fund was up to one-quarter higher than the best annuity on the open market.

Equitable is a mutual insurer. It is owned by all the policyholders who participate in the with-profits funds. The majority of the pensions invested in this fund. Equitable had made no special reserves to meet the costs of these guarantees. It tried to hedge the cost by paying a reduced maturity bonus to savers who wanted to use its guarantee. The impact of the reduced bonus was to make the income their fund produced the same as if the saver had received a standard final bonus and purchased an income at today's lower annuity rates on the open market. A group of policyholders challenged this approach through the courts and, after a protracted legal battle, won in the House of Lords.

The insurer tried and initially failed to find a buyer who could bail it out by injecting cash into its funds to pay for the guarantees. It also stopped paying annual bonuses to all savers, whether they had guarantees or not. Rather than going to boost savers' funds, any investment growth now had to go to pay for the unexpected cost of these guarantees.

Finally, Equitable shut the doors to new business in December 2000. Existing policyholders could carry on paying into their funds, but no new savers would be accepted. The insurer also announced that future investment growth would be reduced because it would have to adopt a more conservative investment policy and it slapped a 10 per cent penalty charge on anyone who wanted to try to transfer out of the with-profits fund. This left many savers, who are the ultimate owners of Equitable, looking at a certain loss on their funds. Either they stayed put and saw the money suffer slow growth, or they transferred out and took the pain of an immediate 10 per cent penalty.

Many customers decided to bite the bullet and started transferring out immediately.

Equitable brought in new managers and started selling off what it could to try and raise funds to meet the cost of its guarantees. In February 2001 it negotiated a deal with Halifax, selling its sales force, ongoing business and non with-profit business. Equitable members received a £500 million down payment, with the prospect of a further £500 million if they agreed a deal to buy-out guaranteed policyholders.

Meanwhile, further problems came to light. The new management discovered that Equitable had been paying inflated bonuses for several years, and in July 2001 reduced the value of all with-profit policies by 16 per cent overnight. Combined with the transfer penalty, it meant that anyone who wanted to bail out now faced the loss of around a quarter of their fund.

Problems with occupational pensions

Problems with occupational pensions are less common than those with personal pensions. However, when things go wrong with a pension arranged through your employer, they can go very wrong indeed. Mention the words 'company pensions' and 'trouble' and many savers think back to the Maxwell scandal in the early 1990s, when disgraced media tycoon Robert Maxwell was found systematically to have looted company pension schemes of hundreds of millions of pounds to try to keep his business empire going.

The rules on company pensions have been dramatically tightened since then, but problems can still occur. Again, it is important to split problems into different categories, which have different implications for the saver. Workplace pensions may cause worry because of:

- poor investment and slow growth;
- changing rules;
- administrative bungling;
- the employer hitting financial problems;
- fraud and theft.

Poor investment

Where an employer is running a money-purchase pension scheme, the value of pensions will depend on how well the money invested grows. If investment performance is poor, pensions will be lower.

Individual employees cannot choose directly how their main

company pension invests. This is a decision for the pension trustees. They will appoint a pension fund manager or managers to invest the money on the scheme's behalf. If investment is continually poor, the trustees will choose a new manager. If you are worried about the investment performance of your pension, talk or write to the trustees and ask whether they are planning to make changes.

The trustees may be able to bring a different perspective on your fears. You may find that even though a fund has lost value over a twelve-month period, so has the rest of the stock market. What you think is a poor-performing fund because it has lost 5 per cent in value may actually be a star performer because the average fund is down 10 per cent. The trustees and senior managers of your company are also likely to be members of the pension, so they have a common interest in the fund doing well. Members of a company pension have the right to nominate and elect trustees, so you have a chance to get involved that way.

Individual employees may have some choice over how any money they pay into a company AVC scheme is invested. If this is the case you can choose to move to a different fund if you are not happy with current performance. Alternatively, you might want to opt for a free-standing AVC in the hunt for higher growth, though this might have other disadvantages such as higher charges.

Of course, you ultimately have the right to leave a company pension and transfer your money elsewhere. However, quitting your company pension is rarely likely to be justified on the grounds of poor investment performance. You may lose employer contributions and other valuable benefits.

Changing rules

Company pension schemes are not set in stone for ever. The scheme's rules can be changed. Often changes appear to be to the disadvantage of members.

There is nothing illegal about changing a pension scheme's rules. A company pension is offered by an employer as part of the terms and conditions of your employment. In most circumstances these terms and conditions can be changed by giving you the appropriate notice. However, while some terms and conditions can be individually negotiated, the rules in a pension scheme have to be the same for all those who are members of the scheme at that time. So if the scheme rules change, they change for everyone in the scheme at the same time.

Many employers have tried to move away from final salary pensions towards money-purchase schemes. Money-purchase schemes are generally cheaper to run and expose the employer to less financial risk.

Where an employer is thinking about changes to the pension scheme, it may first try to negotiate these with employees or with their representatives such as unions. If the employer does want to change the rules of the pension, existing rights have to be preserved. The new conditions apply for service going forward. Otherwise a change would have the effect of giving you a retrospective pay cut. Box 17.4 gives an example of how a rule change might work.

Such changes to pension schemes can be worrying for staff. They can also leave them with less attractive pension conditions than they had before. To soften the blow the employer might offer other benefits. However, if you are one individual in a company pension scheme of many thousands, there is little you can do to resist change. The ultimate sanction is to move job to somewhere with better conditions.

Box 17.4: Changing times for a company pension

Phil, forty-six, works for a commercial bakery. The company runs a final salary pension scheme and Phil has been a member since he joined ten years ago. Members pay 5 per cent of salary, but the company pays the rest.

The company is now going to introduce new pension arrangements. It wants to move to a money-purchase scheme. Instead of Phil's pension being linked to his salary when he retires, it will depend on how well money invested throughout his working life grows.

Under the new plans, employees still have to pay in 5 per

cent of salary and the employer will pay 5 per cent. As a concession to staff, the company will agree to match further voluntary contributions up to another 3 per cent of salary. And to help win acceptance for the scheme, the employer is willing to give a one-off extra 3 per cent pay rise to everyone.

What does this mean for Phil's pension?

His ten years of existing service are still protected. Part of his pension will be based on his salary at retirement, multiplied by ten-sixtieths for his years of service. On top of this, Phil will receive a pension based on how well the money both he and his employer have invested has grown.

Rocky finances, administrative bungling and worse

Employees are naturally worried about both their jobs and their pensions when companies start getting into financial difficulties. Fortunately, a series of safeguards exist which give occupational pensions some protection against the financial misfortunes of an employer.

Firstly, the pensions exist separately from the finances of the employer. Where the scheme is a money-purchase scheme, the cash is often invested with third parties such as fund managers or insurance companies. Likewise, the pension fund of a final salary scheme is also a separate entity. Most pensions are set up as trusts, with trustees to make decisions about how the pension is run.

Money already paid into a pension is safe from creditors of the company, except for very limited circumstances where directors' pensions might be targeted if they are believed to have stuffed money into them solely to put it out of reach of creditors. This means that if a business does go under, whatever is in the pension will not disappear down with the business. However, money that has been promised by an employer for the future – for example, in a targeted money-purchase pension or unapproved retirement benefits scheme – may never be paid.

Most public-sector pension schemes are called statutory schemes. Set up by an Act of Parliament, they are effectively backed by the government. They are mostly unfunded, so the security for members is that future taxpayers will have to pay their pensions.

There are strict rules to ensure that money intended for a pension actually gets there and to ensure that final salary schemes are putting away enough cash to be able to honour their promises.

All occupational pensions, whether they are money-purchase pensions or final salary schemes, come under the umbrella of the 1995 Pensions Act. This Act was a direct consequence of the Maxwell affair. It set up the Occupational Pensions Regulatory Authority (Opra) to act as a watchdog for workplace pensions. It tightened up the rules for pension scheme trustees – they are now much more responsible for day-to-day monitoring of the scheme and can be prosecuted if they fail to alert the regulator to any irregularities they find. Independent professionals like actuaries, auditors and insurance companies also have a duty to blow the whistle on suspected wrongdoing.

The Act also ensured that members of the pension can elect a trustee, which is supposed to improve employee representation. In practice, many elected trustees are still nominated by senior management and get in unopposed.

Opra has powers to ensure company pension schemes are well run, to appoint extra trustees to oversee troubled pensions, to impose fines on companies which break the rules and to initiate prosecutions.

Employers who take money from your wages to pay into an occupational pension have to make sure the money is paid over to the pension by the nineteenth day of the month following the pay day. So a deduction made at the end of January must be in the pension by 19 February. If not, the company can be prosecuted by Opra. This is designed to stamp out the practice of employers using pension contributions to ease cash flow problems.

The Act also imposed a set of rules on final salary schemes called the Minimum Funding Requirement. This is a test placed on the pension to ensure that if a business were wound up tomorrow, there would be sufficient funds in the pot to pay the appropriate benefits to members. Winding up a scheme overnight is much more expensive than paying out pensions gradually as people retire, and benefiting from long-term investment growth to meet the bills.

The MFR, which was introduced in 1997, has been controversial from the start. In many cases it has required employers dramatically to increase contributions into their funds, although they can phase this over ten years to soften the blow. And it has prompted other company pensions to take a more cautious approach to investment to be certain of meeting immediate liabilities. Some companies have abandoned final salary schemes altogether.

The government is consulting on alternative ways to ensure that final salary schemes meet their promises and the MFR rules will be changed again.

Where do you go for help?

If you have a complaint about your company pension, the first port of call should be the administrators of the scheme itself, typically the company's pensions office or personnel department.

If the complaint cannot be resolved, or you are worried about more fundamental issues such as potential wrongdoing, the next step is to contact Opas – the pensions advisory service. Opas can also assist with day-to-day matters, such as helping you understand a pension benefits statement, or with getting extra information from a scheme. The service is run by volunteer advisers, all pensions professionals, who work across the UK to help members of company pension schemes. Contact Opas on 020 7233 8080 or log on to www.opas.org.uk. The Opas adviser may be able to help directly and resolve your problem. Sometimes Opas will put you in touch with another organisation. If there is a suspicion that rules have been broken, it will involve Opra.

If you are unable to resolve your problem with the help of Opas, the next step is to take your case to the Pensions Ombudsman. This Ombudsman is distinct from the Financial Ombudsman Service. It deals only with company pensions schemes. It has the power to make a final decision on issues which cannot be settled through Opas, without an employee resorting to the courts. The Ombudsman will not usually take cases until they have been referred to Opas. To contact the Pensions Ombudsman call 020 7834 9144 or write to:

The Pensions Ombudsman
11 Belgrave Road
London SW1V 1RB

Where money has been dishonestly taken or withheld from a pension fund and the employer is not able to pay it back – for example, because it is insolvent – the Pensions Compensation Board exists to make good employees' losses. This Board is funded through a levy on all occupational pensions.

In summary:

- It pays to keep a regular eye on pensions.
- This will give an early warning of poor investment performance and might alert you to more serious problems.
- Hundreds of thousands of savers are due for compensation over personal pension and FSAVC mis-selling. Are you one of them? If your case is not being investigated, should it be?
- The law now gives wide-ranging protection for members of company pensions. A dedicated watchdog is there for your benefit, but it needs members of schemes to help act as its eyes and ears.
- Make use of the Opas pensions advisory service, either for day-to-day queries on workplace pensions or as the first port of call for more serious problems.

CHAPTER 18 Running your own business

Read this chapter if:

- You are self-employed or have some self-employed income.
- You own and run a business.
- You are thinking of starting a business.
- You are a company director.
- You are a partner in a firm.
- You want to know more about the specialist pension options open to business owners.

We live in an entrepreneurial society. This is the age of working for yourself and of starting business empires in the back bedroom. An estimated one in five of the workforce will be self-employed by 2005.

Many of the basic principles of retirement saving apply to all, whether you are running your own business or whether you are an employee working for someone else. The golden rule of saving early and saving often still holds true. But there are some extra complications to consider when you are working for yourself.

If you are self-employed or are running your own business you will have savings opportunities that are not normally open to others. You will generally have more control over how much income you take from a business in a given year and you sometimes have options over how this income is taken; for example, as salary or dividends. Such flexibility can both help and hinder your retirement plans.

How much do you need to save?

It is vital for those in charge of their own business to be realistic about how much income they need to have in retirement.

Both the self-employed and owner-managers subsidise their own lifestyle through the business, following, of course, the Inland Revenue rules on what expenses are allowable and what are not. This means that a host of items such as personal transport, telephone bills, Internet access and clothing may be paid for in part or in full by work rather than by yourself. It can become difficult to disentangle all the costs and spending, and to determine exactly how much you will need when you cease working. Even small things add up. If, for example, your business buys a daily paper which you can read, buying one from private income after retirement will cost you around £180 a year after tax.

Rather than using the level of earnings that you have taken from a business as a benchmark for retirement planning, instead look at what it would cost you to buy the same standard of living once you retire. You may find the second figure is 10 to 20 per cent higher. The planning chart in Chapter 2 can help you make this forecast.

Self-employment

The self-employed are a huge army of workers, ranging from painters and plumbers to GPs and dentists. They have their own tax rules and their own National Insurance regime. And they have separate challenges in pensions and retirement planning.

If you are self-employed you are completely on your own in building a retirement fund. You cannot rely on an employer to set up a pension scheme and to subsidise contributions into it. And you even draw the short straw on state pensions. This means that personal pensions and other investments, such as Isas, are the key towards a comfortable retirement.

The self-employed do not qualify for additional state pensions. You are not eligible to take part in the State Earnings Related Pension Scheme. And you will not participate in its successor, the State Second Pension, either. This means the only state pension you may receive is the basic state pension. However, this will depend on your National Insurance contribution record.

A self-employed person pays Class 2 National Insurance contributions at the flat rate of £2 a week (tax year 2001/02) unless their profits are less than £3955 a year and they choose not to. Class 2 contributions will build you credit to the basic state pension, so opting not to pay these will mean a smaller pension. On top of this you may have to pay Class 4 National Insurance contributions. These are charged at 7 per cent on profits of between £4535 and £29,900 a year. But these Class 4 payments do not entitle you to any basic state pension or additional pension.

Though National Insurance charges for the self-employed have increased dramatically over the past few years, they remain less than for employees. An employee earning £29,900 a year or more would pay £2537.55 in National Insurance, the highest charge possible. Someone who is self-employed with profits/earnings of £29,900 a year or more would pay only £1879.55 in National Insurance. Logically, the cash saved through this lower payment should be the first part of a self-employed worker's saving plan.

Personal pensions are likely to form the backbone of your retirement savings while you are self-employed. Money paid into the pension qualifies for income tax relief and will grow tax-free. You can pick and choose from the vast range of pensions on offer including the traditional personal pension, a stakeholder pension or a self-invested personal pension (SIPP). A SIPP can be particularly advantageous for the self-employed who might be making sizeable but irregular contributions. See below for more details on a SIPP.

You can also carry on making payments into an existing retirement annuity plan, although it has not been possible to start a new plan since 1988.

These personal pensions are portable. You can move back into an employed job, for example, leaving the money invested in the fund. It may be possible to carry on paying into the pension while you are an employee. Alternatively, you might be able to transfer savings from a personal pension into any future employer's scheme.

How much you can pay in will depend on your net relevant earnings. For a self-employed person net relevant earnings are the profits you make after all allowable business costs are set again your income. This is the same figure that you will pay income tax on. Each tax year you can contribute a maximum of the higher of:

- a percentage of profits, which increases with age as set out in the table below, or
- £3600 a year, regardless of profits.

Payments into a personal pension, but not a retirement annuity plan, are also limited by an annual earnings cap. This means that only earnings up to a certain level count (£95,400 a year in tax year 2001/02).

Maximum contributions into a personal pension for the self-employed:

Age at start of tax year	**Percentage of profits which you can save into**	
	A personal pension	A retirement annuity plan
35 or less	17.5 per cent	17.5 per cent
36 – 45	20 per cent	17.5 per cent
46 – 50	25 per cent	17.5 per cent
51 – 55	30 per cent	20 per cent
56 – 60	35 per cent	22.5 per cent
61 – 74	40 per cent	27.5 per cent

One of the advantages of being self-employed is the ability to have more control over both business costs and your earnings. The majority of people structure their business to be tax-efficient and keep profits as low as possible without depriving them of necessary income. However, this tax efficiency can work against your pension planning. The lower your profits, the less you can pay into a pension.

Until April 2001 the self-employed had to pay gross pension contributions from income and then claim back any tax relief via their annual tax assessment. In years where earnings were low, it could mean that a self-employed person got tax relief at only 10 per cent on their pension contributions. Employees, by contrast, always automatically benefit from basic-rate tax relief on payments into a personal pension, even if they did not pay the basic rate. From April 2001 onwards pension contributions by the self-employed automatically have got basic-rate tax relief. This means that up-front pension contributions can be smaller to save the same gross amount, but there is less scope for reducing the end-of-year tax bill.

Partnerships

Business partnerships can face a problem over how to provide retirement benefits for outgoing partners.

Traditionally, they have used an arrangement called a partnership annuity. The partnership continues to make a payment to a retired partner. The payment is treated as an allowable business expense for the partnership and is taxed as earned income for the partner.

Provided someone has been a partner for at least ten years, the annuity income can be a maximum of half the average partnership profit over the best three of the previous seven years. Once in payment, this sum can be increased in line with inflation.

However, the retired partner is forced to rely on the partnership continuing to be a success and must hope it can go on maintaining the payments.

Increasingly, another option for partners is to make their own separate arrangements through personal pensions. If all partners agree to pay in a minimum sum, they can accept reduced or even no income from the partnership in retirement. This policy allows the partnership to afford bigger distributions to the partners while they are still working.

Owning and running your own firm

Many owner-managers see the business itself as a key ingredient in their retirement plans. They hope that the proceeds of selling the business when they quit will fund a large part of their retirement needs.

There is nothing wrong with looking to release value from the business when you retire, but it is unwise to rely completely on this. Depending on market conditions at the time, the business may not fetch what you are hoping for. This is particularly the case for service-based industries, such as estate agencies or insurance brokerages, where much of the value depends on the input of one or two key people. When they retire, the price for the business may diminish. And worse can happen. If technology changes, or markets dry up or key customers go bust, the business itself may not last until you hope to retire. So it is prudent to build retirement savings that are not dependent upon the health of the business itself.

Pensions should form one part of your alternative savings. They remain tax-efficient, both for the individual and the employee. Employers are not charged National Insurance on payments they make into either company or personal pensions, which means it is cheaper for a director of a business to pay into a pension than to pay money to themselves.

Directors of a company have a wide range of pension options open to them. They can opt for a personal pension. Self-invested personal pensions (SIPPs) can have particular advantages for those running their own businesses (see below). Alternatively, the simplicity of a traditional personal pension, a group personal pension or even a stakeholder pension may appeal.

Or their company can run its own occupational pension scheme. This can be open to all staff or restricted to only one or two directors. Small self-administered schemes (SSAS) and executive pension plans (EPP) are frequently used by small businesses and entrepreneurs. They offer more flexibility than conventional company pension schemes and allow benefits to be tailored to an individual's requirement.

Many of those running their own businesses are known as controlling directors. This means that special rules apply to how they can save for their pensions. Box 18.1 explains more.

The potential advantages for a business owner of SIPP, EPP and SSAS are set out below.

Self-Invested Personal Pensions

SIPPs are a personal pension. They are governed by the general personal pension rules on how much you can pay in, when you can retire and what you have to do with the fund when you have retired. Like other personal pensions, they are money-purchase funds. The money you invest grows over time and the final value of the pension depends on how well stock markets and other investments perform.

The key difference with a SIPP is that you are much more involved in making investment decisions. The pension can invest in a wide range of assets, including commercial property. You decide what to buy and when to buy it.

SIPPs are sold by both insurance companies and specialist providers such as stockbrokers. Charges tend to be higher than for conventional personal pensions and will be a mixture of annual administration charges plus a fee or commission for each investment transaction undertaken. The minimum level of investment is usually higher than for a personal pension. In practice, SIPPs are usually only economic for someone able to invest £5000 to £10,000 per year, or who is able to transfer in an existing pension fund of at least £50,000 to £100,000.

Assets that a SIPP can invest in include:

- shares and other securities quoted on recognised stock exchanges;
- cash deposits;
- UK authorised collective funds such as unit trusts, oeics or investment trusts;
- insurance and pension company funds;
- offshore unit trusts or managed funds that are regulated for sale in the UK;
- commercial land or property.

SIPPs can also borrow to make property purchases. But a SIPP must not buy assets from, or sell to, a connected person. Connected people and organisations include the member, their family or partner, or any company they control. A SIPP cannot hold shares in an unquoted company.

Box 18.1: Controlling directors

Are you a company director? If so, are you a controlling director? You need to be sure, because specific rules apply to how controlling directors conduct their pension savings. These are applied to limit the ability of business owners to arrange the company's affairs for their personal benefit.

Controlling directors are defined by the Income and Corporation Taxes Act of 1988. In brief, it means any director who since March 1987 and within ten years of retirement, or of leaving the company, has owned or controlled 20 per cent or more of the ordinary shares of the company.

A broad view is taken of ownership and control; it applies not only to the director, but to individuals associated with them; for example, including shares held by a spouse or partner, sibling or parents. The definition also extends to shares put in trust by relatives, even if the director did not originally own them. For instance, a director who owned 15 per cent of the shares of a company and had a brother owning another 15 per cent would be classified as a controlling director. This is irrespective of whether or not the brother is himself a director.

Some of the key restrictions on controlling directors include:

- Controlling directors cannot belong to an occupational pension scheme and contribute to a stakeholder pension at the same time.
- Controlling directors of an investment company cannot usually fund pensions via an occupational pension scheme.
- Controlling directors cannot pay into a free-standing AVC.
- The spouse of a controlling director cannot become a member of a company's Executive Pension Plan unless the Revenue is satisfied that they are a genuine employee of the company.
- When a controlling director retires, the level of final salary on which their pension benefits are calculated must be averaged over at least three years. This is to stop directors inflating their pay in the final year to boost the maximum pension they can take.

Holding commercial property in a SIPP is one of the main attractions of the product. Frequently, the pension fund buys a property, which is then let to the pension saver's business. The purchase may additionally be backed by a bank loan or mortgage, which the pension takes out.

Buying a property through a pension can be to a director's advantage because rent that their business would have to pay to a landlord instead goes to their pension, where profits can accumulate tax-free. Any capital gains on the property when it is sold are also free of tax. Some conditions apply: it is not possible for the pension to buy a property already owned by you or your business and the rent paid must be on commercial terms, often backed up by an independent assessment.

Two or more SIPPs can jointly own the same property; for example, where a husband and wife are in partnership together.

There are potential risks with this transaction. The property can represent the bulk of the pension fund's assets. It ties the fate of the pension more closely to the fate of someone's business. If the business fails and rent is not paid, there can be losses on the property. It can also be difficult to time the sale of the property to mesh with when a saver wants to retire or move into income drawdown.

Box 18.2 shows one example of how a SIPP could help fund a property transaction.

A new breed of slimline SIPPs is starting to emerge. These are managed using the Internet and offer lower charges than conventional plans. However, at the moment they restrict investments to assets that can easily be traded on-line, generally shares and some collective funds. More complex deals, such as property transactions, are not available. Try www.sippdeal.co.uk or www.nothing-ventured.com for details.

Box 18.2: Self-invested personal pensions and property transactions

Bethany, thirty-seven, is a director of her own antiques business. It is growing and she wants to acquire bigger premises. She has her eye on a shop with lots of storage space attached. To rent it would cost her business £25,500 a year. Alternatively, she or the business can buy it for £300,000.

Bethany already has £150,000 saved through a personal pension. Her adviser recommends transferring her pension into a self-invested personal pension. The pension then borrows another £150,000 from a bank and buys the shop. Bethany's business then signs a ten-year lease to rent the shop. It will pay the pension fund £25,500 a year in rent, which the business can claim against corporation tax as a normal trading cost.

The pension has to pay the bank interest on the £150,000 loan, but the rent from the shop more than covers this. The renting profit accrues in the pension fund.

Seven years later, Bethany's business is ready to move to even bigger premises. It buys itself out of the lease. The pension fund then spends £20,000 refurbishing the property. It relets this to a new tenant at £40,000 a year. Again, the rental income more than covers bank interest on the original £150,000 loan.

Three years later the property market is booming. Bethany and her financial advisers decide that it is time to sell the shop. They find a buyer willing to pay £550,000. The pension repays the bank loan. The rest of the money can be reinvested as part of the pension, free of any capital gains tax.

The shop has provided both income and capital growth for the pension fund.

Executive Pension Plans

These are a special type of money-purchase company pension scheme. They can be set up for a single employee. Alternatively, one scheme can cover several directors and other senior staff. The money in an EPP is invested by an insurance company on behalf of the members of the scheme. The money goes into insurance company managed funds; it cannot normally be used to buy shares directly, or property.

One key difference between the EPP and a conventional money-purchase pension is that money in it is earmarked for a specific person. Each member of the scheme can have their own level of contributions made by the employer and their own level of personal contributions.

Individuals can contribute into an EPP, subject to the 15 per cent of salary cap that applies to all occupational pensions. But the bulk of the money usually comes from the employer. This contribution is allowable against corporation tax and does not attract National Insurance.

What makes an EPP attractive is that it permits funding of a pension at much higher levels than personal pensions. The rules were tightened in 1994, and then changed again in 1996. These changes have reined back the scope for enormous contributions; at one stage it was possible for employers to be putting up to 130 per cent of salary into a pension on behalf of employees in their thirties. Nevertheless, funding is still permitted at between 35 per cent and 55 per cent of salary depending on the employee's age.

Members of an EPP are still subject to Inland Revenue rules on maximum benefits. These limit the overall value of the final pension that can be paid, pegging it to a maximum of two-thirds of final salary and, for those who joined a scheme after 1989, applying an earnings cap. However, those in an EPP can earn the maximum pension with far fewer years of service than can employees in an ordinary scheme. This means that an EPP can suit someone who is aiming for early retirement. And falling annuity rates mean that savers have to accumulate more money in their funds to buy the maximum permitted income anyway. Chapter 19 has more details on the maximum-benefit rules.

Other features of EPPs that can appeal to business owners include:

- Some schemes offer the facility for the pension to lend money to the business. This can reduce the need to borrow elsewhere. The loan must be on commercial terms, must be for a fixed term and must be for a genuine business purpose. Nevertheless, it is better for your pension to profit from making a loan than for a bank to profit.
- An EPP can be the sole pension for an individual or it can act as a top-up pension, running alongside another scheme open to all employees in the company.
- The EPP can provide added features such as lump sums and pensions for dependants if you die before retirement, and ill health pensions.

At retirement, the EPP fund needs to be converted into an income in the most efficient way. Typically, a person will take the maximum tax-free cash lump sum they can up to the top limit of one and a half times final salary.

Like other money-purchase pensions, the rest of their fund is converted into an income by either purchasing annuities or moving into income drawdown. If drawdown is the chosen route, it may be more attractive to transfer money into a personal pension first to take advantage of more flexible drawdown rules. Not least, the personal pension rules give more generous treatment to a person's dependants if they die during drawdown than do the EPP drawdown rules. It is technically possible to run a drawdown scheme from an EPP, but not all pension providers have updated their rules to facilitate it. Chapter 9 gives an introduction to annuities and drawdown; they are discussed in detail in Chapter 22.

In general, an EPP will appeal over a personal pension where:

- a director or senior employee wants to see their pension funded at a high level, particularly if they have made little or no pension provision in early years of employment. The more generous contribution regime of an EPP can allow this;
- the ability for the business to borrow back from the fund is important;
- an employer wants to try to target a pension to a particular level.

Personal pensions too have their advantages by comparison with EPPs.

- If a director or senior employee already has built up a decent pension pot from previous employment, it might be better to opt for a personal pension. The maximum pension that can be paid out through an EPP will be limited by what you have already got. But the only limit on personal pensions is what is paid in; the final pension value can be as high as stock market growth and annuity rates will allow.
- Personal pensions are simpler to set up and easier to administer than EPPs.

- Personal pensions, particularly stakeholder pensions, are cheaper to run.
- Personal pensions can provide a higher level of life cover for younger employees.
- Personal pensions are usually an easier and more cost-effective way to contract out of Serps.

Small self-administered schemes

The SSAS is a company pension aimed primarily at controlling directors. It cannot usually have more than eleven members and typically will have between one and four members. In addition, some of the money in the pension must be invested in assets other than insurance company funds.

Each employer can only have one SSAS, but one SSAS can cover staff in several associated companies.

A SSAS is run as a money-purchase occupational pension scheme. But unlike an EPP, the money in the funds is pooled. It is not earmarked for a particular member. In normal circumstances each member of the pension is also made a trustee.

Like other types of occupational pension schemes, there are limits on the maximum value of pension benefits that can be taken. These are the normal rules of a maximum pension of no more than two-thirds final salary and a maximum tax-free lump sum of one and a half times final salary.

The attraction of a SSAS for company directors is the high level of control it gives them over their pensions. A small self-administered scheme can invest in a wide range of assets. These include:

- quoted and unquoted shares;
- cash deposits;
- insurance company funds;
- financial futures and options;
- commercial property.

Assets cannot be purchased directly from any member of the scheme or from any other person or organisation connected with the scheme. This definition of 'connected' includes spouses, other relatives, business partners and controlling directors. It does not include the company itself. This means that the scheme can buy assets from the firm itself; usually property.

The scheme can also make loans to the sponsoring company (the employer), provided that the loan is made on commercial terms. The rule of thumb on this is that if a company could not get a loan from normal sources such as a bank, the pension cannot give it a loan either. This rules out loans to businesses which are struggling to stay afloat or which are already insolvent. A maximum of half the pension fund can be loaned to the company.

A SSAS can also borrow to buy an asset, such as commercial property. Such property transactions are one of the main attractions of a SSAS. Unlike an EPP, a SSAS allows the directors of a company to make a company's property part of their pension fund. The main attractions for this sort of deal are:

- The property is paid for out of pension contributions, which are allowable against corporation tax.
- Any capital gain on the property is free from tax.
- The property can be a part of a SSAS for a long period, in effect allowing several generations of a family firm to use it as part of their pension planning.
- Rent paid to the pension is allowable against corporation tax.

The downside of putting property into the fund is that it can form a significant part of the total value of the fund, rather than having a fund of diversified investments. It can also be difficult to sell when money is needed to pay retirement benefits.

Small self-administered schemes are closely monitored by the Pension Schemes Office at the Inland Revenue. This is to ensure that the extra investment flexibility and control given to members is not being abused. The PSO will also make sure that the company and members of the scheme are not putting more into the pension than is actuarially justified to produce the maximum permitted pensions.

Each scheme has an appointed actuary who must report to the PSO every three years. The PSO may order the company to scale back or even stop contributions.

Unapproved pension schemes

There is one other type of pension which can sometimes appeal to those running their own businesses or senior employees. Unapproved retirement benefit schemes can give extra income in retirement to high earners who are otherwise caught by the earnings cap. The cap, remember, restricts the portion of your salary which can be considered for calculating contributions into a personal pension or for calculating the maximum pension at retirement from an occupational scheme. It was £95,400 in tax year 2001/02. The cap applies to all those who joined a new pension on or after 1 June 1989 and to all those in pension schemes set up after 14 March 1989.

The cap means that a higher earner, who has moved jobs since 1989, will frequently not be able to claim a pension on the whole of their salary. In some cases other forms of remuneration, such as share options, may more than compensate. But in other cases an employer and employee may choose to set up a scheme to offer unapproved retirement benefits. Here 'unapproved' means not that a benefit is illegal or underhand; simply that a scheme does not qualify for all the normal pension tax breaks.

Unapproved retirement benefit schemes can offer a lump sum and or a regular income when someone retires. They may also pay death in service benefits and a spouse's pension. They are usually run alongside approved pension schemes and provide an additional benefit for employees.

There are two types of unapproved retirement benefit schemes – unfunded and funded.

Where the scheme is unfunded there is no pension fund and no pot of assets. The employer simply creates an accounting liability to pay a pension or lump sum as agreed. Effectively, the money due to an employee is considered as a long-term debt. The employee pays no tax on this sum due, but the employer cannot claim any tax relief to offset the cost of making this promise to pay. When the employee retires and starts getting the money, it is taxed as earned income. However, National Insurance does not need to be paid on this. The employer can claim the cost of each payment as if it were paying any normal employee.

The big disadvantage of an unfunded scheme for an employee is the lack of security. If your employer goes bust, you get no pension from the scheme. And if there is a falling out and you leave in bitter circumstances there could be a nasty legal tussle to ensure you get the pension you have been promised.

The alternative is a funded unapproved retirement benefit scheme (FURBS). Here the employer pays money into a fund which is invested to grow on behalf of the employee. When the employee retires, the fund can be taken as a lump sum or converted into an annuity. Here the employer's contribution into the fund is treated as a benefit in kind. The employee pays income tax on the full value of it. The employer, and possibly the employee, also has to pay National Insurance on the contribution. FURBS have become less attractive to most firms since National Insurance started to be levied on employer contributions in 1998.

A generous employer can choose to pay the employee's tax too, by increasing their salary. But this becomes very expensive for the employer. For example, the normal tax charge for an individual on a £10,000 contribution into a FURBS is 40 per cent or £4000. To cover the tax on this the employer would have to pay £6667 in extra salary – the £4000 plus tax on that. The company would also have to pay almost £2000 in National Insurance contributions. So the total cost of putting £10,000 in an employee's pension could be around £18,500.

A FURBS fund will be taxed on any investment income and capital gains, which means your money will grow more slowly than in a conventional pension.

When the employee retires, no further tax is due if they take the fund as a lump sum. But they will be taxed if they convert the fund into an annuity income.

The Inland Revenue keeps a close eye on FURBS, which are run for the benefit of shareholding directors and their families. It will check to see that benefits paid into the fund are not excessive.

WARNING

Those running their own businesses have the widest choice of retirement options. The specialist pensions outlined above, such as EPP, SSAS and SIPP, are complex. Professional financial and tax advice is highly recommended. You should ideally seek out a financial adviser who has passed the G60 pension exam, the advanced professional qualification in this area.

Alternatives to pensions

As an owner-manager of a business or someone who is self-employed you also have the full range of alternatives to pension saving open to you. These are discussed more fully in Chapter 11.

In summary:

- Business owners and the self-employed have many savings choices.
- By all means consider the business itself as part of your retirement pot, but making it the whole pot is a risky option.
- Controlling directors need to be aware of their special circumstances with regard to pensions.
- The self-employed do not qualify for any additional state pensions.
- Be prepared to pay for professional advice. The cost of advice is negligible by comparison with the cost of getting it wrong in business tax and pension planning.

PART

Four

Getting Under the Pensions Skin

CHAPTER 19
Occupational and company pension schemes

Read this chapter if:

- You want to check the rules governing specific types of workplace pensions.
- You want to know how the different types of workplace pension operate.

The chapter covers:

- final salary occupational pensions;
- money-purchase occupational pensions;
- simplified money-purchase occupational pensions;
- executive pensions;
- small self-administered schemes;
- additional voluntary contributions (AVCs and FSAVCs).

This chapter sets out the general government rules covering occupational and company pensions. These are a framework. Within the framework, each employer is free to set its own terms and conditions. These terms may be less generous than the government rules allow. Once you understand the general framework, check the documentation you have been given for your specific pension or pensions. Alternatively, ask your employer's pension office to see how your scheme applies the rules.

Although group personal pensions and some stakeholder pensions are arranged through the workplace, they are not occupational pensions. They are governed by the personal pension rules. Group personal pensions and stakeholder are discussed in the next chapter.

Rules applying to all types of occupational pension (except simplified money-purchase schemes)

Pension schemes are favoured investments. Employees and employers can pay into them free of tax, and investment growth and income earned by the pension is also free of tax. These are valuable concessions, so the Inland Revenue sets rules to govern how a pension can operate. Among other things, these rules cover how much can be paid into the pension, how much can be taken out and when you can retire.

The rules have been tightened up over the years to limit the maximum income and other benefits that can be taken from pensions. This means there are three different classes of membership of a company pension, depending on when you joined a pension scheme. Each class of member is governed by its own set of restrictions.

The different classes are:

- pre-1987 members: employees who were members of a pension scheme before 17 March 1987;
- 1987/9 members: employees who between 17 March 1987 and

31 May 1989 joined a pension scheme that had been set up by their employer before 14 March 1989;

- post-1989 members: employees who are members of a scheme that was set up on or after 14 March 1989, or anyone who joined any occupational pension scheme on or after 1 June 1989.

It is vital to know which category of membership you fit into to be aware of the maximum pension you can take and how quickly you can earn it.

If you have moved jobs, you may be a pre-1987 member in one scheme and a post-1989 member in another.

Maximum benefits from employers' pensions

The general principle is that the maximum pension you can draw from an occupational pension scheme at the scheme's normal retirement age is two-thirds of your final salary.

This maximum includes any extra pension you earn through making additional voluntary contributions, any company pensions you have from previous employment and the likely income you will get from any personal pensions linked to that occupation. All these extra payments are known as retained benefits (see below). The basic state pension is not included, but some employers may take account of it anyway when calculating the final pension to pay. This is called clawback (see box 19.1).

Although the limit of two-thirds final salary applies to all employees, the rate at which you can earn this pension differs. Pre-1987 members can earn this maximum pension after only ten years of service – if an employer is prepared to fund their pension at this high level. Those who are 1987/9 members need to complete at least twenty years of service to gain the maximum pension.

Post-1989 members also need to complete at least twenty years of service to qualify for maximum pension. But a further limit applies to them. Their pension is subject to an earnings cap, which was £95,400 in tax year 2001/02. This means that any portion of your final salary above £95,400 does not count for pensionable service. At the moment the majority of those retiring joined their pension before 1989, so are not subject to the cap. However, this earnings cap will affect more and more savers as time goes by. The cap usually increases in line with inflation each April.

Your company pension scheme is responsible for ensuring that you do not get paid more than the Revenue rules permit. It must juggle the calculations and work out the effect of retained benefits. But you have to tell your employer about other pensions.

Box 19.1: Watch out for the clawback

Some occupational pension schemes make allowance for the basic state pension when they work out how much to pay pensioners each year. This is called clawback, or integration. It means that some workers get much reduced company pensions when they retire by comparison with someone on the same salary and length of service who worked for a company with a non-clawback pension scheme.

The attraction of clawback is that employees and employers have to pay less into the pension scheme. But it can mean that the company pension left after clawback is of little extra value, especially for part-time or low-paid workers.

Around four in ten pension schemes still run some form of clawback. Some reduce pensions in payment by the full value of the state pension, currently £3770 a year. Other schemes cut the company pension by a percentage of the state pension, for example, half or £1885 a year. Others freeze their clawback at whatever the value of the state pension was when you retired. For example, someone who retired in June 1995 might see the total clawback capped at £3060.20, the value of the basic state pension then.

Take the case of Jack who retires earning £20,000 after thirty years of service. His employer's pension entitles him to one-sixtieth of salary for each year of service, a nominal pension of £10,000 a year. But full clawback is in operation, so this is reduced to a payment of £6230 a year. Adding in the state pension brings Jack's income back up to £10,000 a year. If his employer had not run clawback he could have had an income of £13,770 – the full £10,000 from his company pension plus his state pension.

Clawback is very unpopular with many employees and with trade unions. And it is gradually falling out of favour with employers too. A number of high-profile employers such as Shell, BP, Nestlé and the Post Office have changed their scheme rules in recent years to scrap clawback or to make it less punishing.

A pension scheme's rules should make it clear whether or not it operates any form of clawback. If you are in any doubt check with your employer's pension department. Where clawback is still in force, saving through AVCs can help bolster the value of the company pension.

How is final salary defined?

The Revenue rules allow quite a generous interpretation of final salary, although most pension schemes have far more restrictive limits.

The Revenue says final salary can either be:

- total remuneration on which you have been taxed in any one of the five years before normal retirement age. This includes basic salary plus the average of variable payments (such as commission, overtime, profit sharing etc.) over the three years up to and including the year chosen, or
- the annual average of total earnings on which you have paid tax over three or more consecutive years ending no earlier than ten years before you retire.

Controlling directors of a company have to use the second definition because they have a greater ability to manipulate their earnings. If the first definition gives a figure of more than £100,000, then you have to use the second definition. Box 19.2 illustrates an example of how the final salary calculation might work.

Where your earnings have failed to keep pace with inflation, it is possible to use earnings from a much earlier year and revalue these in line with inflation to calculate final salary. This process is known as dynamisation. However, it is irrelevant for most because, on average, earnings have grown much faster than inflation in recent years.

Box 19.2: Calculating final salary for maximum-benefit purposes

Pip is retiring in 2002. She sells advertising for a glossy women's magazine. Her earnings are heavily linked to commission on her annual sales. Her employer is generous and uses the full definition of final salary permitted by the Inland Revenue to help calculate Pip's pension. Her basic salary and commission over her last six years of work are:

Year	Salary	Commission
2002	£33,300	£11,600
2001	£32,300	£15,500
2000	£31,000	£18,000
1999	£29,500	£26,000
1998	£28,500	£28,000
1997	£27,500	£16,000

In 2002, her basic salary is higher than in previous years, but her commission earnings have been low as she has eased down towards retirement. Together they total £44,900. In Pip's case it is most advantageous to calculate final salary based on a previous year, 2000. In 2000 her basic pay was £31,000 and she earned £18,000 in commission. But she can also count her commission in the two previous years – both of which were bumper years. The average of commission over the three years is £24,000. Added to her pay from 2000, this gives a total salary of £55,000. This is the level of final salary on which her maximum pension can be calculated in 2002.

Retained benefits

These are taken into account when calculating your maximum pension. They include pension benefits that you have from:

- previous membership of an employer's pension scheme, including AVCs and FSAVCs;
- current memberships of AVCs/FSAVCs;
- previous and continuing contributions to a personal pension based on income from this job;
- any other pension arrangements that have taken a transfer from one of the above, such as a pension buy-out bond, also called a Section 32 or Section 226 plan.

Some types of pension can be ignored:

- Trivial pensions – those that are worth less than £260 a year to you, whether they are being paid or have not yet been drawn.
- Pension you have earned from a totally separate occupation, which you have carried on at the same time as your main employment; e.g. someone who simultaneously farms and works part-time as an employee in another business would not have any farming-linked pension taken into account when their other employer was calculating their maximum pension benefits.
- Retained benefits of an employee who earns less than one-quarter of the earnings cap in the year they join the new pension scheme. In 2001/02 this means anyone earning less than £23,850 a year.
- State pensions including Serps and SSP, plus any income from a contracted-out rebate-only personal pension.

Lump sum payments

Virtually all occupational pensions offer the option of a tax-free lump sum payment in addition to your annual pension. The process of swapping pension for lump sum is known as commutation.

Again, there are rules limiting how big this lump sum can be and how quickly you can become entitled to it.

In general, the maximum tax-free lump sum at normal retirement age is one and a half times final salary. The definition of final salary can be as broad as was discussed above, though most company schemes are less generous.

If you take any tax-free cash, the value of your annual pension is reduced. The lump sum cannot be on top of a two-thirds final salary pension. The rate at which your pension is converted to a lump sum may vary with age and sex. The Revenue sets out tables of conversion rates to guide pension schemes. For example, a man retiring at sixty-five has his lump sum divided by nine to calculate the amount of annual pension he loses. A woman aged sixty has the lump sum divided by eleven. Post-1989 members usually have their pensions reduced at the rate of £1 of pension income for each £12 of lump sum they take, regardless of sex.

Normally, an employee will earn entitlement to this lump sum at the rate of three-eightieths of final salary for each year of service. So after forty years, you would accrue a hundred-and-twenty-eightieths or one and a half times final salary.

A pre-1987 member can earn entitlement more quickly, using an accelerated accrual rate. This would give them the maximum tax-free lump sum after only twenty years of employment.

An 1987/9 member is normally restricted to three-eightieths of salary per year unless they are earning their main pension at an accelerated rate. If this is the case, the accelerated rate also applies to their lump sum. For example, if your employer were willing to credit you with two-sixtieths of salary per year of service for your main pension, double the normal rate, you could build up lump sum at six-eightieths of salary per year – also double the normal rate.

If you are a post-1989 member you are allowed a maximum tax-free lump sum which is the greater of:

- three-eightieths of final salary (including any restriction imposed by the earnings cap) for each year of employment, or
- two and a quarter times your actual annual pension, including AVCs or FSAVCs, but before any reduction is made for buying the lump sum or any dependants' pension.

It is important to understand that although all these limits are expressed in fractions of salary as suited for final salary pension schemes, they also apply to money-purchase pensions. So it is possible that spectacular investment growth could leave you with a money-purchase pension fund that provides an income above the limits.

Likewise, it is possible to over-fund your pension if you consistently make big payments into AVC or FSAVC schemes. If your pension is over-funded the amount of income you draw is restricted and you may have some contributions returned, with a tax charge levied on them. The section on AVCs below explains this further.

Retirement ages

Pension schemes are free to set a scheme's normal retirement age anywhere between sixty and seventy-five. Sometimes it can be set lower where this is normal for a particular occupation; for example, in military service or deep-sea diving.

The limits are more restrictive for pre-1987 and 1987/9 members. Here normal retirement ages for men are set between sixty and seventy and for women between fifty-five and seventy. If you leave the pension at the scheme's normal retirement age, the maximum benefits the Revenue allows you to have are as set out above. However, early retirement is both possible and popular. In this case the amount of pension you can have can be restricted.

Early retirement is allowed by the Revenue from the age of fifty onwards. A consultation paper published by the government in 2000 suggested lifting this age to fifty-five, phased in gradually between 2010 and 2020. But this is not yet a definite plan.

For pre-1987 and 1987/9 members, the maximum permitted early-retirement pension is either:

- one-sixtieth of salary for each year of service up to your actual retirement date, including the optional lump sum worked out as three-eightieths of salary per year of service, or
- where a pension scheme allows for more generous accrual, e.g.

one-thirtieth of salary per year, you can get the normal maximum pension and lump sum but scaled down in proportion to your early retirement.

This is calculated by dividing the number of years you have worked by the maximum possible number of years you could have worked and then multiplying that by the pension you would have got if you retired at normal retirement age. For example, if you had joined a pension and would have had twenty years of service at normal retirement age, but you quit five years early, the maximum value of the pension is fifteen-twentieths of the pension if you had worked to normal retirement age.

For post-1989 members the maximum early-retirement pension is the larger of:

- one-sixtieth of capped final salary multiplied by your years of service – up to forty years can count – or
- one-thirtieth of capped final salary multiplied by your years of service – up to twenty years can count.

The maximum lump sum is calculated in the standard way, but with only years of service to the early retirement date counting.

In all these calculations the final salary used is the one when you retire, not how much you might have earned had you carried on working until normal retirement age.

In practice, many employers running final salary pensions are far less generous in calculating early-retirement pensions. They frequently scale back the pension by a percentage, typically 4 – 6 per cent, for each year you quit ahead of normal retirement age. This is because the employer has to pay the pension for a longer period.

Early retirement through ill health is possible at any age. Maximum benefits are calculated in the same way as for other early retirement.

Enhanced retirement terms are permitted if an employee is forced to retire through redundancy, but these cannot increase the pension beyond the two-thirds of final salary limit.

It is also possible to retire late and to remain a member of a pension scheme beyond normal retirement age. This is rare, though.

If you are a pre-1987 or 1987/9 member with long service and carry on working beyond normal retirement age, you can boost your pension above the two-thirds final salary cap. You can earn an extra sixtieth of final salary *for each year of service above forty years that you work after the pension scheme's normal retirement date.* You can earn a maximum of an extra five years or five-sixtieths of salary in this way. Alternatively, you can opt to have the pension you would have earned at normal retirement deferred. This means it will grow in value each year in line with a formula set out in the scheme rules.

But post-1989 members who have already earned entitlement to the maximum two-thirds of final salary by the pension scheme's normal retirement age cannot get any extra pension by staying on in work.

Other benefits

The Revenue rules also cap the value of other pension benefits.

The maximum lump sum paid to your estate if you die before retiring is four years' salary (capped for post-1989 members), plus a refund of any contributions the member has made themselves. These contributions can be returned with interest, or, in the case of a money-purchase scheme, with actual investment growth.

The definition of final salary here is more generous than for calculating the actual pension. It can include other items such as gains on share options. Salary for controlling directors can be calculated in whatever way is most advantageous.

Any lump sum death benefits from retained pensions must be taken into account if an employer pays more than twice final salary as a lump sum.

Pensions paid to a widow or widower and to any dependent children are also limited. A spouse, or other designated partner, can get a maximum of two-thirds of the pension which you would have received had you continued working to normal retirement age, but calculated using current salary. For someone with at least twenty years of projected service, this gives a maximum of four-ninths of salary when you die. Retained benefits are ignored when calculating widows'/widowers' pensions.

Where you are a post-1989 member, the final salary on which any dependant's pension is calculated is again limited by the earnings cap.

If you have joined a scheme late in your career and so would have been unable to attain twenty years of service by the normal retirement date, survivors' benefits are worked out as follows: pre-1987 members' service is assessed using the table below. The maximum survivors' pension is based on the total number of years of prospective employment, that is, employment you would have accumulated if you had survived to the normal retirement age.

Years of prospective employment	Proportion of final salary for maximum survivors' pension
1 to 5	$\frac{1}{90}$ for each year
6	$\frac{8}{90}$
7	$\frac{16}{90}$
8	$\frac{24}{90}$
9	$\frac{32}{90}$
10 or more	$\frac{40}{90}$

For 1987/9 members and post-1989 members the calculation is more straightforward. The widows' or widowers' pension is calculated as a maximum of one-forty-fifth of final salary for each year of service up to twenty years.

Additional pensions can be paid for other dependants such as children. There are no specific limits on how these are calculated, provided that:

- no single dependant draws a pension of more than two-thirds what you could have got yourself;
- the total of all dependants' pensions is a maximum of the pension you would have received at normal retirement age;
- where the dependant is a child, the pension must stop at the age

of eighteen or when they cease full-time education, whichever is later.

Pension increases after you retire or after a dependant's pension is paid

The maximum rate at which your annual pension can increase is laid out by the rules. Increases can be either:

- 3 per cent a year;
- the rise in inflation, as measured by the Retail Price Index (RPI). Such a pension is known as an RPI-linked pension;
- the lesser of RPI or 5 per cent a year. So this means that a pension would increase in line with RPI unless RPI were over 5 per cent. This formula is known as Limited Price Indexing or LPI. All final salary pension benefits accrued since April 1997 have to be increased by at least LPI.

If a pension scheme has increased the pension by less than the maximum permitted in one year or years, it can then catch up in subsequent years by making discretionary increases.

Contributions

Your contributions into a company pension are also regulated. An employee cannot pay more than 15 per cent of salary into a pension. This includes the value of all compulsory contributions, plus any AVC or FSAVC payments you make. For post-1989 members the earnings cap applies when calculating your salary for contributions too.

Simultaneously belonging to a company pension and making payments into a personal pension in respect of the same income used not to be permitted. But someone with two jobs could be in a company scheme with one and pay into a personal pension with income earned out of the second.

However, new contribution rules introduced in April 2001 changed this. It is now possible both to belong to a company pension *and* to pay into a personal or stakeholder pension provided that you earn less than £30,000 a year and are not a controlling director. So an employee aged thirty earning £28,000 a year could pay up to £3600 into a stakeholder pension, on top of the 15 per cent they pay into a company scheme – a maximum of almost 28 per cent of salary. Chapter 20 has full details of personal pension contribution rules.

How the different types of pension work

Final salary pensions

Final salary schemes are generally recognised as the Rolls-Royce of occupational pensions. They are also known as defined-benefit schemes, because the value of the pension that you earn in retirement is pre-set. The advantage for an employee is that the employer takes the bulk of the investment risk. If stock market growth is good, the company can pay less into the pension and sometimes can go years without making contributions. But if investments grow slowly the employer may have to pay far more to ensure that workers receive the pensions they were promised.

The value of your pension is linked to the number of years you work. Employees earn entitlement to a pension income at a pre-set rate, called the accrual rate. Historically, the standard rate of accrual has been one-sixtieth of your final salary for each year of service. Other schemes accrue at one-eightieth of salary per year or one-thirtieth of salary per year, or they may use a decimal fraction such as 1.6 per cent per year. The maximum value of a pension is governed by the maximum-benefit rules set out above.

Employees may have to chip in a proportion of their pay to the scheme as a condition of being a member. A typical level is 5 per cent of salary, but it can be higher or lower. These kinds of pensions are called contributory pensions. If the whole cost of the pension is paid by the employer it is called a non-contributory pension.

Where the employer is a private company the pension fund

exists as a separate entity, usually governed under trust rules. The money in the pension fund is controlled by the pension trustees and invested on behalf of members of the pension scheme. Some big funds have their own investment departments. Others subcontract the investment to specialist fund managers. The money may be invested in shares, bonds, cash and property. Such schemes are known as funded pensions.

The money in the fund is matched to the projected liabilities of paying pensions for staff who have already retired and for those who are about to retire. Where it appears that the fund might be stretched to do this an employer, by law, has to put more money in to make sure that all liabilities can be met.

In the public sector some of the final salary schemes are unfunded. This means there is no central reserve kitty and the pension costs have to be met each year from current income, which means, ultimately, that today's taxpayers pay the pensions of those in retirement. The pension costs of some public services, such as fire brigades or some police authorities, have become so big and use up such a large proportion of the annual budget that their primary services are under pressure.

The vast majority of final salary schemes are contracted out from Serps. This means members of the scheme do not earn entitlement to a Serps pension. Instead, the scheme itself promises to deliver an equivalent income as part of the total pension it pays. Chapter 21 explains contracting out in detail.

At retirement, any tax-free lump sum and the annual pension income are paid out directly by the pension scheme.

Each final salary scheme will set its own terms and conditions within the limits of the Inland Revenue overall pension rules. Some employers are generous in how quickly your pension builds up and how early retirement is treated. Public-sector pensions, for example, tend to be more generous on ill health retirement and generally increase all pensions in payment by RPI. Other employers' pensions pay less than the limits permitted, which makes them cheaper to run.

Changing investment conditions and stricter rules have made final salary pensions more expensive for employers to provide. Over the past decade many have converted their pensions into money-purchase schemes.

Money-purchase pensions

Money-purchase pensions switch a lot of the investment risk in producing a pension from the employer to the employee. Also known as defined contribution pensions, the sum that is paid into the pension is fixed, but the value of the final pension depends on how stock markets grow.

Employers have to make payments into the pension. Employees usually contribute too. These contributions are invested in a fund which grows until the member retires. At retirement, the value of the pension is determined by what income that fund can purchase on the annuity market. If contributions have been generous and investment growth has been good the income may be higher than you would get from a similar number of years of membership of a final salary pension. It may be lower. But if it is lower, no one will top it up. So the employee carries the risk.

Money-purchase schemes can be invested in a wide variety of ways. They may be insured schemes, where the investments are restricted to the funds and insurance policies offered by pension companies. In turn, these insured schemes can invest in:

- non-unit-linked policies; for example, insurance company with-profit funds or deferred annuity contracts. Here, the value of the fund does not automatically move up or down in line with stock market changes;
- unit-linked policies; for example, a range of stock market pension funds. Here the value of the pension fund can move up or down in line with the daily fluctuations of the market.

Members of the scheme usually get some choice over which of these funds their money is invested in and may be able to split contributions between two or more funds. For example, a saver might put half their contribution into a UK index tracking fund, one-quarter into a US growth fund and one-quarter into an ethical fund.

Each person's pension benefits are linked to the value of the units and funds that their contributions have purchased. These insured funds will carry their own series of charges, entry fees, exit fees etc. The cost of these charges will directly affect the valuation of the pension.

A money-purchase pension scheme can be directly invested too (also known as self-administered). Here the fund itself invests the money directly, under the watchful eyes of the trustees. The money may be spread across a wide mix of assets, including shares and property. A notional accounting system keeps track of each person's entitlement to a share of the fund. Individuals can still express a preference for what they want their money to be invested in, but do not directly own the investments.

When you reach retirement age the fund that has been accumulated in your name is converted into an income and possibly a tax-free lump sum. Again, this process is governed by the overall limits set out earlier in this chapter.

If the pension is an insured scheme, the fund will be used to buy a compulsory purchase annuity in your name. The annuity provides a guaranteed income and can be tailored to provide specific benefits such as increasing income or a spouse's pension after your death. Where the scheme is directly invested it may also buy an annuity for you, or convert your fund into an income paid out by the scheme itself. The formula for converting fund to income will be laid down in the scheme rules. Where schemes have such set payment terms it can help protect members from fluctuating annuity rates.

From 1999 it has also been possible for occupational money-purchase pension schemes to offer an income drawdown option to members. However, not all schemes have adopted this in their rules. Income drawdown allows you to keep your pension fund invested and hopefully growing, while cashing in a modest element each year before retiring. An annuity would still have to be purchased by the time you reach seventy-five.

If the pension scheme is contracted out from Serps, an element of your fund will have what are called protected rights. This means it has to be converted into a pension income according to a pre-set formula. Chapter 21 explains more.

Hybrid pension schemes

A few company pension schemes mix features of final salary and money-purchase pensions. This can work in several ways. The two most common are money-purchase underpin and final salary underpin.

With money-purchase underpin, the main pension is a final salary scheme. Both employer and employee pay in. Benefits accrue with years of service as usual, with the pension linked to final salary. However, alongside this runs a notional money-purchase scheme. This calculates a money-purchase pension as if both employee and employer were paying in, although no extra money is paid in. At retirement, the employee gets whichever method produces the biggest pension. So if the stock market has done very well, the money-purchase calculation may produce a bigger pension. If not, the final salary calculation is used and the employee gets that pension.

Where the scheme adopts the final salary underpin the opposite happens. The employer and employee both invest a fixed proportion of salary. This fund grows and is reserved for the employee when they retire. However, a minimum level of pension, linked to final salary, is guaranteed. If when you come to retire there is not sufficient in the money-purchase fund to pay at least this guaranteed amount, your pension is topped up from a separate fund, which only the employer has paid into.

Some company pensions operate a special scheme for younger employees, also known as a nursery scheme. Typically, all those staff up to a certain age, for example thirty-five, are members of a money-purchase scheme. Both employee and employer contribute, which makes it more attractive than a personal pension. At the threshold age employees can then transfer into a final salary scheme. They will earn credit for years of service beyond this age, while their money-purchase funds can continue to grow.

The theory behind nursery schemes is that younger employees

are most likely to move jobs; money-purchase benefits can be more attractive and more portable for this class of employee. But older workers who are going to stick with a firm might prefer final salary pensions. However, as the workforce has become more mobile and people have switched jobs at later ages, the nursery concept has begun to look outdated.

Simplified money-purchase pensions

A few company pensions are also set up under an Inland Revenue concession for simplified money-purchase pension schemes. Here the scheme can be run in a streamlined way and employees can be exempt from the maximum-benefit rules. The key difference, though, is that contributions into the pension are strictly limited. Total payments in by employee *and employer* must not be more than 17.5 per cent of salary. This includes anything paid into an AVC, FSAVC or towards the cost of life insurance. No more than 5 per cent of salary can be used for life insurance.

Like a personal pension, retirement from a simplified money-purchase scheme can be between the ages of fifty and seventy-five. Up to 25 per cent of the value of the fund can be taken as tax-free cash.

Executive pensions

Executive pension plans, or EPPs, are a special type of money-purchase company pension scheme. They can be set up for a single employee, though one scheme can cover several directors and other senior staff. The money in an EPP is invested by an insurance company on behalf of the members of the scheme. The money goes into insurance company managed funds; it cannot normally be used to buy shares directly, or property.

One key difference between the EPP and a conventional money-purchase pension is that money in it is earmarked for a specific person. Each member of the scheme can have their own level of contributions made by the employer and their own level of personal contributions.

Both employee and employer contributions into an EPP are

allowed. The vast bulk of the cash is usually provided by an employer. Funding by an employer can be at a very generous rate. This means that employees can build up their maximum pension far more quickly than they might be able to in a conventional scheme.

EPPs also have other special features that appeal to directors and senior managers within a firm.

- Some schemes offer the facility for the pension to lend money to the business.
- An EPP can be the sole pension for an individual or it can act as a top-up pension, running alongside another scheme open to all employees in the company.

At retirement, the pension fund is converted to income through buying an annuity or through income drawdown. The maximum-benefit rules set out above apply. There are further details on EPP in Chapter 18.

Small self-administered schemes

This is a special version of a self-administered money-purchase pension aimed at company directors. It cannot have more than eleven members and may have only one or two members.

A small self-administered scheme (SSAS) is run as a money-purchase pension scheme. But unlike an EPP, the money in the funds is pooled. It is not earmarked for a particular member. In normal circumstances each member of the pension is also made a trustee.

The attraction of a SSAS for company directors is the high level of control it gives them over their pensions. A small self-administered scheme can invest in a wide range of assets. These include quoted and unquoted shares, cash, property and insurance company funds.

Assets cannot be purchased directly from any member of the scheme or from any other person or organisation connected with the scheme. This definition of 'connected' includes spouses, other relatives, business partners and controlling directors. It does not include the company itself. This means that the scheme can buy assets from the firm itself; usually property.

The scheme can also make loans of up to half the value of the pension fund to the sponsoring company (the employer), provided that the loan is made on commercial terms. A SSAS can also borrow to buy an asset, such as commercial property.

Such property transactions are one of the main attractions of a SSAS. Unlike an EPP, a SSAS allows the directors of a company to make a company's property part of their pension fund.

When you retire, your share of the fund is used to buy an annuity or can be transferred into an income drawdown scheme. Again, the maximum-benefit rules apply.

Top-up pension schemes: AVC and FSAVC

Employees are allowed to make extra payments into a special top-up pension to run alongside their main company pension. These payments are called additional voluntary contributions (AVC). There are two versions of AVC. All employers have to offer an in-house AVC scheme. This runs in conjunction with the main pension, with contributions being deducted direct from weekly or monthly pay before tax.

Money paid into an in-house AVC can either:

- buy added years of service to a final salary pension, or
- be invested to grow in a money-purchase fund, or
- be used to produce extra pension at a predetermined flat rate, e.g. for every £1000 saved by retirement you get £60 a year of extra pension.

Some occupational schemes may offer a choice of two or three different investment options within their AVC.

The alternative is a free-standing AVC, also called FSAVC. This is run by an independent pensions company and is invested on a money-purchase basis. Here contributions are paid from the saver's after-tax salary. The FSAVC provider automatically claims back basic-rate tax relief. Higher-rate taxpayers claim back extra tax relief via the tax self-assessment process.

It is possible to pay into both an AVC and an FSAVC at the same time. But controlling directors are not permitted to have an FSAVC.

An employee can pay up to 15 per cent of salary into a company pension including all AVC or FSAVC contributions. So if your employer requires you to pay 6 per cent of salary into its pension, you have a further 9 per cent available for AVCs.

Contributions may also be restricted if they threaten to take the value of your pension above the maximum benefit levels outlined earlier in this chapter. For the vast majority of savers this will not be an issue; their pensions will be much less than the maximum allowed. But a few savers with long service, high salaries or a combination of both might butt up against this ceiling. The organisation receiving either AVC or FSAVC contributions is responsible for making what is called a 'headroom check' to test whether the level of AVC payment might take you anywhere near maximum-benefit levels.

In normal circumstances money paid into an AVC or FSAVC must be used to boost your final annual pension, or to provide extra life insurance. It cannot be taken as a lump sum when you retire. There are a few exceptions to this rule, including:

- In-house AVCs which you started paying into before 8 April 1987.
- If you retire early through very serious ill health and are taking the whole pension as a lump sum, AVC contributions can also be taken as a lump sum. The whole pension, including AVC, is taxed at 20 per cent.
- If the value of the whole pension including AVCs is trivial, that is less than £260 a year, then it can be taken as a lump sum. This sum is taxed at 20 per cent.

However, the AVC can help boost the size of the tax-free lump sum for those who are post-1989 members of their pension. Here the maximum tax-free lump sum is two and a quarter times your annual pension. The value of the AVC pension income can be taken into account for this calculation, giving a bigger potential lump sum.

Benefits from most in-house AVCs can only be drawn at the same time as you retire from the main pension scheme. A concession introduced in 1999 allows money-purchase AVCs to be cashed in at any time between fifty and seventy-five, providing the main pension scheme rules are rewritten to allow this. They can also be used alongside an income drawdown from occupational pension schemes, though the rules are complex. In practice, few pension schemes have got round to changing their rules to facilitate either use of an AVC.

FSAVCs are more flexible. You are free to specify any retirement date between fifty and seventy-five when you sign up to the scheme and can take the proceeds when you reach this age.

When you retire, the AVC and FSAVC providers will again check to make sure that the size of the pension does not exceed the two-thirds of final salary limit. If it does, your AVC or FSAVC has produced a surplus. This surplus may be eliminated by taking an enhanced pension; for example, one that increases faster or one with a larger spouse's pension. This would reduce the size of your initial income and might get it back under the two-thirds of final salary limit. Alternatively, the surplus can be repaid to you as a lump sum, minus a 32 per cent tax charge. Top-rate taxpayers have to pay extra tax on this.

AVCs can be added to the value of your main pension if you are transferring between funds. FSAVCs can also be transferred into another FSAVC or into the employer's main scheme if that scheme is happy to accept the transfer.

CHAPTER 20 Personal pensions

Read this chapter if:

- You want a reminder of the different types of personal pension.
- You want to check the rules of how each pension operates.

The chapter covers:

- traditional personal pensions;
- group personal pensions;
- stakeholder pensions;
- self-invested personal pensions (SIPPs);
- retirement annuity plans (RAPs);
- Section 32 policies.

There are hundreds of different personal pension schemes on the market. This includes some which are no longer open to new savers, but which remain open to those who have already started one.

This chapter sets out the general rules governing personal pensions. Many of the rules and principles are common to different types of pension. Within the framework of these general rules, each pension company will set its own terms, conditions and charges. These will vary widely between different providers. Providers include insurance companies, banks, building societies, friendly societies and investment managers.

All personal pensions share two key principles. Firstly, they belong to and are controlled by the saver. You decide what to save, where to save it, when to retire and what sort of an income to take from the pension – albeit subject to the restrictions of the overall personal pension rules and the rules of your pension contract. Your employer may contribute into a personal pension too, but the majority of the money saved in these schemes is paid in directly by individuals. You can take a personal pension with you from job to job and, in many cases, can carry on saving into a personal pension even if you have a company pension.

Secondly, personal pensions are all money-purchase pensions. Money paid into the pension is invested on your behalf into shares, bonds, property and other assets. There are no guarantees about what sort of income this pension will provide when you retire. The value of a saver's pension depends on how well the markets grow and how a saver chooses to convert their fund into an income at retirement. The saver takes all the risk, with neither employer nor government underwriting the pension.

General personal pension rules

These are set out by the Inland Revenue and govern the framework within which all personal pensions operate. They apply to all types of personal pension, except for retirement annuity plans.

Personal pensions are now open to anyone from birth to age seventy-five. Money saved into the pension will qualify for tax relief. That means that any contribution you make into the pension, or that is made into the pension on your behalf, will be topped up by money from the government as if you were a basic-rate taxpayer. So if you pay in £78, the government rounds this up to £100 by paying in an extra £22. This tax relief applies even if you pay no tax, or pay tax at only the 10 per cent rate. It also applies to the self-employed, who previously obtained tax relief at only their actual rate of tax.

Higher-rate taxpayers can claim back extra tax relief through their tax returns. A higher-rate taxpayer who paid in £78 to a personal pension would see their tax bill reduced by an extra £18. So the true cost of them paying £100 into their pension is £60.

Once invested in a pension, the money will hopefully grow, free of tax. But it is locked away until you 'retire'. The word retire has a special meaning in the case of personal pensions. It does not mean the date at which you stop work, or the date when someone becomes entitled to a state pension. It simply means the time that you decide to start drawing on those personal pension savings. It is possible to take an income from a personal pension while you are still working.

Under normal circumstances you cannot draw on a personal pension until the age of fifty. The pension has to be taken by the time you reach seventy-five. How and when you access the money between these ages is up to the saver.

How much can be paid into a personal pension?

Payments into a personal pension are strictly controlled. The rules changed with effect from April 2001, which has given savers more flexibility and opened up personal pensions to more savers. The contribution rules for retirement annuity plans are different (see below).

The maximum that can be paid into a personal pension is the higher of £3600 per tax year, or a percentage of your relevant earnings in that year. Relevant earnings are income from employment, including perks on which you can be taxed, but not income from investments such as bank interest or share dividends, or income from existing pensions.

The percentage limits vary with age as set out in table 20.1. It is important to note that the limits are gross, that is income before tax. Tax is refunded on personal pension contributions, so the actual sum you pay in will be less. For example, a basic-rate taxpayer, subject to the £3600-a-year limit, will be able to pay a maximum of £2808 a year into their pension. The other £792 is paid by the government directly to the pension company.

Table 20.1: Maximum permitted contributions into a personal pension

Age on 6 April of tax year	per cent of relevant earnings *	
	Stakeholder, traditional personal pension, GPP	Retirement annuity plans
35 or less	17.5	17.5
36 to 45	20	17.5
46 to 50	25	17.5
51 to 55	30	20
56 to 60	35	22.5
61 to 74	40	27.5

*Or £3600 per year from any income if greater. Relevant earnings are capped at £95,400. No cap applies on retirement annuity plans.

Someone with no relevant earnings would be able to pay up to £3600 per year into a personal pension. Table 20.2 shows the threshold earnings levels below which the flat-rate allowance of £3600 allows more generous pension contributions than the percentage of earnings formula. In other words, if you earn more than the figures listed, you can pay more than £3600 a year into your pension.

There is one other important factor. If you stop working or switch to a lower-paid job – for example, to bring up a family – you can carry on making pension payments based on your previous earnings for up to five years. This is only to a saver's advantage if their previous earnings meant that they could pay in more than £3600 a year – and, of course, if they have the resources to keep paying into a pension. Those who can benefit from this concession will include high earners who take a career break for a few years but want to keep some pension savings going, plus those who are made redundant with big lump sum pay-offs.

The maximum sum that can be paid into a personal pension is also limited by a cap on earnings. This cap is set at £95,400 in tax year 2001/02. It means that any earnings above this level are disregarded when calculating the maximum pension contribution. Someone aged fifty-five earning £120,000 a year, for example, could pay up to £28,620 into their pension (30 per cent of £95,400), rather than £36,000 which would be 30 per cent of their earnings. This cap normally increases in line with inflation each year.

Table 20.2: Income levels at which the percentage earning rules permit a higher contribution into a personal pension than £3600 a year

Age	Annual earnings
35 or less	£20,572
36 to 45	£18,001
46 to 50	£14,401
51 to 55	£12,001
56 to 60	£10,286
61 to 74	£9001

Money going into the pension does not have to come directly from the individual. It can be paid on your behalf. So an employer can pay on behalf of an employee; a husband on behalf of his wife; or a grandparent on behalf of a grandchild. But contributions from all sources must not exceed your individual limit. No National Insurance is charged on employers' payments into a personal pension.

National Insurance rebates paid by the government into contracted-out personal pensions do not count when calculating contribution limits. They are in addition to your annual limit.

In the past it was not permitted to pay into a personal pension if you were already a member of a company pension scheme. This rule has now been relaxed. Employees who are members of company pension schemes can now pay up to £3600 a year into a stakeholder pension or other company pension, as well as contributing to their company scheme, provided they

- do not earn in excess of £30,000 a year;
- are not controlling directors of the company.

There are a few other special circumstances when someone with a company pension might still be permitted to have a personal pension. These include:

- when a money-purchase occupational pension is contracted in to Serps or the State Second Pension, in which case an individual can opt to contract out of Serps using an appropriate personal pension (see Chapter 21);
- when the company scheme is an unapproved retirement benefit scheme (see Chapter 18).

Other benefits

The majority of the money paid into a personal pension is used to provide an income in retirement. But it is possible to use some of the premium to buy insurance against ill health and/or death. For traditional personal pensions, up to 5 per cent of net relevant earnings can go towards buying life insurance. This 5 per cent comes out of the total annual allowance for contributions into a personal pension. The 5 per cent limit is also subject to the earnings cap.

In stakeholder pensions the maximum that can be used to buy life insurance has been changed to 10 per cent of the total premium. For all but those earning less than £7200 a year this is a reduction in the amount of the pension contribution that can be used for life insurance.

The other insurance purchased through a personal pension is

waiver-of-premium cover. This is insurance which continues paying your pension premiums if you are unable to work through accident or ill health. This is not possible with new pensions started after April 2001, but remains an optional benefit on many personal pensions purchased before then.

For pensions sold after April 2001, waiver-of-premium cover is now sold as an add-on, purchased alongside a pension.

As a pension contribution is made free of tax, insurance purchased through a pension is cheaper than comparable cover purchased from ordinary taxed income. However, every penny of premium used to buy insurance is a penny which does not get invested for future income.

Retirement ages

As already mentioned, the earliest age at which it is normally possible to draw money from a personal pension is fifty. A Cabinet Office discussion paper in 2000 suggested gradually raising this to fifty-five, to encourage people to stay in work longer. But no such proposals have been confirmed.

For some occupations, where retirement at earlier ages is considered normal, the Inland Revenue has agreed special early-retirement concessions. Box 13.3 on page 248 lists many of these occupations. Here, savers can start taking benefits from their pensions at an earlier age, *provided the money in the pension was earned only through that occupation.*

There are two other important conditions to be aware of. The protected-rights portion of any personal pension, the fund that has been built up by contracting out of Serps, cannot be taken before the age of sixty. Chapter 21 has more details on protected-rights funds.

It is also permitted to take money from a personal pension before the age of fifty on the grounds of ill health. Savers have to show that through mental or physical illness they are unable to carry on with their normal occupation or another of a similar nature for which they are trained and are able to do. Doctors' reports are essential and a medical examination may be necessary before a pension company will release money before fifty on ill health grounds. But even for those in ill health the protected-rights funds cannot be accessed before the age of sixty.

Death before retirement

If you die before drawing some or all of your personal pension, whatever is in the fund is used to benefit a spouse or other nominated individuals. Typically, the value of the fund is paid as a lump sum. Depending on the pension scheme rules, this may go to:

- nominated beneficiaries, who do not have to be dependants. You can nominate whoever you like as a beneficiary by contacting your pension company and completing a form;
- the saver's legal representatives;
- trustees, if the scheme is written under trust. The trustees then decide where the money goes.

Sometimes the scheme rules will say the death benefit has to be paid as an annuity, an income for life. If so, the value of this annuity cannot exceed what the deceased could have had as an annuity income if they had retired the day before they died.

If some or all of the money in the personal pension is the result of a transfer from an occupational pension, special conditions apply if the saver dies before retiring. If the saver has a surviving spouse, a maximum of 25 per cent of the value of this money can be paid as a lump sum. The rest must be used to buy an annuity for the spouse. If there is no spouse, the whole fund can be distributed as a lump sum.

If some or all of the money in the personal pension is a protected-rights fund built up by contracting out from Serps, special conditions also apply. All of the protected-rights fund must be used to buy an annuity to pay a spouse's pension if the saver was married and their spouse is either aged over forty-five or is under forty-five but still in receipt of Child Benefit.

What happens when you retire?

Once someone decides to start drawing on their personal pension, they usually face a number of options.

Firstly, it is not necessary to capitalise on all of the pension at the same time, although many savers will want to. The vast majority of existing personal pensions are written as segmented policies. This means that the plan is made up of hundreds of identical segments, each of which can be cashed in at different times if necessary. Whatever is not cashed in, or vested to use the pension jargon, remains in the pension fund and can continue to grow free of tax.

New rules which came into force from April 2001 will allow pensions to be partially vested without the need for segments, so the use of segmented pensions will gradually cease.

A saver firstly has to decide how much of their pension they want to cash in. Secondly, they have to decide how much, if any, of that they wish to take as a tax-free cash lump sum. Inland Revenue rules permit up to 25 per cent of a personal pension to be taken as tax-free cash. The valuation of the fund must exclude any protected-rights money, all of which has to be used to provide an annuity on specified terms. There can be some other restrictions on the lump sum, depending on where the money in your personal pension has come from.

- In some cases funds arising from a transfer in from an occupational pension may have to be excluded when calculating the lump sum.
- Where the transfer comes from a contracted-out final salary pension scheme, any money derived from service after 5 April 1997 has to be used to provide an income and no lump sum is available.
- If the personal pension was started before 27 July 1989, different rules apply. Here the lump sum cannot exceed 25 per cent of the fund including protected-rights, but excluding all transfers in from an occupational pension and excluding money that will be used to provide any pension for a spouse or other dependant.

Once a saver has established how much tax-free cash, if any, they are entitled to and whether they want to take it, the rest of the pension must be used to provide an income. This is done by either:

- purchasing an annuity, or
- going for pension fund drawdown, also called income drawdown.

The income from either option will be taxed. Annuities, drawdown and phased retirement are discussed in detail in Chapter 22.

Special types of personal pension

The conditions set out above apply to all personal pensions, except retirement annuity plans. These are discussed below. There are, however, several categories of personal pension which have extra and specialised terms and conditions.

Stakeholder pensions

Stakeholder pensions are the newest type of personal pensions. They are designed to be an attractive proposition for many ordinary savers, by making pensions simple, cheap and flexible. Stakeholder pensions have to meet with standards set out by the government. Unless they match the standards, they cannot be added to the official register of stakeholder pensions and promoted using the stakeholder name.

Stakeholder pensions are flexible. You can stop or start payments into a stakeholder pension at any time, or change the amount you save – all without penalty. And you are allowed to transfer the entire value of the stakeholder pension to another provider at any time, again without penalty.

Pension companies are only allowed to levy one charge for running stakeholder. This must cover the costs of investing your money and administering the pension scheme. The charge cannot be higher than 1 per cent per year of the value of your fund. So someone who has built up a fund with an average value of £10,000 over a year would pay a maximum of £100 in charges that year. In fact, many of the companies offering stakeholder charge less than 1 per cent. Others reduce their annual charge as the fund gets bigger. So a £5000 fund might be charged 0.95 per cent a year. But a £100,000 fund might be charged 0.65 per cent a year.

If you use the services of a financial adviser to help you arrange a stakeholder pension, you may be asked to pay a separate one-off fee to cover their time.

There may also be extra charges for extra benefits; for example, for waiver-of-premium insurance or life insurance. You cannot be forced to take any of these extras, but will pay for them separately if you do.

The stakeholder charges are designed to be much more simple to understand than traditional pensions charges (see box 20.1).

Employers have a key role in providing stakeholder pensions. By October 2001, all qualifying firms – broadly companies with five or more employees that do not already offer a pension to all staff – had to make a stakeholder pension available. This does not mean that stakeholder is a company pension. The employer simply must designate a pension provider as its chosen stakeholder scheme. If you want to join this scheme, employers will deduct pension contributions direct from your salary and pass them on to the pension company. The employer does not have to pay anything else into the pension, but many are already choosing to. Total contributions from employee and employer must not exceed the annual limits set out above.

Employees do not have to join their employer's designated stakeholder scheme. They can join another, or may decide not to save into a pension at all.

The rules on when you can retire and what you have to do with the fund at retirement are the same for stakeholder as for normal personal pensions.

Box 20.1: Personal pensions charges

A useful rule of thumb is: the older a personal pension, the more confusing and tortuous the charges are. And the more expensive the pension is.

Stakeholder pensions have the simplest charges. Only one charge can be levied. This is based on a percentage of the value of your pension fund. It is taken each year and can be no more than 1 per cent of the value of the fund. That is it.

Older personal pensions can have complex layers of charging. Types of charges include:

- A bid-offer spread: this is the difference between the price at which you buy units in a pension fund and the price at which you can sell them back to the pension provider. The difference could be as much as 5 or 6 per cent. Such a spread is also a form of initial charge, in that the money is gone from day one.
- A reduced allocation rate: rather than all your money being allocated to buy units in the fund, a lesser percentage is allocated for investment, with the difference being the pension company's charge. For example, an allocation rate might be 98 per cent, an initial charge of 2 per cent. Confusingly, allocation rates can be higher than 100 per cent, such as 103 per cent. Enhanced allocation rates are a way of attracting transfers or new business.
- An annual management fee: this is a charge levied on your fund each year. Different funds may have different management fees. A cash fund might have a small fee, say 0.3 per cent a year. A technology fund might have an annual fee of 1 per cent or more.
- A set-up or installation fee: this is a flat charge – for example, £100 – levied when a pension is started. It is notionally to cover the paperwork costs of setting up a pension but is, in fact, just an extra charge.
- A monthly policy fee: this is a flat fee – for example, £2 –

levied on the pension for each month that the plan is in force.

- Capital units: these, now rare on new pensions, are a special type of pension fund unit. They carry a much higher annual charge than ordinary units, perhaps 6 or 8 per cent a year. This higher charge applies throughout the life of the pension. Often, the contributions in the first year or two years of the life of a pension were used to buy capital units. Thereafter, money was invested in ordinary units. They are effectively another form of initial charge.
- Switching fees: these are one-off administration charges if savers switch their money between different pension funds managed by the same company. Many companies offer one or two free switches per year, thereafter charging a fixed fee, typically £20–50 per switch.

Some of the charges can blend together. For example, you might have a pension with an enhanced allocation rate of 103 per cent and a bid-offer spread of 5 per cent. The end result of this is that for every £1000 you pay in, £1030 is allocated to your fund, but the value if you want to transfer or cash in your pension is £978.50 – an overall initial charge of 2.15 per cent.

Charges have historically differed depending on whether you made a lump sum contribution, called a single premium, or whether you paid in monthly instalments, called regular premiums. Generally, regular premiums carried higher charges than single premiums.

The advent of stakeholder pensions has caused many of the bigger pension companies to reassess charges. Some have even repriced older pensions so that if the old-style charges add up to more than stakeholder charges, customers get the difference refunded.

Group personal pensions (GPP)

A group personal pension is a special type of personal pension arranged by an employer on behalf of its employees. It is not a company pension, although the employer may negotiate special terms and may handle some of the administration, for example, collecting employee contributions through the payroll.

A group personal pension is a series of individual personal pensions set up with the same pension provider. Typically, the employer chooses the provider. The employer may negotiate charges and other terms which are better than an individual saver could obtain themselves. But the pension fund is the property of each individual and they can take it with them if they move to another job.

The employer typically agrees to make a payment into the pension, often conditional on the employee sacrificing a proportion of salary. For example, the employer may agree to match employee contributions up to 5 per cent of salary. Employees are free, then, to pay in more, subject to the overall annual contribution limits. In most cases employees' contributions are collected direct from salary and passed on to the pension company on their behalf.

Employers may also arrange for enhanced life insurance as part of the pension. Because they are buying in bulk for the whole workforce, the terms of this are usually better than if an individual were buying themselves.

With a GPP, employees can make their own decisions about whether they contract in or out of Serps and State Second Pension.

The rules on when you can retire and what you have to do with the fund at retirement are the same for GPPs as for normal personal pensions.

When someone leaves the employer they can continue paying into the GPP, although without employer contributions, transfer the fund into a new personal pension or new occupational pension, or make the pension paid-up.

GPPs are not the same as stakeholder pensions. There is no requirement for them to conform to an annual 1 per cent charging limit, though in practice most schemes are already below that level.

However, GPPs do offer a wider choice of investments than stakeholder and potentially more generous life insurance benefits. Also, employers that would rather offer a GPP to staff than offer stakeholder pensions have to pay in at least 3 per cent of salary. Under stakeholder rules there is no requirement for the employer to pay anything.

Self-invested personal pensions (SIPPs)

As the name suggests, the key difference with a SIPP is that the saver is much more involved in making investment decisions. The pension can invest in a wide range of assets, including commercial property. The saver decides what to buy and when to buy it.

SIPPs are sold by both insurance companies and specialist providers such as stockbrokers. Charges tend to be higher than for conventional personal pensions and will be a mixture of annual administration charges plus a fee or commission for each investment transaction undertaken. The minimum level of investment is normally higher than for a personal pension. In practice, full SIPPs are usually only economic for someone able to invest £5000 to £10,000 per year, or who is able to transfer in an existing pension fund of at least £50,000 to £100,000. A number of streamlined SIPPs administered through the Internet have been launched which have lower charges, so this may bring the pension to a wider audience (see below).

Assets that a SIPP can invest in include:

- shares and other securities quoted on recognised stock exchanges;
- cash deposits;
- UK authorised collective funds such as unit trusts, oeics or investment trusts;
- insurance and pension company funds;
- offshore unit trusts or managed funds that are regulated for sale in the UK;
- commercial land or property.

SIPPs can also borrow to make property purchases. But a SIPP must not buy assets from, or sell to, a connected person. Connected people and organisations include the member, their family or partner, or any company they control. A SIPP cannot hold shares in an unquoted company.

Holding commercial property in a SIPP is one of the main attractions of the product. Frequently the pension fund buys a property, which is then let to the pension saver's business. The purchase may additionally be backed by a bank loan or mortgage, which the pension takes out.

Buying a property through a pension can be to a director's advantage because rent that their business would have to pay to a third party instead goes to their pension where profits can accumulate tax-free. Any capital gains on the property when it is sold are also free of tax. Some conditions apply: it is not possible for the pension to buy a property already owned by you or your business. And the rent paid must be on commercial terms, often backed up by an independent assessment.

Contribution limits and retirement ages are exactly the same on a SIPP as for other personal pensions.

A new breed of SIPPs is starting to emerge. These are managed using the Internet and offer lower charges than conventional plans. However, at the moment they restrict investments to assets that can easily be traded on-line, generally shares and some collective funds. More complex deals, such as property transactions, are not available. Try www.sippdeal.co.uk or www.nothing-ventured.com for details.

Retirement annuity plans

These pre-date modern personal pensions. It has not been possible to start a Retirement Annuity Plan (RAP) since July 1988. However, those who have a RAP can still make payments in and can usually increase the level of payments too. If you do not already have a RAP, the rest of this section is irrelevant to you.

Contribution rules for RAPs are different from those for personal pensions. Firstly, the percentage of relevant earnings which can be paid in appears to be less generous than for personal pensions. A glance at table 20.1 shows that the annual contribution into a RAP varies from 17.5 per cent to 27.5 per cent of earnings, depending on age. For older ages this is a lower percentage than for payments into personal pensions. However, payments into a RAP are not restricted by the earnings cap. This means that higher earners may be able to contribute more into a RAP than they can into a personal pension. For example, someone aged fifty-five earning £150,000 a year can pay a maximum of £28,620 into a personal pension but can pay £30,000 into a RAP. Savers paying into a RAP can also benefit from concessions known as carry-forward and carry-back, which allow them to juggle contributions between different tax years.

You cannot retire with a RAP until the age of sixty. If you want to take benefits from a RAP before this, you will have to transfer into a personal pension or stakeholder pension. This may involve additional charges.

At retirement, money in a RAP can be used to buy an annuity, to provide a lump sum or for a combination of both. For a RAP, the maximum tax-free lump sum is calculated by reference to the size of the annuity your fund can buy. The lump sum must not be greater than three times the pension the remaining fund can buy. This calculation is done using an annuity rate most favourable to the person retiring, i.e. using a single-life annuity, payable annually in arrears, with no guarantee and no escalation in the income paid. This will produce the biggest notional income and hence the biggest possible tax-free lump sum. The actual annuity purchased may be entirely different and give the saver a lower income, especially if they are aiming to provide a pension for a spouse after their death.

What all this means is that the size of the maximum tax-free lump sum for a RAP saver depends on their age, sex and on annuity rates when they retire. For those who leave retirement to their seventies, it could be one-third or more of the fund.

If a RAP saver wants to have the option of income drawdown, they will first have to transfer into a personal pension.

Section 32 Policies

These are a special type of personal pension policy used for transfers out of company pension schemes. They are a way of securing a lump sum transfer paid by the employer and then investing it for growth. However, although a Section 32 policy is held in the name of the individual, it is still bound by many of the restrictions which governed the original pension scheme.

The pension paid when you retire is capped by the Inland Revenue maximum-benefit rules (see previous chapter). These limit both tax-free cash and the size of the final pension. Likewise, the maximum lump sum paid if you die before retirement is typically four times salary at the date of leaving the company pension scheme plus a return of your own contributions. Anything left in the fund has to be used to pay a pension for a spouse.

If your fund has grown well and there is enough in the kitty to provide more than the maximum benefits, the surplus has to go back to the original employer. If this firm is no longer in business, the insurer running the policy keeps the extra.

Most advisers generally use personal pensions for transfers, rather than Section 32 policies. However, there are some advantages to a Section 32 policy. For example, when someone is transferring contracted-out benefits from a final salary scheme, the Section 32 policy allows more flexibility on when you can retire and allows for the possibility of tax-free cash. A personal pension converts all such transfers into a protected-rights fund, which does not allow retirement before the age of sixty and there is no tax-free cash.

When considering a transfer, specialist advice is strongly recommended.

CHAPTER 21 Contracting out

Read this chapter if:

- You want to understand what contracting out is.
- You want to know whether it is worth contracting out.
- You want to know what you can do with a contracted-out pension.

Contracting out affects millions of workers, yet is poorly understood. However, it can have a significant effect on both the value of a future pension and how that pension can be taken.

In simple terms, contracting out means opting out of a state-run system which gives you additional income to the basic state pension and instead trying to build a similar, or better, income through private means.

Contracting out applies to the Serps pension and to the new State Second Pension (SSP), which is being introduced to replace Serps from April 2002. Both schemes are additional state pensions. They give an income over and above the basic state pension, based on the number of years you work and the income you have earned during these years. Chapter 3 explains how Serps and SSP work if you need a reminder.

Each year that you remain a member of Serps or SSP, you are building a bigger pension entitlement for the future. No money is invested directly into a pension fund, but credits are totalling up in your name, which will entitle you to an income paid by the government when you reach state retirement age.

When you contract out of Serps or SSP, you cease to earn entitlement to future pension for each tax year you remain contracted-out. Entitlement that you have already earned is preserved. In return for contracting out, the government arranges for money to be paid into either a personal or company pension in your name. That money can then grow over time and will hopefully provide you with a pension at least as good as the one you would have earned by staying a member of Serps or SSP.

Contracting out was also possible before Serps under the graduated-pension scheme. Here an employer's pension undertook to replace the additional income you would have got from the graduated scheme.

There are risks with contracting out. If investment growth is weak and annuity rates decline, the value of the pension your fund buys may be less than the equivalent Serps pension. In practice, it is unlikely that you will suffer much loss if you contract out through an employer's final salary pension scheme. Contracting out through money-purchase company pensions or through personal pensions is more risky.

But there are also dangers in remaining in the state schemes. The value of additional pension can be cut at the whim of politicians. The value of Serps has already been reduced fourfold since the scheme was started. Real money invested in your name is much harder for politicians to take away at a future date.

Contracting out is not an issue for the self-employed. They are not eligible for Serps or SSP, so cannot contract out of it.

It is also possible for someone who is contracted out to change their mind and rejoin the state system. This is called contracting in.

How someone contracts out depends on what kind of company or personal pension, if any, they are in and how long they have worked for an employer. Each type of pension has its own rules.

Final salary pensions

The vast majority of final salary company pensions are contracted-out schemes. This means that everyone who belongs to the scheme is automatically contracted out of Serps, or in future, out of SSP. If you are a member of such a pension scheme you cannot opt to be different and remain part of Serps.

In return for contracting out and forsaking the right to future pension from the state, the National Insurance contributions paid by both an employer and the employees are reduced. This gives both employee and employer extra money each month, which can be invested to produce a company pension to replace or better what Serps would have provided.

Exactly what you get instead of Serps/SSP depends on when you were contracted-out. For each year of service before 6 April 1997 your employer undertakes to pay you a guaranteed minimum pension or GMP. This GMP must be broadly the same as the pension you would have earned by being in Serps for the same period. There is a compulsory half-pension for widows (and since 1988 for widowers) and the GMP element of your company pension must be increased in line with inflation each year. This is a more generous rate of increase than many company schemes offer for the main pension.

There is also a valuable safety net provided by the Department of Work and Pensions. When you retire, the DWP calculates the maximum Serps pension you would get if you had stayed in Serps throughout the period. If the GMP from an employer's pension is less than this, the government pays the difference. It can add the money to any Serps pension you might be entitled to from other periods of employment, or pay it as a modest Serps pension if all your employment has been contracted-out.

If the GMP is more than what your maximum Serps pension would have been, you keep the difference.

When you retire, any GMP will be shown separately on your employer's pension documentation. And it may be treated differently from other parts of the pension; for example, it may increase by more than the rest because it is fully linked to inflation.

A Serps pension would not normally be paid until you reached state retirement age. But many people want to retire early from a company pension. So if you quit before state retirement age, the GMP portion of your pension is revalued and reduced to reflect the fact that you are leaving early. If the GMP forms the bulk of your pension, this revaluation might restrict other benefits you take and may even mean you cannot afford to retire early.

Contracted-out employment after 6 April 1997 is treated differently. Rather than GMP, employers now have to run a pension which pays at least a reference level of income. This reference level is a benchmark. It says:

- By the age of sixty-five the pension must pay at least one-eightieth of 90 per cent of your earnings in the National Insurance middle band for each year of service. The middle band is your earnings, including overtime, above the NI lower earnings limits (£72 per week) and below the upper earnings limit (£575 per week).
- The pension must increase by Limited Price Indexing, that is the lesser of RPI or 5 per cent per year.
- There must be at least half-pension paid after you die for any survivor, such as widow or widower.
- This reference test must be matched for at least 90 per cent of the people in the pension.

The result of this change is generally to produce a pension which is higher than GMP when you retire, but which does not increase as rapidly against inflation once you have retired.

If you have some contracted-out employment before April 1997 and some after April 1997, the replacement for your Serps or SSP pension will be a mix of GMP and post-1997-rules pension.

In a contracted-out final salary scheme your employer has taken on the risk of providing you with the GMP or post-1997 contracted-out pension. If investment conditions are poor, the employer may have to pay more in. Your contributions remain the same.

The introduction of the State Second Pension in April 2002 will change the mechanisms for contracting out through final salary schemes (see section on SSP below).

Money-purchase company pensions

Contracting out is also possible through a money-purchase company pension. The crucial difference is that your employer no longer makes any guarantee about the size of pension you will get instead of Serps or SSP. Your income will largely depend on how well investment markets grow.

When your employer is running a contracted-out money-purchase pension (also known as a COMP scheme), it has to guarantee to pay a set amount of money into the scheme. This will be invested to build up your pension fund.

Again, when you are contracted-out, both you and your employer qualify for National Insurance discounts, called rebates. The sum paid into a COMP scheme equals the value of your rebate. Rebates vary with age and with earnings (see box 21.1).

The fund that these rebates build up is known as a protected-rights fund. Although it can be invested in the same way as other pension contributions, it must be accounted for separately because there are strict rules over how the protected-rights fund can be used. These include:

- Money in the fund can only be taken from the age of sixty, the same age for both men and women. Early retirement is not possible using this fund.
- If you die before sixty, the whole fund can be used to buy a pension for your spouse.
- No tax-free cash can be taken from a protected-rights fund.
- When the fund is converted to a pension, the pension must increase each year in line with a set formula. This is 3 per cent a year for any of the pension earned by rebates paid in relation

to employment before 6 April 1997 and 5 per cent a year for any of the pension earned by rebates paid in relation to employment after 5 April 1997.
- The annuity your fund buys on retirement must make provision for a half-pension to be paid to any surviving spouse after your death.

If you transfer from one pension scheme to another, the protected-rights fund can move too. But it remains a protected-rights fund, still subject to the restrictions outlined above.

The fund is invested as any normal money-purchase pension. The amount of pension when you retire will depend on how well the money has been invested, what charges are levied on the pension scheme and what annuity rates are at the time. There are special terms quoted for protected-rights annuities. In particular, these are the only annuities where men and women get the same income at the same age. This is because the annuity is trying to replicate a state pension, which pays the same to both sexes.

Even if your money-purchase company pension is not contracted-out, you can choose to contract out yourself. You can set up a special type of personal pension called a rebate-only plan (see below).

Box 21.1: Contracting-out rebates

The government rewards those who have contracted-out by reducing the amount of National Insurance they have to pay. These reductions are known as rebates. Rebates recognise that you are giving up future state pension, so are intended to match the cost of paying for this pension privately. Both employers and employees get a rebate.

For final salary pensions the rebate is the same for each employee. The employer's NI contribution is cut by 3 per cent and the employee's NI contribution is cut by 1.6 per cent. This gives a total of 4.8 per cent, which can be paid into their pension.

Where someone is in a contracted-out money-purchase pension scheme or in a personal pension, the rules on rebates have changed over the years. This in turn has made contracting out either more or less attractive to certain groups of people.

Between 1988 and April 1997, rebates for contracted-out money-purchase pensions and personal pensions were also flat; that is, they were the same proportion of earnings regardless of age. This meant that contracting out was perceived as very attractive for younger employees: they had the longest time to retirement and so the most time for the rebate money that was invested on their behalf to grow into a healthy pension. But those near retirement only had a few years for the money to grow. So it was worth much less to them.

The process led many employers and pension companies to calculate pivotal ages, typically between the late forties and early fifties. Those below the pivot age were recommended to contract out of Serps, while those above were told to stay in or to rejoin, because the forecast value of their private pensions would be lower than the state pension.

To try to level the playing field, in April 1997 the government introduced age-related rebates. This ties the level of your annual rebate much more closely to the cost of matching a Serps pension through investing. Older employees get a higher rebate because the money only has a few years to grow. Younger employees get smaller rebates, which can be invested for a longer period. Both are calculated to produce the same pension. The table below gives examples of the value of rebates for employees in different age groups for tax year 2001/02.

The change to age-related rebates means the decision on whether to contract out or not is much more finely balanced.

Age on 5 April 2001	Rebate as a percentage of earnings on which NI is paid	
	COMP pension*	Personal pension
15	2.2	3.8
20	2.4	4.0
25	2.7	4.3
30	3.0	4.5
35	3.3	4.8
40	3.8	5.3
45	4.8	6.2
50	9.0	9.0

*This is the value of the employer's rebate. Employees get an additional 1.6 per cent discounted from their NI bill.

Personal pensions

It is possible to contract out of Serps/SSP through a range of personal pensions including group personal pensions and stakeholder pensions. Contracting out through personal pensions works differently from contracting out through a company scheme.

Both employer and employee pay National Insurance contributions at the standard rate. But the employee sets up an 'appropriate' personal pension. This pension is any qualifying pension that is willing to accept a payment in from the Department of Work and Pensions. Each year that you are contracted-out, the DWP pays a National Insurance rebate directly into this personal pension. The element of the rebate based on your own National Insurance contributions also qualifies for basic-rate tax relief, which boosts the value of the money going into your pension by 0.45 per cent of your earnings. The size of the rebate itself depends on your age and earnings (see box 21.1).

You can choose to top up the DWP rebate with additional

payments from your own income, which will also attract tax relief in the normal way. If the only money going into a personal pension is the National Insurance rebate from the DWP, the pension is known as a rebate-only plan. Many savers choose to have a rebate-only plan and a separate personal pension running alongside. This can give more flexibility about when you retire (see below).

Once invested in a personal pension, the money from a National Insurance rebate is under your control. It can be invested in a wide range of funds, switched between these funds and even moved to a different pension if you like. On retirement, the fund is used to buy an annuity to give you an annual income, which may be more or less than you would get if you had stayed within Serps.

However, there are restrictions on how and when you can take advantage of a contracted-out pension. Any portion of a personal pension fund made up of NI rebates is known as a protected-rights fund. There are strict government rules over how protected-rights are treated when you retire. These include:

- The fund can only be used at the age of sixty, the same for men and women. Early retirement is not possible using this fund.
- If you die before sixty, the entire fund can be used to buy a pension for your spouse.
- No tax-free cash can be taken from a protected-rights fund.
- When the fund is converted to a pension, the pension must increase each year in line with a set formula. This is 3 per cent a year for any of the pension earned by rebates paid in relation to employment before 6 April 1997 and 5 per cent a year for any of the pension earned by rebates paid in relation to employment after 5 April 1997.
- The annuity rate for protected-rights pensions has to be the same for both men and women.
- The annuity your fund buys on retirement must make provision for a half-pension to be paid to any surviving spouse after your death. There is a small concession for those who are single when they retire; all pension built up from April 1997 onwards can be used to buy a single-life annuity. But anything earned

from rebates pre-April 1997 must go to a joint-life pension, even if you are single.

Where you have a personal pension which is a mixture of protected-rights money and your own contributions, it is usually not possible to split the pension in two. This means that you may have to wait until at least sixty to access any of the money in the pension. Hence many save into a separate personal pension alongside a rebate-only personal pension, so that they have the option of cashing in their own savings at an earlier date.

State Second Pension

The arrival of the State Second Pension (SSP) in April 2002 will gradually change the equation on contracting out. In the longer term it is likely to benefit the vast majority of employees to contract out.

SSP will be introduced in two phases. Under phase one, from April 2002 until possibly April 2007, additional state pension will still be linked to earnings. Those earning above approximately £21,600 will receive the same SSP as they would have under Serps. Those earning below approximately £9500 a year will be treated as if they earned £9500, getting a much bigger entitlement to SSP than under Serps. And those in the middle, earning between £9500 and £21,600, will do a little better than under Serps, though the improvement will diminish as earnings rise.

In order to replicate this, the government is introducing an entirely new rebate structure to make sure that anyone contracting out is not disadvantaged. Otherwise all those earning less than £21,600 would immediately be better off rejoining the new SSP. Box 21.2 explains this in detail.

In phase two of SSP the pension will drop the link with earnings. Instead, it will become a flat-rate benefit. The intention is that those on low earnings, defined as below £9500 in today's income, will get an enhanced SSP. But this pension will not be any higher for those who earn more. However, National Insurance rebates are still expected to increase with earnings. This means that it will clearly benefit anyone earning more than £17,000–18,000 in today's money to contract out. There could still be a grey area on earnings of £14,000–16,000 in which it is hard to know whether contracting out is wise or not.

The Department of Work and Pensions produces a detailed guide on contracting out, called 'Contracted-out pensions – Your guide (PM7)'. This free guide is available by calling 08457 313233, or by writing to DWP Pensions, Freepost BS5555/1, Bristol BS99 1BL. It can also be downloaded from the Internet at www.pensionguide.gov.uk.

Box 21.2: Contracting out under SSP

The arrival of the State Second Pension in April 2002 means the whole structure of contracting-out rebates has to change.

Rather than simply being linked to a percentage of earnings, as for Serps, they have to also reflect the aims of the new pension – which is to be more generous to lower earners. So the level of the rebate will vary with how much you earn, as well as with age.

There will be three bands of rebate for each age; the most generous rebate will apply to the first slice of earnings up to £10,500*. Then a middle rebate will apply to earnings between £10,500 and £23,700. Finally, earnings above £23,700 qualify for a third level of rebate. So someone whose earnings hit the top band will have their rebate calculated at three different rates. However, the end result is to leave them with a payment into their pension worth roughly the same as they would have got under Serps. Lower earners get a bigger rebate than they would have got under Serps, reflecting the greater value of state pension they are now giving up by contracting out.

The level of earnings at which each earnings band kicks in will change year-by-year. The table below sets out the examples of the rebates paid for personal pensions. Different values will apply to those in contracted-out occupational pensions.

Value of rebates paid for contributing out of State Second Pension in 2002/03:

Age on last day of previous tax year	Earnings less than £10,500*	Earnings between £10,500 and £23,700*	Earnings more than £23,700*
20	8.8 per cent	2.2 per cent	4.4 per cent
30	9.6 per cent	2.4 per cent	4.8 per cent
40	10.8 per cent	2.7 per cent	5.4 per cent
50	19.8 per cent	4.95 per cent	9.9 per cent
60	21 per cent	5.25 per cent	10.5 per cent

* The exact bands were not finalised at the time of writing. These figures are estimated values provided by the Department of Work and Pensions.

CHAPTER 22 Converting a pension into an income

Read this chapter if:

- You want to know what an annuity is.
- You want to find out about different types of annuities.
- You want to know about income drawdown.
- You want to know about phased retirement.

When you retire, some pensions are paid to you in a predefined way. This includes state pensions and some company pensions, including final salary schemes. But many other pensions require the saver to make some important decisions about how they convert the funds they have accumulated in their pension into an income.

This chapter explains the rules for converting a pension into an income. If you want a general overview of this topic, see Chapter 9.

Introduction

Savings built up through a pension have benefited from generous tax relief. To avoid these tax advantages being abused, the government imposes strict rules on how a pension fund can be converted into an income. Chapter 19 sets out the general rules on maximum benefits that can be taken from a company pension. Chapter 20 does the same for personal pensions.

The government also dictates how this pension is paid; it does not want savers taking huge lump sums from their pension. Instead, it insists you take the bulk of a fund as a sustainable and regular income through retirement. Many occupational pensions automatically do this. They pay a regular income to members each year from accumulated funds. All final salary schemes work in this way and so do many of the larger money-purchase company pension schemes.

But other pensions give the saver choices over how they structure their income. These choices apply to those with personal pensions, including stakeholder, and to some types of company money-purchase pensions. It may also be possible for those in other kinds of company pension to transfer their funds into a personal pension before they retire to gain more flexibility about how they take their income in retirement.

Tax-free lump sums

All pension savers will have some entitlement to a tax-free lump sum from their pension when they retire. The size of this sum will vary.

For long-standing members of company pensions, the maximum tax-free lump sum is likely to be one and a half times their final salary. For those who joined a pension after April 1997 it can be a maximum of two and a quarter times the annual pension they will get on retirement. If you have only been a member of a company pension scheme for a few years, the tax-free lump sum will be far less than these maximums.

With personal pensions, the tax-free cash can be up to 25 per cent of the value of the pension fund when you retire. Chapters 19 and 20 have fuller details about how this lump sum is calculated.

The lump sum is optional, but most of those retiring take the cash.

After taking any tax-free cash, the remainder of your pension must be turned into an annual income. Buying an annuity is the most common way to convert a pension into income. Annuities are used by the majority of those retiring to give a secure and sustainable income in retirement. Those with personal pensions buy annuities for themselves while company pension funds buy them on behalf of their members.

There are some approved alternatives to buying an annuity, but under current rules they cannot operate indefinitely. Even if you use these alternatives, such as income drawdown or phased retirement, an annuity has to be purchased before your seventy-fifth birthday.

What is an annuity?

An annuity converts a pension fund lump sum into an income. In the majority of cases this income is guaranteed until you die.

Only insurance companies are allowed to sell annuities. The business is closely regulated to ensure that companies offering these annuities have sufficient money to honour their promises. Insurers back their annuity promises by investing in gilts: government bonds. These are the most secure type of investment available.

Another way to think about an annuity is like life insurance in reverse. With life insurance, you pay a regular monthly premium which produces a lump sum on your death. With the annuity you give the insurer the lump sum and it pays you this money back in monthly, or annual, instalments. The longer you live, the more the insurer has to pay back. But once you buy an annuity, your capital is gone for good. So the total benefits that you get from the annuity depend on how long you live. Those who die soon after retirement will have got back far less than they paid in and will subsidise those who live for thirty or forty years. This subsidy between short-lived and long-lived is a key strength of an annuity for those who survive long after retiring.

How much income an annuity produces depends on several factors, not least the size of your pension fund. Bigger funds give bigger incomes. The next most important issue is age. The older you are when you buy an annuity, the more income you will get, because your life expectancy is lower. Men get higher incomes than women of the same age because they are expected to die sooner.

Annuities are also affected by general economic conditions, such as long-term interest rates. The lower rates are, the more it costs an insurer to provide the absolute guarantee of future income. The size of income an annuity will produce also depends on the added extras a pensioner can build into their annuity. Annuity rates change from day to day, but once you have signed up and purchased an annuity, the rate on that day of purchase will govern your pension for the whole of your retirement.

Pension annuities are taxed at source through the PAYE tax system. When you sign up for an annuity, the insurer is given a tax code for you. It then deducts a slice of each payment it makes on behalf of the Inland Revenue. Income tax is taken at the basic rate. Non-taxpayers have to claim this back and higher-rate taxpayers pay more through the annual self-assessment process.

You are not obliged to buy an annuity from the company which has managed your pension fund up to retirement. Indeed, some pension companies do not offer annuities. Savers can use what is called the 'open-market option' to take an annuity from another company. You should shop around and obtain alternative annuity quotes through independent financial advisers. A number of firms specialise in this market including Annuity Direct and The Annuity Bureau in London and Bridgegate Annuities in Chester.

Annuity options

A basic annuity will give the person who buys it a set income from now until the day they die. The income will not increase; the same will be paid every year. But there are a range of different options that can be chosen to customise an annuity to a buyer's needs. Adding options will reduce the annual starting income you get from an annuity. Optional extras include:

- A spouse's or partner's pension – you extend your annuity to cover two lives, not just one. This means that when one partner dies, the annuity goes on paying out until the second death. This is the most common add-on for an annuity. Though it is sometimes called spouse's pension or widow's pension, it can cover a partner of any sex. You can pick different levels of pension for a spouse, from nothing through to 100 per cent of what the main annuitant gets. Most couples opt for between one-third and two-thirds of the original pension. The cost of providing a partner's pension depends on their age. The younger they are, the more expensive it will be. For example, a man aged sixty-five, with a wife of sixty-two, would see his starting income fall by around 14 per cent if he opted for a 50 per cent widow's pension.
- Guarantees – a period over which the annuity is guaranteed to pay out, even if the holder dies. This guards against the danger of someone handing over tens of thousands of pounds and then dying a few weeks later with very little return. Guarantees are typically for five or ten years. The cost depends on age. The older you are, the more expensive the guarantee because there is more chance of it having to pay out. For example, a five-year guarantee for a man aged sixty would reduce the starting income by 1 per cent. This cost would rise to 3 per cent of starting income for a man aged seventy. Do not confuse guarantees with guaranteed annuity rates, offered by some types of personal pension (see box 22.1).
- Income in advance or arrears – you can pick whether you get paid in advance or at the end of a period. Being paid in advance reduces the income; an income paid annually in advance is likely to be around 8 per cent less than one paid annually in arrears. Where the income is being paid in arrears you can also choose the option of a proportional payment. This means that

when you die your estate is paid a proportion of your annuity income from the date of your last payment to the date of your death. If you are on annual income and die just before the next payment is due this could be a significant sum.

- Frequency of income – you can also pick how often you are paid an income. Options are usually monthly, quarterly, half-yearly or annually. Being paid monthly in arrears gives you 4 per cent less than being paid annually in arrears.
- Escalation or inflation proofing – the basic option is a level annuity, where the income is unchanged. Alternatively, you can pick an annuity where income will increase each year. Typically, you can nominate any level of increase between nothing and 8.5 per cent a year. You can also pick the Retail Price Index, which matches increases to inflation, or a Limited Price Index increase. LPI is the lower of inflation or 5 per cent a year. All these annual increases are guaranteed. But they are costly. On average, a man aged sixty opting for 5 per cent a year increases would receive a 40 per cent lower income at the start than for a level annuity.
- A dependant's pension – similar to the partner's pension but for other dependants, such as children or aged relatives. Costs vary dramatically, depending on the age of the dependants.

There are special annuity rates paid to those in poor health. This is called an impaired-life annuity. It is available to those who can demonstrate that they have a medical condition which has reduced their probable life expectancy. Buyers will need to be prepared to complete a medical questionnaire and to submit doctors' reports. They may even have to undergo a medical examination. But in return, insurers can be willing to pay annuity incomes up to 30 or 40 per cent higher than they would for someone in perfect health. If you defy the doctors' expectations and live for many years, you carry on receiving the higher income. That is the gamble the insurer has taken.

Another variation on the impaired-life annuity are special annuities available to smokers (and the partners of smokers), to those who live in certain areas of the UK and to those who worked in higher-risk occupations such as mining. All these groups have statistically shorter life expectancy, so can qualify for more generous incomes.

Specialist annuity advisers can talk you through all these options.

Box 22.1: Guaranteed annuity rates

Some insurance companies have in the past sold pensions with a guaranteed annuity rate. This promises savers that their pension fund will be converted into an income at a pre-set rate. A common guarantee for men is an income of one-ninth of the fund value per year. For women the most common number used is one-eleventh of the fund value per year. But for both sexes guarantees can be higher.

For most of the time guarantees were offered, they were less generous than prevailing annuity rates. In other words they were a promise that pension companies never expected to have to keep. However, as annuity rates have fallen, the guarantees have become more and more valuable. The guarantees can now produce an income 20 or 30 per cent higher than a similar fund could buy on the open market.

Where a pension has a guaranteed annuity rate attached to it, shopping around and using the open-market option may not be a wise move. However, it is not a completely black-and-white issue.

Frequently the guarantees only apply to certain types of annuity. So the guarantee may apply to a single-life annuity for the pension holder, but not to a joint-life annuity to give their spouse an income after they die. In such circumstances the open-market option might appeal. It can even make sense to split the fund and use some of it to make the most of the guarantee, and some of it to shop around for another annuity. Again, specialist advice is essential to capitalise on a guarantee.

Companies that have sold pensions in the past with guaranteed annuity rates include:

Company name	Years when pensions with annuity guarantees were sold
Axa Sun Life/Axa Equity & Law	Early 1970s to mid-1980s
Equitable Life	1956 to 1988
Legal & General	Early 1970s to 1987
Scottish Amicable	1970 to 1987
Scottish Equitable	1960 to 1988
Scottish Mutual	Early 1970s to mid-1980s
Scottish Widows	1983 to 1994
Standard Life	Early 1970s to 1989

Investment annuities

There is one other important family of annuity. This is the investment annuity. Here the money you give to an insurer is invested not in gilts but on the stock market for growth. The amount of income you receive is not guaranteed to stay the same. It depends on how well stock markets grow. In good years the pension will rise. But in years of poor stock market growth the income may be static or even fall. Investment annuities are not always available to those buying an annuity from a money-purchase company pension fund.

The attraction of investment-linked annuities is the chance to increase your income over a number of years. They will not appeal to those who need every penny of pension income to get by and so cannot afford to have a year or two when income dips. Advisers do not usually recommend investment annuities unless you have other savings or sources of income on top of your pension.

With-profit annuities

There are two types of investment annuity. The most commonly used is a with-profit annuity. The money that you give to an insurer is invested in the company's with-profit fund. This fund invests in a mix of shares, bonds, property and cash. It is designed to produce steady, sustainable growth, smoothing out the worst shocks of the stock market. Growth is returned to investors by declaring a bonus on the fund each year.

The insurer gives you a starting income which is guaranteed in year one. Each year thereafter, the level of your income depends on how well the insurer's fund has done and what bonus has been declared on the with-profit fund.

When you buy a with-profit annuity you are asked to select a level of growth which you think is realistic for the fund. This is called an anticipated bonus rate. Insurers typically let you pick rates between 0 per cent and 5 per cent growth a year. The higher the level of bonus you select, the bigger your starting income will be. Table 22.1 shows how this might work.

The income in the second and subsequent years depends on how the insurer's declared bonuses match up to the growth you have chosen. If the declared bonus is more than your anticipated bonus, the income will rise. If it is the same, your income is unchanged. But if the insurer declares a lower bonus than you have anticipated, your income will fall.

Most insurers have a base level below which the income cannot fall – this is typically the income you would get if you had opted for 0 per cent growth at the start.

The lower the anticipated bonus rate that you select at the start, the lower your starting income will be but the greater the chance of increasing it. The higher the anticipated bonus rate, the higher your starting income, but the greater the risk of that falling in future years.

Some newer versions of with-profit annuities have scrapped the requirement to select a bonus rate. You get a standardised income which will rise or fall in line with the bonuses from the insurer's fund.

Some with-profit annuities can also be converted into a conventional annuity if the saver chooses. But the annuity has to be with the same insurer, which may not be the most generous rate on the market.

On your death, the annuity has no cash value. If you have a

spouse's option and they are still alive, the annuity will carry on paying them. If not, there is no money paid to your estate.

Table 22.1: Starting income on a with-profit annuity

Annual bonus rate you choose	Annual income in first year
0 per cent	£5503
1 per cent	£6131
2 per cent	£6782
3 per cent	£7453
4 per cent	£8141
5 per cent	£8843

Based on a male, aged sixty-five, with a fund of £100,000 buying an annuity from Prudential.

Unit-linked annuities

The unit-linked annuity ties your income directly to how well an investment fund performs. When you retire, your annual annuity income is calculated in the normal way, depending on age, sex etc. You receive this income for your first payment. At the same time you are then credited with units of that monetary value in an investment fund of your choice run by that pensions company. The next payment you get depends on what happens to the value of that fund; if the fund rises by 10 per cent, the payment rises by 10 per cent. If the fund falls by 10 per cent, so does your income.

Many insurers also offer a variant of the annuity where you select an anticipated growth rate from a range of rates on offer. This works in much the same way as anticipated bonus rates on with-profit annuities. The higher the growth rate you pick, the higher your initial income. But if growth fails to live up to this benchmark, your income is pegged back each year.

The attraction of a unit-linked annuity is the wide choice of investment funds. You can opt for aggressive-growth funds, spread your money around the globe in different regional funds or punt on technology or smaller company stocks. Alternatively, you can go for the more cautious options of bond funds or an insurer's managed fund. Active investors can switch money between funds as market conditions change. But the income from such an annuity will fluctuate on a month-by-month basis. Again, it will not suit those who need a minimum sum each month.

For experienced investors there is a self-invested annuity option. Here you retain full control of where your annuity invests. The annuity fund can hold shares, collective funds such as unit trusts, bank deposits and gilts. Your income depends on what income these investments can produce. However, you are still bound by the constraints of an annuity. Starting income is defined by your age and sex; and the funds belong to an insurer not your estate when you die.

The self-invested annuity is available up to the age of seventy-five, after which you must switch into a unit-linked annuity or a conventional annuity. Anyone attracted to this should also consider the option of income drawdown (see below).

Some unit-linked annuities can also be converted into a conventional annuity if the saver chooses. But the annuity has to be with the same insurer, which may not be the most generous rate on the market.

It is strongly recommended that you take independent financial advice before buying any investment annuity. These are complex products with some risk to the saver.

Alternatives to annuities

Annuities have a number of advantages for those in retirement. In particular, the income is absolutely guaranteed (unless you opt for an investment annuity). The money will go on being paid until the day you die. If you like, you can consider an annuity as insurance against the cost of a very long lifespan. Many insurers have annuities that they have been paying for more than forty years.

But critics point to a number of drawbacks. They say that annuities offer poor value. Certainly, the income that a given fund can produce has fallen dramatically over the last decade. A fund which could produce a gross annuity income of over £10,000 a year in 1991 will produce less than £6000 a year today. Moreover, critics argue that an annuity is not an efficient investment because you lose control of your capital. There is nothing left to pass on to dependants. Critics say that with retirement commonly lasting thirty or so years, it is foolish to lock yourself into an income level determined by the economic conditions at the particular moment you retire.

There is a growing campaign for the compulsory annuity purchase rules to be scrapped. Many investors would rather take their chances with some of the alternatives to annuities.

Some reform of annuity rules is highly likely in the next few years. At the time of writing, several proposals had been aired and the matter had received a lot of debate in Parliament, including a Private Member's Bill which ran out of time. But the government itself has made no firm proposals for change. For the moment, pensioners can use other methods to produce an income from their pensions before they have to bite the bullet and get an annuity when they become seventy-five.

The two main alternatives to annuities are income drawdown and phased retirement.

Income drawdown

This is an option for those with personal pensions and for some money-purchase company pensions which have changed their rules to build in a drawdown option. It may also be possible to arrange a transfer out of a company pension into a personal pension scheme and then go into income drawdown from that second pension. But the charges you face to do this might be prohibitive.

Personal pension income drawdown schemes are run by a handful of specialist pension companies. They allow you to take up to your maximum entitlement of tax-free cash when you retire. The remainder of your pension fund is then reinvested to carry on growing. A drawdown fund is classed as a pension, so growth remains free of tax.

Each year you are allowed to draw an income from this fund. The amount of income is strictly regulated by the Inland Revenue. It must lie between 35 per cent and 100 per cent of the approximate income you would get from a single-life, level annuity for a person of your age with your fund. It will also be taxed by the pension company at the income tax basic rate.

The idea is that growth in your funds provides you with enough money to live off, while preserving the capital for years to come. The drawdown process can continue until your seventy-fifth birthday, when the remaining money in the fund has to be used to buy an annuity. However, you do not have to wait until seventy-five. You can buy an annuity with some or all of a drawdown fund at any time.

Every three years the drawdown plan is reviewed, at extra cost to yourself. If investment growth has been poor, the fund value will have been eroded and the amount of income you will be allowed to take in future years is reduced. Conversely, if your money has grown well, or if general annuity rates have improved, then you may be allowed to take a higher income. You will also be three years older, which helps boost the permissible income.

Once you have invested in a drawdown fund, it is not possible to make any further contributions to the fund.

One of the attractions of income drawdown is that you retain ownership of the funds. If you die while your fund is in drawdown, the money does not just disappear into some insurance company black hole. If you have no dependants and die, the income ceases being paid out and your estate gets the value of your fund, less a 35 per cent tax charge. Your estate may then be subject to inheritance tax, although the drawdown fund can be written under trust to avoid this second tax charge.

If you are married at the time of death, your spouse has three options:

- They can carry on drawing down an income from the funds, within the overall income limits set out above. This process can continue until they reach seventy-five, or until the time when you would have reached seventy-five if earlier. Then they must use the remaining fund to buy an annuity.
- They can cancel the income drawdown and take all the remaining fund as a lump sum. This lump sum is taxed at 35 per cent. But once this tax charge has been paid, your spouse is free to do what they like with the money. Taking the lump sum is possible for up to two years after your death. Thereafter, the option lapses.
- They can buy an annuity with the fund straight away.

Drawdown is not normally recommended for those with pension funds of less than £200,000 to £250,000. This is because you need a reasonable-sized fund to bear the administration costs of drawdown and to provide a good spread of different investments. Those with substantial funds may use some to buy an annuity at retirement and put the rest into drawdown, hedging their bets both ways.

The charges on drawdown can be complex and vary widely between different types of scheme and through different advisers. Initial charges can be as high as 6 or 7 per cent of the fund value, although specialist firms will usually charge a more competitive 2 or 3 per cent. Annual running costs of a drawdown plan are between 1 and 1.5 per cent of the fund value. Those with bigger funds may find it more economical to pay their advisers through fees.

Among others, drawdown may appeal to:

- those who do not want to buy an annuity;
- those who are going into semi-retirement or part-time work and do not need to collect a full income from their pension. They would draw as much as they need and leave the rest to grow;
- those who are retiring at a young age and want to defer buying an annuity until they are older and they will get a higher annuity income;

- those who are already running a self-invested personal pension or a small self-administered pension scheme and who want to continue to be involved in investing their own funds.

It will not appeal to those who are risk averse or who want absolute security of income. Like investment annuities, the income that you get from a drawdown plan is not guaranteed. It may fluctuate up or down. You can choose to change your income from year to year, but reductions may be forced on you by the three-year review process. Ultimately, future income depends on how well the underlying funds perform.

Protected-rights funds built up through contracting out of Serps can be also be used for income drawdown, but special rules apply. Protected-rights funds cannot be accessed until the age of sixty at the earliest for both sexes, so any drawdown cannot start before then. They must be converted into a protected-rights annuity by the age of seventy-five. And if you die before age seventy-five, there is no option of a lump sum for a spouse. They either continue in drawdown or convert to an annuity directly. Protected-rights funds in drawdown cannot be written under trust.

Not all income drawdown companies accept protected rights into a drawdown scheme. In practice, most of those with protected-rights money put this into a separate scheme, so have two drawdown funds running in parallel. See Chapter 21 for a definition of protected rights if you are uncertain about these funds.

Drawdown from an occupational pension scheme uses similar principles, though some of the detailed rules are different. Specifically, any company pension is governed by company pension rules, so the calculation of how much tax-free income you can take is different. And the maximum size of your pension is capped. So it is possible that your income could hit this limit if funds grow well.

Not all company pensions have written drawdown provisions into their scheme rules. If you are a member of such a scheme and are keen on using drawdown instead of an annuity, it may be necessary to transfer the whole company pension into a personal pension before retiring.

How income drawdown funds are invested is also an important part of the equation. There are three investment strategies:

- Hands-off investment – here the saver hands control of their funds to someone else, typically a pension company. They decide how and where to invest the money in accordance with your chosen investment goals. You get annual updates on how the funds are performing. The costs of this service are contained within the pension company's charges.
- Hands-on investment – you work actively with an investment manager, independent financial adviser or stockbroker deciding how to invest your money. The pension company provides the administration but you and your advisers decide where the money goes. The advisers will charge you separate fees for this work.
- Self-managed – you make the decisions and are ultimately responsible for how well your pension performs. You only pay the basic pension administration charges, plus any costs of buying and selling the investments you make.

If you want to follow either a hands-on or self-managed strategy, you will need to use a self-invested income drawdown product. This is an administration wrapper within which you hold your investments. Drawdown funds can be invested in a wide range of different assets including insurance company pension funds, quoted shares, gilts, bonds, property, unit trusts and stocks and shares from recognised overseas investment markets.

New rules introduced early in 2001 mean that it is now possible to transfer a drawdown fund from one scheme to another. You might want to switch if you were unhappy with the investment performance or administration of your existing scheme. However, there will be an extra set of charges involved in any transfer and advisers would generally caution against it if you are ten or fewer years away from having to buy an annuity. Transfers are not permitted where a drawdown scheme has been running for less than a year. At the time of transfer, the maximum income that can be taken from the scheme will have to be assessed again, even if it is less than three years since it was last reviewed.

Phased retirement

This is an alternative to income drawdown, or can be used alongside drawdown to give complete control over how you convert a fund into income. It is suitable for those who are invested in a personal pension plan. To move into phased retirement from a company pension you would have first to transfer into a personal pension. The combination of charges for initially switching into a personal pension and then moving to phased retirement may make this poor value.

With phased retirement you split a pension fund into many separate segments. Typically 1000 segments are used. Each year you 'retire', or vest, a certain number of segments. Each segment gives the saver a chunk of tax-free cash, plus money to be invested in an annuity or in a drawdown plan.

In the early years, the majority of the income comes from tax-free cash and only a little from the annuities or drawdown fund. But as more money is used to purchase annuities or goes into drawdown, the proportion of the annuity or drawdown income increases.

The portion of the pension which has not been vested remains invested and hopefully continues to grow free of tax. By the time you reach seventy-five, all the funds must be converted into an annuity.

Table 22.2 shows an example of how the first five years of a phased retirement process might work. It looks daunting but read it through a couple of times to get the feel of the process.

Table 22.2: Example of how phased retirement works for a man aged sixty with a fund of £500,000

Pension fund	Year 1	Year 2	Year 3	Year 4	Year 5
Available fund	£500,000	£452,000	£410,000	£372,000	£338,000
Value of segments vested	£72,000	£65,712	£59,800	£54,248	£49,056
Remaining fund	£428,000	£386,228	£352,200	£317,752	£288,944
Income					
Tax-free cash	£18,000	£16,428	£14,950	£13,562	£12,264
Annuity income from vested segments	£2564	£2708	£2580	£2354	£2186
Annuity income from previous years	£0	£2640	£5456	£8276	£10,950
Total gross income	**£20,564**	**£21,776**	**£22,986**	**£24,192**	**£25,400**
Income tax on annuities	£564	£1176	£1768	£2339	£2889
Effective tax rate	2.74%	5.4%	7.69%	9.67%	11.38%
Total net income	**£20,000**	**£20,600**	**£21,218**	**£21,853**	**£22,511**

Key assumptions: all annuities are 3 per cent income escalating, with 50 per cent spouse pension. Fund grows at 7 per cent a year before charges. Income tax is 22 per cent.

Annuity rates are: age sixty, 4.75 per cent; age sixty-one, 5.49 per cent: age sixty-two, 5.75 per cent; age sixty-three, 5.79 per cent: age sixty-four, 5.94 per cent.

Source: Income Drawdown Advisory Bureau, with thanks.

In year one, a man aged sixty retires with a substantial personal pension fund of £500,000. This is placed into a phased retirement scheme. Of this, he vests £72,000 at the start. This gives £18,000 of tax-free cash (25 per cent of £72,000). The other £54,000 is used to buy annuities. These pay £2564 of income in the first year. So our saver's total income in the first year is £18,000 plus £2564 – a grand total of £20,564. This income is mainly made up of tax-free cash. Only the annuity income is taxed, so his after-tax income is almost the same at £20,000. The effective tax rate shows the total tax charged as a proportion of this saver's income.

Over the course of the first year the remaining pension fund grows in value by £24,000 – the equivalent of 7 per cent a year before charges. So at the start of year two, our saver has a total fund worth £452,000. Again, a slice of segments is vested, this time worth £65,712. This gives £16,428 of tax-free cash and buys £2708 a year of annuity income. But there is also the £2640 of income from his annuity purchased in the previous year. So the total income before tax rises to £21,776.

As the table shows, as the years go by a larger proportion of the income is made up from annuity money and a smaller proportion from tax-free cash.

Phased retirement will appeal to those with substantial pension funds and for similar reasons to those listed for income drawdown. There are a few crucial differences between income drawdown and phased retirement. With phased retirement:

- Tax-free cash is released gradually, rather than up front.
- It is possible to carry on paying into a phased retirement pension if you are still working.
- If you die before the whole fund is vested personal pension rules still apply. So whatever is left passes to your spouse with no tax charge. If you have no spouse, it forms part of your estate. However, if some or all of the money came from an occupational pension, then the maximum lump sum is only 25 per cent of the remaining fund and the rest must be used to buy an annuity on behalf of the spouse.

Again, phased retirement is not suited to those who are nervous of stock market risk or who want a guaranteed income. The value of the income produced in future years depends on how well your fund grows and on what happens to future annuity rates.

The investment choices for phased retirement are similar to those for income drawdown. There is no legal requirement for a formal review, but most plans are monitored on an annual basis.

Phased retirement policies can be switched from pension company to pension company if you become dissatisfied with your existing provider. But annuities already purchased remain with the organisation that you first bought them from.

Protected-rights funds do not suit phased retirement because no tax-free cash can be taken from them. If your pension is substantially made up of protected-rights money, phased retirement may not be possible.

There is nothing to prevent a wealthy saver who has two or three different personal pensions using one to buy an annuity for a guaranteed income and then using either drawdown or phased retirement with other pension funds.

Phased retirement and income drawdown are sophisticated products. Independent advice from a specialist is essential.

APPENDIX 1a

Earnings growth calculator

Number of years	Value of £1 at different growth rates			
	1%	2%	3%	4%
1	1.010	1.020	1.030	1.040
2	1.020	1.040	1.061	1.082
3	1.030	1.061	1.093	1.125
4	1.041	1.082	1.126	1.170
5	1.051	1.104	1.159	1.217
6	1.062	1.126	1.194	1.265
7	1.072	1.149	1.230	1.316
8	1.083	1.172	1.267	1.369
9	1.094	1.195	1.305	1.423
10	1.105	1.219	1.344	1.480
11	1.116	1.243	1.384	1.539
12	1.127	1.268	1.426	1.601
13	1.138	1.294	1.469	1.665
14	1.149	1.319	1.513	1.732
15	1.161	1.346	1.558	1.801
16	1.173	1.373	1.605	1.873
17	1.184	1.400	1.653	1.948
18	1.196	1.428	1.702	2.026
19	1.208	1.457	1.754	2.107
20	1.220	1.486	1.806	2.191
21	1.232	1.516	1.860	2.279
22	1.245	1.546	1.916	2.370
23	1.257	1.577	1.974	2.465
24	1.270	1.608	2.033	2.563
25	1.282	1.641	2.094	2.666
26	1.295	1.673	2.157	2.772
27	1.308	1.707	2.221	2.883
28	1.321	1.741	2.288	2.999
29	1.335	1.776	2.357	3.119
30	1.348	1.811	2.427	3.243
31	1.361	1.848	2.500	3.373
32	1.375	1.885	2.575	3.508
33	1.389	1.922	2.652	3.648
34	1.403	1.961	2.732	3.794
35	1.417	2.000	2.814	3.946
36	1.431	2.040	2.898	4.104
37	1.445	2.081	2.985	4.268
38	1.460	2.122	3.075	4.439
39	1.474	2.165	3.167	4.616
40	1.489	2.208	3.262	4.801
41	1.504	2.252	3.360	4.993
42	1.519	2.297	3.461	5.193
43	1.534	2.343	3.565	5.400
44	1.549	2.390	3.671	5.617
45	1.565	2.438	3.782	5.841
46	1.580	2.487	3.895	6.075
47	1.596	2.536	4.012	6.318
48	1.612	2.587	4.132	6.571
49	1.628	2.639	4.256	6.833
50	1.645	2.692	4.384	7.107

5%	6%	7%	8%	9%
1.050	1.060	1.070	1.080	1.090
1.103	1.124	1.145	1.166	1.188
1.158	1.191	1.225	1.260	1.295
1.216	1.262	1.311	1.360	1.412
1.276	1.338	1.403	1.469	1.539
1.340	1.419	1.501	1.587	1.677
1.407	1.504	1.606	1.714	1.828
1.477	1.594	1.718	1.851	1.993
1.551	1.689	1.838	1.999	2.172
1.629	1.791	1.967	2.159	2.367
1.710	1.898	2.105	2.332	2.580
1.796	2.012	2.252	2.518	2.813
1.886	2.133	2.410	2.720	3.066
1.980	2.261	2.579	2.937	3.342
2.079	2.397	2.759	3.172	3.642
2.183	2.540	2.952	3.426	3.970
2.292	2.693	3.159	3.700	4.328
2.407	2.854	3.380	3.996	4.717
2.527	3.026	3.617	4.316	5.142
2.653	3.207	3.870	4.661	5.604
2.786	3.400	4.141	5.034	6.109
2.925	3.604	4.430	5.437	6.659
3.072	3.820	4.741	5.871	7.258
3.225	4.049	5.072	6.341	7.911
3.386	4.292	5.427	6.848	8.623
3.556	4.549	5.807	7.396	9.399
3.733	4.822	6.214	7.988	10.245
3.920	5.112	6.649	8.627	11.167
4.116	5.418	7.114	9.317	12.172
4.322	5.743	7.612	10.063	13.268
4.538	6.088	8.145	10.868	14.462
4.765	6.453	8.715	11.737	15.763
5.003	6.841	9.325	12.676	17.182
5.253	7.251	9.978	13.690	18.728
5.516	7.686	10.677	14.785	20.414
5.792	8.147	11.424	15.968	22.251
6.081	8.636	12.224	17.246	24.254
6.385	9.154	13.079	18.625	26.437
6.705	9.704	13.995	20.115	28.816
7.040	10.286	14.974	21.725	31.409
7.392	10.903	16.023	23.462	34.236
7.762	11.557	17.144	25.339	37.318
8.150	12.250	18.344	27.367	40.676
8.557	12.985	19.628	29.556	44.337
8.985	13.765	21.002	31.920	48.327
9.434	14.590	22.473	34.474	52.677
9.906	15.466	24.046	37.232	57.418
10.401	16.394	25.729	40.211	62.585
10.921	17.378	27.530	43.427	68.218
11.467	18.420	29.457	46.902	74.358

APPENDIX 1b
Inflation calculator

Number of years	Sum needed to have the same buying power as £1000 in today's			
	1%	2%	3%	4%
1	1010	1020	1030	1040
2	1020	1040	1061	1082
3	1030	1061	1093	1125
4	1041	1082	1126	1170
5	1051	1104	1159	1217
6	1062	1126	1194	1265
7	1072	1149	1230	1316
8	1083	1172	1267	1369
9	1094	1195	1305	1423
10	1105	1219	1344	1480
11	1116	1243	1384	1539
12	1127	1268	1426	1601
13	1138	1294	1469	1665
14	1149	1319	1513	1732
15	1161	1346	1558	1801
16	1173	1373	1605	1873
17	1184	1400	1653	1948
18	1196	1428	1702	2026
19	1208	1457	1754	2107
20	1220	1486	1806	2191
21	1232	1516	1860	2279
22	1245	1546	1916	2370
23	1257	1577	1974	2465
24	1270	1608	2033	2563
25	1282	1641	2094	2666
26	1295	1673	2157	2772
27	1308	1707	2221	2883
28	1321	1741	2288	2999
29	1335	1776	2357	3119
30	1348	1811	2427	3243
31	1361	1848	2500	3373
32	1375	1885	2575	3508
33	1389	1922	2652	3648
34	1403	1961	2732	3794
35	1417	2000	2814	3946
36	1431	2040	2898	4104
37	1445	2081	2985	4268
38	1460	2122	3075	4439
39	1474	2165	3167	4616
40	1489	2208	3262	4801
41	1504	2252	3360	4993
42	1519	2297	3461	5193
43	1534	2343	3565	5400
44	1549	2390	3671	5617
45	1565	2438	3782	5841
46	1580	2487	3895	6075
47	1596	2536	4012	6318
48	1612	2587	4132	6571
49	1628	2639	4256	6833
50	1645	2692	4384	7107

money at different inflation rates

5%	6%	7%	8%	9%
1050	1060	1070	1080	1090
1103	1124	1145	1166	1188
1158	1191	1225	1260	1295
1216	1262	1311	1360	1412
1276	1338	1403	1469	1539
1340	1419	1501	1587	1677
1407	1504	1606	1714	1828
1477	1594	1718	1851	1993
1551	1689	1838	1999	2172
1629	1791	1967	2159	2367
1710	1898	2105	2332	2580
1796	2012	2252	2518	2813
1886	2133	2410	2720	3066
1980	2261	2579	2937	3342
2079	2397	2759	3172	3642
2183	2540	2952	3426	3970
2292	2693	3159	3700	4328
2407	2854	3380	3996	4717
2527	3026	3617	4316	5142
2653	3207	3870	4661	5604
2786	3400	4141	5034	6109
2925	3604	4430	5437	6659
3072	3820	4741	5871	7258
3225	4049	5072	6341	7911
3386	4292	5427	6848	8623
3556	4549	5807	7396	9399
3733	4822	6214	7988	10245
3920	5112	6649	8627	11167
4116	5418	7114	9317	12172
4322	5743	7612	10063	13268
4538	6088	8145	10868	14462
4765	6453	8715	11737	15763
5003	6841	9325	12676	17182
5253	7251	9978	13690	18728
5516	7686	10677	14785	20414
5792	8147	11424	15968	22251
6081	8636	12224	17246	24254
6385	9154	13079	18625	26437
6705	9704	13995	20115	28816
7040	10286	14974	21725	31409
7392	10903	16023	23462	34236
7762	11557	17144	25339	37318
8150	12250	18344	27367	40676
8557	12985	19628	29556	44337
8985	13765	21002	31920	48327
9434	14590	22473	34474	52677
9906	15466	24046	37232	57418
10401	16394	25729	40211	62585
10921	17378	27530	43427	68218
11467	18420	29457	46902	74358

Contact information

There are a wealth of organisations that can provide further help and advice on the issues discussed in this book, much of it for free. The organisations listed here include charities, government bodies, financial regulators and finance industry trade bodies.

Age Concern
Age Concern Information Line
Freepost (SWB 30375)
Ashburton
Devon
TQ13 7ZZ
Telephone: 0800 009 966 (7a.m.–7p.m.)
Website: www.ageconcern.org.uk
Services: Charity which provides advice to elderly people and their families on a wide range of issues including pensions, state benefits, long-term care and equity release schemes. Also publishes a range of useful free fact-sheets.

Age Concern Scotland
113 Rose Street
Edinburgh
EH2 3DT
Telephone: 0131 220 3345 (Monday–Friday, 9a.m. to 5p.m.)

Services: Provides advice to elderly people and their families on a wide range of issues including pensions, state benefits, long-term care, with specific reference to how the rules work in Scotland.

Association of British Insurers
Consumer Information Department
51 Gresham Street
London
EC2V 7HQ
Telephone: 020 7600 3333
E-mail: *info@abi.org.uk*
Website: www.abi.org.uk
Services: Provides useful fact sheets and booklets on a wide range of insurance issues including health and life covers, and income replacement insurance. Is also the trade body representing most pensions companies, so has lots of information and comment on personal pensions.

Association of Investment Trust Companies
Durrant House
8–13 Chiswell Street
London
EC1Y 4YY
Telephone: 0800 085 8520
E-mail: info@ait.co.uk
Website: www.aitc.co.uk
Services: Trade body for investment trust companies. Provides information and fact sheets on investment trusts, including performance figures.

Association of Private Client Investment Managers and Stockbrokers
112 Middlesex Street
London
E1 7HY
Telephone: 020 7247 7080

E-mail: info@apcims.co.uk
Website: www.apcims.co.uk
Services: Trade body for stockbrokers and portfolio managers. Provides general information on share ownership and dealing and can help you to find a local stockbroker.

Association of Residential Letting Agents
Maple House
53–55 Woodside Road
Amersham
Bucks HP6 6AA
Telephone: 01494 431680
Website: www.arla.co.uk
Services: Trade body representing professional lettings agents. Useful source of information on investing in and managing letting property.

Association of Solicitor Investment Managers
Baldocks Barn
Chiddingstone Causeway
Tonbridge
Kent
TN11 8JX
Telephone: 01892 870065
E-mail: hmna@clara.co.uk
Services: Trade body representing solicitors who are also qualified to offer financial and investment advice. Can provide contact details of members local to you.

Association of Unit Trusts and Investment Funds
65 Kingsway
London
WC2B 6TD
Telephone: 020 8207 1361
E-mail: autif@investmentfunds.org.uk
Website: www.investmentfunds.org.uk

Services: Trade body for investment managers who run unit trusts and open-ended investment companies (Oeics). Provides useful fact sheets and booklets about how to invest using these funds.

Citizens Advice Bureaux
Website: www.nacab.org.uk
Services: More than 750 local offices across the UK. They can provide face-to-face help and advice on money issues including debt, state benefits and state pensions. Look in the phone book for your local office or use the on-line search facility on the website.

Department of Work and Pensions (formerly the DSS)
Correspondence Unit
Room 540
The Adelphi
1–11 John Adam Street
London
WC2N 6HT
Telephone: 020 7712 2171
Website: www.dwp.gov.uk
Services: The main government department covering state pensions and the wide range of state benefits. It administers services through local job centres and Benefits Agency offices, plus runs a range of centralised helplines and information services. It runs a series of specialist services, some of which are listed below. Local Benefits Agency offices can help with most other general enquiries. Alternatively, use the general address and phone number listed above. To find your local Benefits Agency office, use the phone book or log on to www.dss.gov.uk/localoffice/search/index.

Specialist services
Minimum Income Guarantee helpline: 0800 028 1111
Pensions information helpline (for leaflets on state pensions): 08457 313233
Retirement pension forecast and advice service: 0845 731 3233
General pension guidance: www.pensionguide. gov.uk
See also entry for the Pensions and Overseas Benefits Directorate

Disability Alliance
Universal House
88–94 Wentworth Street
London
E1 7SA
Telephone: 020 7247 8776
Services: Information on welfare benefits available to disabled people and their carers.

Ethical Investment Research Service
60–84 Bondway
London
SW8 1SF
Telephone: 0845 606 0324
Website: *www.eris.u-net.com*
Services: Specialist organisation advising charities and others on ethical investment. Provides general fact sheets, plus lists of advisers who specialise in ethical investments and pension funds.

The Financial Ombudsman Service
South Quay Plaza
183 Marsh Wall
London
E14 9SR
Telephone: 020 7964 1000
Website: www.financial-ombudsman.org.uk
Services: A complaints investigation and mediation service for a wide range of financial products including personal pensions, Isas, endowments and other packaged investment products. The Ombudsman will not consider a case until you have gone through a company's own complaints procedure.

The Financial Services Authority (FSA)
25 The North Colonnade
Canary Wharf
London
E14 5HS
Telephone: 0845 606 1234
E-mail: enquiries@fsa.gov.uk
Website: www.fsa.gov.uk
Services: The UK's main financial regulator, responsible for supervision of the selling and prudent running of a wide range of products including personal pensions, endowments and unit trusts. Provides booklets and fact sheets on a wide range of general finance topics, plus extra information on specifics such as the pensions mis-selling review.

Help the Aged
207–221 Pentonville Road
London
N1 9UZ
Telephone: 0808 800 6565 (9a.m.–4p.m.)
Website: www.helptheaged.org.uk
Services: Free advice on state pensions and benefits, funding of residential care and other benefits.

IFA Promotion
113–117 Farringdon Road
London
EC1R 3BX
Telephone: 020 7833 3131 (Find an Adviser helpline: 0800 085 3250)
Website: www.unbiased.co.uk
Services: Can put you in touch with local independent financial advisers and provides generic help and advice on working with an IFA.

Inland Revenue
Website: www.inlandrevenue.gov.uk
Services: Provides a wide range of fact sheets, booklets and advice relating to taxation and pensions legislation. It also runs some customer helplines which can assist with basic enquiries:

For Occupational Pension Schemes General technical/procedural enquiries (including small self-administered schemes): 0115 974 1600 9a.m.–5p.m. (Mon–Fri); *Personal Pension Schemes, Retirement Annuity Contracts and Free Standing Additional Voluntary Contribution Schemes*: 0115 974 1777 9a.m.–5p.m. (Mon–Fri)

Institute of Financial Planning
Whitefriars Centre
Lewins Mead
Bristol
BS1 2NT
Telephone: 0117 945 2470
Services: Can provide contact details for independent financial advisers who hold its qualifications.

National Association of Bank and Insurance Customers
PO Box 15
Caldicot
Newport
NP26 5YD
Telephone: 01291 430009
E-mail: insurance.help@virgin.net
Website: http://free space.virgin.net/bank.help
Services: Fact sheets and booklets on the workings of banks and insurance companies.

National Directory of Fee-Based Advisers
Matrix Data Services
Freepost
Gossard House
7–8 Savile Row
London
W1X 1AF
Telephone: 0870 013 1925
Services: Details of financial advisers who are paid by fees, rather than by commission.

Occupational Pensions Regulatory Authority (OPRA)
Invicta House
Trafalgar Place
Brighton
BN1 4DW
Telephone: 01273 637600
Website: www.opra.org.uk
Services: Regulator of company and other workplace pension schemes. Provides information relating to company pension schemes.

Office of the Pensions Advisory Service (Opas)
11 Belgrave Road
London
SW1V 1RB
Telephone: 020 7233 8080
Website: www.opas.org.uk
Services: Independent help and advice service to assist those who have a problem with either a workplace or a personal pension. Runs a nationwide network of volunteer advisers.

OPRA Pension Schemes Registry
PO Box 1NN
Newcastle upon Tyne
NE99 1NN

Telephone: 0191 225 6316
Website: www.opra.gov.uk./registry/regmenu.shtml
Services: Tracing of pension schemes for members of the public.

Pensions Compensation Board
11 Belgrave Road
London
SW1V 1RB
Telephone: 020 7828 9794
Services: Compensation scheme covering occupational pensions.

Pensions and Overseas Benefits Directorate
Tyneview Park
Whitley Road
Benton
Newcastle upon Tyne
NE98 1BA
Telephone: 0191 218 2000
Services: Deals with payments of state pensions to those living overseas.

The Pensions Ombudsman
11 Belgrave Road
London
SW1V 1RB
Telephone: 020 7834 9144
Services: Resolves disputes between company pension schemes and their members. Does not deal with personal pensions (see **Financial Ombudsman Service**).

Pre Retirement Association
9 Chesham Road
Guildford
Surrey
GU1 3LS
Telephone: 01483 301170

Website: www.pra.uk.com
Services: Help in preparing for retirement, both financial and lifestyle.

Proshare
Centurion House
44 Monument Street
London
EC3R 8AQ
Telephone: 020 7394 5200
E-mail: info@proshare.org.uk
Website: www.proshare.org.uk
Services: Fact sheets on stock markets, share ownership and information on investment clubs.

Safe Home Income Plans (SHIP)
1st Floor
Parker Court
Knapp Lane
Cheltenham
GL50 3QJ
Telephone: 01242 539494
Website: www.ship-ltd.co.uk
Services: Trade body for companies selling equity release schemes.

Society of Financial Advisers
20 Aldermanbury
London
EC2V 7HY
Telephone: 020 7417 4419
Website: www.sofa.org
Services: Will put you in touch with independent financial advisers holding SOFA's professional qualifications.

INDEX

Notes Entries in *italic* refer to tables and graphs
Entries in **bold** refer to boxed text.